# TABOO!

The Hidden Culture of a Red Light Area

# TABOO!

## The Hidden Culture of a Red Light Area

Fouzia Saeed

Foreword by
I.A. Rehman

OXFORD
UNIVERSITY PRESS

# OXFORD

UNIVERSITY PRESS

Great Clarendon Street, Oxford OX2 6DP

Oxford University Press is a department of the University of Oxford.
It furthers the University's objective of excellence in research, scholarship,
and education by publishing worldwide in

Oxford  New York

Auckland  Bangkok  Buenos Aires  Cape Town  Chennai
Dar es Salaam  Delhi  Hong Kong  Istanbul  Karachi  Kolkata
Kuala Lumpur  Madrid  Melbourne  Mexico City  Mumbai  Nairobi
São Paulo  Shanghai  Singapore  Taipei  Tokyo  Toronto
and an associated company in Berlin

ISBN  0 19 579412 5

Cover Design by Asif Shahjehan
Photography by Sajid Munir
Edited by Paul Lundberg and Judith Amtzis

Second Impression 2002

Typeset in Times
Printed in Pakistan by
New Sketch Graphics, Karachi.
Published by
Ameena Saiyid, Oxford University Press
5-Bangalore Town, Sharae Faisal
PO Box 13033, Karachi-75350, Pakistan.

# Contents

# Foreword

Shahi Mohalla, the red light area of Lahore, is one of the battlefronts where the Pakistani woman has been fighting for her freedom, dignity, and a decent place in society. But it is seldom recognized as such. Identified by various names, it represents one of the oldest flesh markets in the land, where prostitution and the performing arts are linked in a complex web of human relations. Hardly any informed citizen can plead ignorance of the residents of this area, but they are considered the least entitled to be understood by their fellow beings. Anyone who visits them, regardless of the excuse proffered, risks his standing with the vigilantes of public morality, and anyone who tries to discuss their condition, risks much else in both their world and his own. This was amply confirmed by the gentlemen of the Press who pretended to be scandalized by Fouzia Saeed's plans to study the culture of Shahi Mohalla. They did not belong to any special vice squad; indeed they merely reflected the dominant social view.

It is also the area, which reveals the state in a microcosm. The Offence of Zina (Enforcement of Hudood) Ordinance, promulgated in 1979 by the country's third military ruler, General Ziaul Haq, made extra-marital sex a penal offence liable to a variety of stiff punishments, ranging from a few years in prison to stoning to death. This law implies abolition of brothels. But neither religion nor law has ended prostitution in Pakistan. The brothels of Lahore, as of other cities and towns across the country, are not only still there; they are, by all accounts, increasing at a rapid rate. The spread of prostitution at an unprecedented scale raises critical issues regarding the rationale for laws that cannot be enforced, and about the element of bigotry in treating social issues as matters of law and order. Those living by prostitution have found accessories and means to live outside the law. An elaborate network of recruiting agents, brokers, pimps and the so-called enforcers of law has developed to keep the trade going. This network does not serve the practitioners of the world's oldest profession as much as it serves their clients, though their partnership in the flesh trade is only marginally admitted. They always enjoy a higher social status than that of the Shahi Mohalla prostitutes.

The obvious reason for the survival of the Shahi Mohalla's brothels is their traditional role as places of amusement where female professionals entertain their customers with song and dance, where indigent musicians ply their trade, and where film-makers and theatre-producers come looking for attractive bodies and acting talent. These activities have not yet been added to the list of offences drawn up in the penal code, despite the clamour of pseudo-religious zealots for shutting down all art platforms, which they deprecate under the single label of obscenity.

The nexus between prostitution and the performing arts is as old as prostitution itself. In whatever form their calling may have originated, the prostitutes were at the same time victims of patriarchy as well as the rebels who challenged it. Those who were not forced into prostitution by religious or temporal authority[1] sought freedom from societal bondages, and the independence not only to do with their bodies and charms as they wished, but also to follow their own rules about freedom of movement and style of living. Music and dance were the principal means to such independence.

Lahore, and other urban centres in Pakistan, were inducted into the culture of prostitution much later than the older capitals in the subcontinent—Mahabalipuram, Lucknow, Delhi. But courtesans were there and some matched the influence of their patrons as king makers and exhorters to war. The establishment of Muslim rule in the then Northern India, the north-western part of which now constitutes Pakistan, brought a radical shift in the prostitutes' status. Whereas the earlier religious clergies had accepted prostitutes as an unavoidable evil, the advocates of Islam pronounced anathema on them without any reservation.

The space for the courtesan who kept a salon and conquered kings and princes with her wit contracted and that for the confined-to-the-harem concubine increased. But throughout the Sultanate period we find references to the existence of prostitutes and *gaikas* (female singers), whose order was presided over by the favourites of kings and princes. They provided entertainment at all royal ceremonies. Their beauty and professional skills were considered a measure of the grandeur and worth of a court. But in the ultimate analysis, woman—as a wife gained forcibly from the vanquished enemy, as a courtesan from another land, and as an ordinary whore—was used to denote power—power of authority as well as of wealth. Thus, we find Ibn Batuta noticing that the women leading the dancing girls at the court of Mohammed Tughlaq belonged to the families of rajas he had subjugated a little earlier.[2] Jehangir's harem was said to have 6,000 mistresses, including women from China, the Caucasus, and Africa, as if they were tokens of the king's superiority, if not his sovereignty, over the countries of their origin. However, the Mughals patronized the performing arts and this kept open the possibility of an accomplished singer or dancer rising to the highest echelon of prostitution. Under the Mughals, prostitution flourished considerably.

The decline of the Mughal power and its replacement by Sikh rule in the Punjab and Frontier lowered the social taboo against prostitution and brought it out into the open. After the end of the Sikh rule, the arrival of the British brought a new breed of prostitutes' patrons. The Shahi Mohalla witnessed a major shift in the ranks of the elite. Literary and cultural values and norms changed. After brief attempts to publish newspapers in Persian and Arabic and to teach medicine in Urdu, the English language, dress, lifestyle supplanted the earlier modes of living and cultural expression. The apex of the prostitutes' hierarchy crumbled. The earlier standards of literary and cultural accomplishment that had helped the prostitute to rule over men with her wits became irrelevant. The scene came to be dominated by prostitutes of the lower categories.

During the five decades of independence the Shahi Mohalla has undergone several changes in patronage and clientele. The rajas have been replaced by politicians, who are comparatively much lower on the cultural scale, more interested in sexual gratification, and less capable of valuing prostitutes for skill in essential performing arts. A new class of businessmen, entrepreneurs, and officials has replaced the old patrons of Shahi Mohalla. There has been a sharp decline in the quality of singing and dancing and a consequent fall in the ranks of pure *gaikas*, and an increase by a wider margin in the crowd of ordinary whores. Forty years ago it was possible for a music lover to choose a *kotha* from several maintained by classical singers, but today the search may be limited. The *gaika* of two decades ago could oblige a client if he insisted on the poetry of Ghalib, Iqbal, or Hasrat Mohani. That breed has thinned, and if you hear verses of Faiz or Faraz that is because they were added to the repertory courtesy *ghazal* singers like Mehdi Hasan or Ghulam Ali via the cinema. The main inspirations now are Indian films or Cable TV. The nexus between performing arts and prostitution has become tenuous. Cinema, theatre and the liking of the *noveau riche* for variety shows keeps hopes of *gaikas* and *gaikas*-cum-prostitutes alive as they keep die-hard musicians tied to their posts. As for brothels, Shahi Mohalla has been left far behind by new establishments spreading all over the town. Still, for cheaper sex for periods as short as half-an-hour, Shahi Mohalla remains unbeatable.

The inner structure of the group that includes both singers and prostitutes has changed little over the centuries. What Fouzia Saeed has found is not materially different from the account left by Lahore's eleventh century poet, Masood Saad Salman. In his poem about an evening of revelry at the court of prince Sheerzad the musicians are mentioned earlier than female singers-dancers. The pride of place is occupied by a flute-player, whose troupe comprised several musicians and a prostitute.[3]

Exploration of the culture of Shahi Mohalla is a difficult though fascinating task. That here the birth of a girl is more welcome than that of a boy, who could be totally neglected, is easily understandable as an economic compulsion. Special emphasis on the sale of virginity also falls in the same category. It also helps in making the sale of the body attractive for the novice and in reducing the constraints marriage is supposed to impose on promiscuity. But there is a great deal in this culture that springs from a strategy of defence. Shahi Mohalla is claimed to be a nursery of artists who meet the entertainment needs of a vast multitude, including both rich and poor, who keep the tradition of music and dance alive, and who have brought success and credit to cinema. However, female singers and dancers have been traditionally classed as prostitutes, even when they do not put their bodies on sale, they have to join the prostitutes in relying on a common defence strategy in order to survive authorities efforts to suppress their trade.

Prostitution started getting denounced quite early in history. Manu* put harlots in the category of criminals along with gamblers and thieves. There was a time when a particular regime in the subcontinent declared that killing a prostitute was no offence. But it was soon realized that prostitution was a source of revenue to the state. Thus, while censure of prostitution was not withdrawn, various rulers tried to regulate the trade. Prostitutes could be allowed to live only on the fringe of an urban settlement. Emperor Akbar devised an elaborate plan to monitor visits to brothels, and to ensure some balance between the interests of the state on the one hand and those of the prostitute and the customer on the other hand.

Regulation became necessary to ensure that the functionaries of the state did not surrender completely to their entertainers, to the detriment of the official order. The tradition survived during the British period. The red light areas at many places were declared out of bounds for troops. Irregular regulation continued after independence so long as voluntary prostitution was considered a permissible vice and not a crime, because trafficking in girls and running brothels were considered penal

---

* Manu was the first century Hindu law-giver. The ancient city of Ayodhya, according to the *Ramayana*, was founded by Manu.

offences, and enforced prostitution had to be curbed. Now the question of regulating prostitution does not arise because it has been declared a serious criminal offence. No one can regulate a business that is unlawful. You cannot regulate smuggling, robbery and trafficking in drugs and you cannot regulate prostitution. Hence old practices, such as medical examination of prostitutes, have fallen away. The prostitutes must turn to quacks to secure abortion and relief from the various diseases that are dismissed as professional hazards.

Society has followed the state in putting prostitutes outside its fold. The tradition is to ignore their existence. The chroniclers of old Lahore hardly mention the flesh market. What one can learn about this trade is either from the classical literature of South India, when it was possible to write about prostitution without glamorising or condemning it, or from the travelogues and journals of European travellers in the medieval period who relished dwelling on the hypocrisy of the oriental. The resistance to discussing prostitution is a strong part of the tradition.

Things have improved a little as a result of the new debates on the various forms of violence upon women and on women's right to control over her body. Thus we find the latest commission on the status of women taking note of prostitution in a few lines:

> Enforced prostitution and trafficking in women are forms of violence for profit to which a substantial number of women are subjected ... Enforced prostitution of girls from lower-income backgrounds has always been in existence, with very few being able to escape from the net even if they wish to do so. However, very little has been done to effectively stem the practice or to rehabilitate the victims of the crime.[4]

And yet little is said about steps necessary to curb enforced prostitution, and nothing about women who voluntarily become prostitutes after rebelling against social or family oppression or enforced unhappiness, or those who, having reconciled themselves to trading in flesh, continue to pursue the vocation of their free will. The authors of the National Plan of Action, supposedly drawn up to ensure implementation of the Convention on the Elimination of all forms of Discrimination Against Women (CEDAW), say nothing about ways of dealing with prostitution. The subject is again placed in the category of violence against women. After discussing gang-rape and custodial rape, incest, child abuse, and sexual violence in the workplace, the Plan merely observes that other forms of violence include forced prostitution, trafficking in women, and such customs as demands of price for brides.[5]

No one is prepared to take up the brief for prostitutes because the only alternative to banning of prostitution—tried unsuccessfully by quite a few rulers from Aurangzeb to Ziaul Haq—is the offer of marriage to prostitutes. Firoz Tughlaq asked the pious men who wanted prostitution to be erased if they were prepared to marry the prostitutes and finding no volunteers he settled for regulation. The exercise was repeated during the Zia period when the Punjab Martial Law Administrator reportedly found the anti-prostitution dignitaries unwilling to take prostitutes as their wives. During the intervening years, many a Muslim reformer invited prostitutes to settle down in married life but his zeal for reform vanished the moment a *naika* invited him to marry her.

The idea of asking prostitutes to swap their profession with marriage begs the issue. Besides it envisages replacing a form of bondage, which permits little freedom, with another form of bondage, in which a woman has no freedom (in Pakistan society). Fouzia Saeed finally finds the answer in exposing the patriarchal system by treating 'bad' women and 'good' women as the two sides of the same coin. This is the one occasion when the author gives up the studiously maintained role of an anthropologist and reveals herself as essentially an activist in the cause of woman's rights. Her final fling is preceded by a polemic in which she examines prostitution in a historical perspective and debates with a fellow researcher the relationship between prostitution and the nature of rule and the web of patriarchy. This should mark the beginning of a more thorough research into the whys and hows of prostitution.

This inquiry began by discarding the notion that prostitution is a problem and by accepting the reality that prostitution is only a symptom of the multifaceted problem that society's economic structure and its social mores have created. *Kamasutra* was written for the guidance of well-to-do citizens. It prescribed a gentle existence devoted to the refinement of life for those who had both leisure and the wherewithal for such living. The Pakistan state and society both contribute to prostitution by maintaining an economic system in which some acquire wealth without working, which they can squander as they wish, and then closing the routes to enjoyment of the performing arts. So long as the iniquitous distribution of fruits of labour continues and so long as music, dance, laughter and love are denounced as sinful activities, prostitution will grow.

A more crucial issue is the role a society assigns to its women. In Pakistan, prostitution in its ugliest form is the direct consequence of denial of women's inherent dignity and rights. The first assault is on woman's right to work, as this enables her to break out of the patriarchal trap. One of the words used for a prostitute is *kasbi* (one who earns her living) and in our middle class culture the prostitute indulges in *peisha* (profession). Thus, a woman who earns her livelihood, who has a profession, has to be associated with whores. Next, patriarchy creates a group of 'bad' women and denounces them as seducers, home-breakers, destroyers of the male mind, and corrupters of the youth and then fixes responsibility for all these forms of vice on all womenfolk.

The plight of the Pakistani women will need many more tomes, much deep research into the common social norms and a degree of freedom from belief and deeply ingrained social values that are not visible at the moment. In a situation where women alone are responsible for acts considered immoral, where no husband is ever supposed to rape his wife, where women can be sold under notional marriage, where women's right to work is subject to bargaining, and where women activists are treated as immoral women and must therefore be forced into marriage by clerics, the woman of Pakistan has to fight on many fronts. Shahi Mohalla is only one of them.

I.A. Rehman
May 2001

## NOTES

1. The story of South Indian temple *devadasis* becoming priests' concubines and prostitutes is well known. In parts of Muslim society of Pakistan a woman given over to a pir (a spiritual guide) is still described as *Pir's Oontni* (*pir's* she-camel). She must be a virgin of tender age and she cannot marry anyone after sleeping with a *pir*. At some places the room in which the *pir* ravishes his prey cannot be used for any purpose except for a repeat performance whenever the *pir* chooses to come again.
2. Ibn Batuta, *Travelogue*, translated into Urdu by Mohammad Husain, Takhleeqat, Lahore, 1996, p. 132.
3. Syed Hashmi Faridabadi, *Ma'asir Lahore*, Institute of Islamic Culture, Lahore, 1976 edition, pp. 103–105.
4. Commission of Inquiry for Women, 1997, p. 85.
5. National Plan of Action for Women, Ministry of Women's Development, Islamabad, 1998, p. 27.

# MAP OF LAHORE

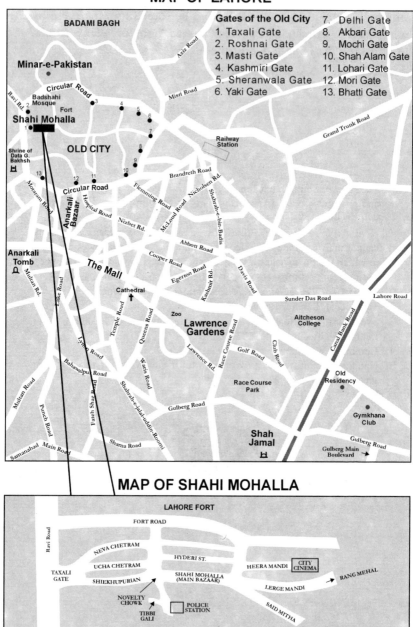

**Gates of the Old City**
1. Taxali Gate
2. Roshnai Gate
3. Masti Gate
4. Kashmiri Gate
5. Sheranwala Gate
6. Yaki Gate
7. Delhi Gate
8. Akbari Gate
9. Mochi Gate
10. Shah Alam Gate
11. Lohari Gate
12. Mori Gate
13. Bhatti Gate

BADAMI BAGH

Minar-e-Pakistan

Circular Road

Badshahi Mosque

Fort

Shahi Mohalla

Shrine of Data G. Bakhsh

OLD CITY

Anarkali Bazaar

Circular Road

Hospital Road

Nizbet Rd.

Flemming Road

McLeod Road

Nicholsen Rd.

Brandreth Road

Shahrah-e-bin-Badis

Aziz Road

Misri Road

Railway Station

Grand Trunk Road

Abbott Road

Cooper Road

Egerton Road

Kashmir Rd.

Davis Road

Anarkali Tomb

Multan Rd.

The Mall

Cathedral

Temple Road

Queens Road

Zoo

Lawrence Gardens

Lawrence Rd.

Race Course Road

Golf Road

Club Road

Sunder Das Road

Aitcheson College

Lahore Road

Lake Road

Lytton Road

Bahawalpur Road

Waris Road

Shahrah-e-Jalal-uddin-Roomi

Gulberg Road

Race Course Park

Old Residency

Canal Bank Road

Multan Road

Fatch Shah

Samanabad Main Road

Shama Road

Shah Jamal

Gulberg Road

Gymkhana Club

Gulberg Main Boulevard

Ravi Rd.

Mozaram Road

Panch Road

# MAP OF SHAHI MOHALLA

LAHORE FORT

FORT ROAD

Ravi Road

NEVA CHETRAM

UCHA CHETRAM

SHIEKHUPURIAN

HYDERI ST.

SHAHI MOHALLA (MAIN BAZAAR)

HEERA MANDI

CITY CINEMA

RANG MEHAL

LERGE MANDI

SAID MITHA

TAXALI GATE

NOVELTY CHOWK

TIBBI GALI

POLICE STATION

# Preface

After completing my doctorate in the United States, I returned to Pakistan, settled with my parents in Islamabad and began to plan my future. I had always wanted to work on women's issues from the time when I was a student in Pakistan. In the United States I gained a great deal of valuable experience by being active in many women's organizations. My firm belief, however, was that strengthening the women's movement in Pakistan required an exploration of our own traditional culture and that we had to build our base on the progressive elements already present in our society. I did not believe in attempting to import foreign concepts that were not strongly rooted in Pakistani culture. I was convinced that change had to come from within our own society and that it needed to be based upon appropriate existing practices.

Personally, I felt a need to learn about our roots, our folk traditions and the values of our country's different sub-cultures and classes. Urban, middle-class Pakistanis like myself rarely experience much of this during their childhood. Despite my conceptual clarity and activist experience, I knew I needed to get in touch with the women in rural Pakistan and those living in traditional contexts in the inner cities. As a researcher, I wanted to study women's role in different traditional communities and to connect with women at several levels. I felt there was much work to be done to truly understand the varied circumstances we women deal with before we could begin restoring our self-respect and status in society. Social taboos associated with any form of women's free and open expression of themselves particularly interested me.

I have long been interested in folk dancing and over the years have learned many Pakistani folk dances. I have often encountered the social taboo associated with dancing, sometimes even at family gatherings. Women who express themselves through the performing arts like singing, dancing or acting, are often, rightly or wrongly, associated with prostitution. In my initial research on folk theatre I learned that women from the red light areas were inducted into the theatre world only when the directors had difficulty recruiting other women whose families would not allow them to perform before an audience. Bali Jatti, whose life I studied as a part of my earlier research, was a theatrical performer. Although she never engaged in prostitution, as a female performer she was still stigmatized. Nevertheless, despite severe social constraints, she was eventually recognized as a prominent Pakistani stage artist and became the first woman to own a theatre company.

The fact that most of Pakistan's musicians, singers and film actors, especially women, come from the country's red light areas made me want to look more closely at this phenomenon. I was curious to study the contradicting values of a society where, on the one hand, women performers can be respected and in some cases, even acknowledged by the President, but where on the contrary, most families refuse to allow women to learn any form of music or dancing.

This book is based on a study I conducted in the Shahi Mohalla, a district of Lahore that maintains the custom of traditional prostitution. Shahi Mohalla means the Royal Bazaar, and it has long been one of South Asia's best known areas for prostitution. Coupling music and dance performances with prostitution has ancient roots in South Asia. Areas where the practice is centred, such as the Shahi Mohalla, have produced many well-known performing artists. These areas, quite different from the typical 'red light districts' in the west, have for centuries been hubs of creativity and nurturing environments for poets, singers, actors, and the *gurus*, musicians and composers of classical music. They also differ from the current trend of crude brothels increasingly found throughout Lahore and other Pakistani cities. In traditional prostitution systems, certain ethnic groups undertake this occupation as their family business. The *Kanjar*, the ethnic group most commonly associated with prostitution, have been involved for centuries. The *Mirasi*, another ethnic group, do not work directly in prostitution, but provide music for the *Kanjars* when they entertain their customers. Several ethnic groups throughout South Asia have these professions as their traditional family heritage; *Kanjars* and *Mirasi* are the typical ones in Pakistan.

To gather the information needed for this research I used the ethnographic methods of anthropologists to chronicle the lives of the Shahi Mohalla inhabitants. I interviewed over two hundred people from many walks of life, all connected, in one way or another, to the profession of prostitution. This background work enabled me to describe the socialization of prostitutes, their traditions, their business and its subtle complications. I also came to know the power dynamics of a household of prostitutes where a woman is the head, where the birth of a girl is celebrated, and where the birth of a boy brings sorrow.

Ethnographies are also useful for taking one aspect of a society as a window into the larger system. Here I have not only analysed the phenomenon of prostitution, but through it have looked at Pakistani society and its gender roles. I began this research in an effort to help Pakistani women understand themselves better. I felt that a straight academic treatment of this subject would not be a good way to achieve this objective. Therefore, I am employing a narrative format that enables the book to provide a picture of the lives of those who live in the Shahi Mohalla and breaks the myths propagated in our society. I show these people as they are—hard working or lazy, good or bad, helpless or powerful, talented or incompetent, with their own sets of sorrows and achievements, problems and challenges, wishes and aspirations. My research reveals them as human beings who struggle to make a living without a clear sense of where they fit in the larger picture of Pakistani society.

I observed and interacted with many of these people over a ten-year period. Through all this work, my own understanding of the issues became clearer and throughout the book I have addressed my own process of education on the subject. A critical aspect of feminist research is to make the researcher visible. In

*Feminism and Methodology*, the editor, Sandra Harding, wrote:

> The best feminist analysis goes beyond the innovations in subject matter in a crucial way: it insists that the inquirer her/himself be placed in the same critical plane as the overt subject matter, thereby recovering the entire research process for scrutiny in the results of research.

Thus, the urge to uncover the basis of the social taboo against women dancing in public became for me an entry point into a journey of discovery, full of surprises and insights. Interestingly, it helped bring to light the most fundamental concepts of gender power relationships in our society and contributed to my understanding of the role of patriarchy in shaping every one of those relationships.

I have attempted to use the study findings to develop a holistic understanding of the sub-culture. These findings are reported back in the stories of the people themselves. The data that were collected over the years are embedded in the stories selected for this book. Thus, some of the characters presented are composites of the area's most representative individuals; through their lives and words is the sub-culture revealed. Some people's names have been changed for their own protection, but all the other information about Shahi Mohalla is true.

All of the original research was conducted using the Punjabi language along with some Urdu. Some of these original words and phrases remain in the text to lend special meaning or where no easy English equivalent exists. A glossary is provided for those unfamiliar with these terms.

Unlike many professionals who prefer to use the term 'commercial sex worker', I chose to use the word 'prostitute' in my study. I think 'sex workers' is too limited a term for these women as they have a rich sub-culture of tradition and art and they have been trained from an early age to provide more than just sex. In the same manner, 'commercial sex worker' would be too limiting a term to replace the Japanese term, *geisha*. However, there is no all-inclusive local term that I could have selected. The local language words used by the women themselves are different for each category of prostitute. The most common words they use amongst themselves are *tawaif*, *Kanjari* and *gashtee*. Others in Pakistani society use polite terms such as *tawaif*, which actually only means a high level prostitute dealing with one or a few customers, but can be used more broadly, and *nachne wali*, for all those who use music for their business. I use 'prostitute' in my book as the term for all classes of women engaged in the sex trade in Shahi Mohalla. The term 'sex worker' might be more applicable to those women who work in brothels or on the streets and only provide sexual services. It might also be more applicable to the western system of prostitution where their role is generally limited to providing sex. In the end, however, my book is about eliminating the social stigma associated with women in this profession. In order to do so, we will have to do more than worry about the political correctness of our semantics.

# Acknowledgements

I would like to acknowledge and thank some important people without whom it would have been difficult for me to complete this book. Words seem too limited to express my gratitude to them.

First I must acknowledge the people of Shahi Mohalla, who opened their homes and lives to me and vested their trust in me. It was only their generosity that made it possible for me to open up their world to others. Due to confidentiality I cannot mention their names individually but would, however, mention *Ustad* Mohammad Sadiq and Mehmud Kanjar Sahib, who specifically allowed me to use their real names in the book, for their help and generosity.

My parents, Saeed Ahmad and Farhat Saeed, allowed me to work on such a tabooed topic, and supported and encouraged me throughout the many years of my research. I am fortunate to have parents who are liberal, and for whom their children's learning and happiness is a high priority. My brother, Dr Kamran Ahmad and niece Sadaf Ahmad gave me substantive comments and encouragement. My sister Maliha actively supported me and prayed for my safety.

Paul Lundberg, my husband and best friend, made his biggest contribution to this book by encouraging me to switch my style from a purely academic one to a more informal one, one that was geared towards a broad based readership. He was a friend and partner throughout the writing process, a sounding board for my ideas. He lifted my spirits, and offered me bowls of chocolate ice cream whenever I was too tired to go on.

Many professionals in the field of culture and other friends gave me feedback and offered comments on the manuscript. My friend Yasser Nomann, not only gave me his expert views on the musical aspects, but also supported me actively through all stages of the book.

Mr I.A. Rehman, believed in my capability to do this research study and continuously pushed me to complete this project over the last several years. He has been important in this process for me from the very beginning and is familiar with all the hardships I faced. He was always there to give me advice whenever I would face a dead end.

My friend, John Krignen, from Swiss Intercorporation, arranged travel funds at the last stage of my data collection, when my personal resources had totally depleted.

Sajid Munir, caught the essence of the Mohalla through his photographs allowing me to concentrate on the unseen details in their social system.

# Glossary

| | |
|---|---|
| *aam* wood | wood of mango tree |
| *achut* | untouchable |
| *affis* | office; performance room of a prostitute, also called *kotha* |
| *afsane* | short stories |
| *alaap* | the beginning of a musical piece, where a musician or a singer sets the parameters of the classical *raga* to be performed |
| *ami* | mother |
| *andrun sheher* | old city |
| *annas* | currency |
| *baithak* | sitting area, for musicians it means living quarters |
| *baji* | addressing elder sister |
| *basant* | kite flying festival; spring |
| *bazaar* | market place. Also used for the red light area, as it is a market of certain services |
| *beta* | addressing a son |
| *beti* | addressing a daughter |
| *bhairvin, bhairo* | ragas of classical South Asian music |
| *bibi* | respectful way of addressing a woman |
| *bindia* | a dot/mark worn on the forehead by Indian or sometimes other South Asian women |
| *biradri* | community |
| *bithana* | to make one sit, implying sexual services (verb) |
| *bongo* | small Cuban drums played in pairs by the fingers and thumbs. They consist of a hollowed out piece of wood with animal skin stretched over one end. Some are tunable, others are not |
| *bura kam* | bad deed, implying 'prostitution' |
| *chaddar* | a sheet of cloth to cover a woman or a bed. Also a decorated sheet of cloth used as offering to put on a grave or a shrine |
| *chakla* | whore house |
| *chandni* | white sheets covering the carpet or the floor |
| *charpai* | light weight portable bed/cot |
| *chat* | a popular spicy snack made of garbanzo beans |
| *chics* | traditional door or window coverings—woven bamboo strips |

| | |
|---|---|
| *chimta* | tongs |
| *chowk* | intersection of roads |
| *congo* | Afro-Cuban barrel drum, long and narrow in shape, played with fingers and palms. |
| *dafli* | tambourine |
| *dai* | traditional birth attendants |
| *dala* | pimp |
| *Data Sahib* | a well known mystic Sufi of South Asia |
| *deg* | big pots used for cooking food at the shrines or weddings |
| *desi* | local |
| *devadasi* | girls given away to a temple as religious servants of a god. This ritual was conducted as an offering to the temple. The girls in return got some share of the temple wealth/ properties |
| *devata* | god |
| *dhanda* | business or occupation. Sometimes used to refer to the occupation of prostitution |
| *dhol wala* | a musician who plays the traditional drum |
| *dholak* | a barrel shaped small drum, played at both ends with hands |
| *dhoti* | folk dress. Wrap-around skirt worn by both men and women in Punjab |
| *dil phaink* | one who easily falls in love |
| *domni* | women who earn their living by singing on the streets. An occupational ethnic cast |
| *dum* | capacity |
| *dupatta* | sheer fabric shawl, worn to cover head or draped over shoulders |
| *gashtee, gashtian* | low class prostitutes |
| *gharana* | family or school of learning in South Asian classical music with a distinct style of singing. |
| *ghazals* | a popular poetic form in Persian as well as Urdu literature. Also used for singing in South Asia and is now considered a most popular genre of light singing |
| *ghungroo* | ankle bells; worn by dancers, usually for a classical dance performance |
| *Haj* | Pilgrimage for Muslims undertaken in Mecca. This is one of the five pillars of Islam |
| *hamam* | public bath |
| *havelis* | large traditional-style houses |
| *iftar* | the time of day during the month of Ramzan when the fast should be broken |
| *jhalla* | a simple-minded person |
| *joras* | clothes |
| *kaam chor* | lazy |

| | |
|---|---|
| *Kanjar/s* | ethnic group/caste which undertakes prostitution as their traditional family occupation |
| *Kanjari/an* | female word for a *Kanjar*, *Kanjarian* is the plural |
| *karo kari* | a tribal tradition of Sindh province which allows both a woman and a man to be killed if they are suspected of adultery |
| *karwai* | action |
| *kathak* | a form of classical dancing |
| *kheer* | rice pudding; a desert |
| *khokha* | small shop on a side-walk or in a park. It usually has a temporary structure and sells snacks and drinks |
| *khusa* | traditional leather shoes with embroidery |
| *koka* | nose stud |
| *kotha* | performing room for a dancer |
| *kothi khanas* | brothels run by pimps |
| *kunda/e* | food cooked as a religious ritual by Shia families |
| *kurta* | loose long shirt |
| *Lahori/s* | born or brought up in Lahore |
| *lehria* | a simple arrangement of keys on a 16 beat cycle |
| *malika-e-ghazal* | queen of *ghazal* singing |
| *malika-e-taranum* | queen of melody |
| *malmal* | sheer cotton fabric |
| *manat* | offering promised to the divine in return of a wish |
| *mehfil* | an eastern-style music gathering |
| *melas* | festivals |
| *Meraj sharif* | religious day. Prophet Mohammed (PBUH) is said to have ascended to heaven on this day. His spiritual experience is celebrated every year |
| *Mirasi* | occupational ethnic group/caste of musicians |
| *miti khani* | mud eaters; prostitutes of the lowest class |
| *mot ka kuan* | *lit.* death well; a fragile wooden well-like structure, with a motor bike running on the vertical walls. Used in circus or folk entertainment shows |
| *moti asami* | rich guys; big catch |
| *Muharrum* | first month of the Islamic lunar calendar. It is also a month of mourning because of a sad historic war in which Hazrat Imam Hussain (RA) (grandson of Prophet Mohammed [PBUH]) was martyred |
| *mujra* | dance performance for an audience/customers by a courtesan or a prostitute |
| *mulazmat* | employment. This was used to refer to a long-term relationship of a courtesan with a customer in return for a monthly stipend |

| | |
|---|---|
| *Multani kafi* | a form of mystic poetry written in the Siraiki language |
| *nachne wali* | the woman who dances |
| *nai* | barbers; occupational ethnic group/caste |
| *naika* | the madam; head of a *Kanjar* household and the manager of the prostitution business |
| *nal* | an elongated drum with skin on both sides, played with hands |
| *nasur* | festering sore |
| *nath utarwai* | taking off the nose ring; de-flowering the virgin |
| *nautch* girls | the dancing girls; a term coined by the British rulers of the subcontinent |
| *Nawab* | title given to a rich landlord or a ruler of an estate |
| *niaz* | religious offering |
| *nikah* | contract of marriage and exchange of vows under the Muslim tradition |
| *pagri* | bribe taken for a specific employment position |
| *pah* | elder brother |
| *paia, paias, paie* | curry made of hooves of cow or goat, a specialty for breakfast |
| *paindu* | a derogatory word for a village person living in a town |
| *pakki seheli* | close female friend |
| *pakorey* | gram flour puffs, a popular snack |
| *paan* | betel leaf |
| *paandan* | container for the betel leaves |
| *parchian* | pieces of paper used for writing messages |
| *parsa* | chaste |
| *Pathan* | A larger tribal ethnic group from the northern part of Pakistan |
| *phitkari* | alum, a double sulfate of aluminum and potassium |
| *piri* | low stool, a part of the traditional furniture |
| *paisas* | Pakistani coins, one hundred paisas to a rupee |
| *pishwaz* | a traditional dress, popular in the times of Mughals. In present times it is worn mostly at formal occasions by dancers for a performance |
| *post-its* | a brand name for small stick-on message slips |
| *puja* | worship |
| *quam* | people with common background |
| *Ramazan* | lunar month of fasting for Muslims |
| *rickshaw* | three wheeler used for public transport |
| *sahib* | Mr. - to address a gentleman |
| *sahiba* | Ms. - to address a lady |
| *salaam* | Muslim greetings |
| *sangat* | accompaniment |
| *semsem* | Sesame, the legendary door in Ali Baba's story |

| | |
|---|---|
| *seth* | a rich gentleman |
| *Shab-e-Barat* | religious day for Muslims. Night of 15th Shaban (8th lunar month) |
| *shadi* | marriage, also used for contracts made between prostitutes and their customers |
| *Shahi Mohalla* | Red Light District of the city of Lahore |
| *shalwar kamiz* | traditional Pakistani dress, loose pants and long shirt |
| *Sham Chaurasi* | A family/school known for a specific style of singing classicial music |
| *sharif* | chaste |
| *sheesham* | rosewood |
| *Shia* | a sect of Islam |
| *shurafa* | nobility, chaste people |
| *sia kari* | a tribal tradition of Baluchistan province which allows both a woman and a man to be killed if they are suspected of adultery |
| *sitar* | one of the most popular string instruments of sub-continental classical music. It is played with a steel plectrum |
| *surma* | antimony |
| *tabaruk* | blessed food |
| *tabla* | a rhythm musical instrument; a pair of kettle drums played by fingers and palms. An essential part of South Asian classical music |
| *tali* | wood |
| *tanpura* | a musical instrument with four strings, used for accompanying a singer or other musical instruments. |
| *thumri* | a genre of semi-classical singing |
| *tawaif* | courtesan, quite high in the hierarchy of prostitutes |
| *Urdu* | language of many Muslim States in the subcontinent and Pakistan's national language |
| *usher* | one-tenth; a tax payable on agricultural produce according to Islamic jurisprudence |
| *ustad* | teacher of a higher rank |
| *vail* | money given away to an artist |
| *wadera* | feudal |
| *wala/wale* | belonging to or from (a city, a field of study or a specific group) |
| *walaikum salaam* | response to the common Islamic greeting |
| *walima* | the wedding reception given by the groom after bringing the bride home |
| *yar* | friend; can be used as a derogatory term |

| | |
|---|---|
| *yazid* | a historic personality who betrayed the grandson of the Prophet (PBUH) and killed him. His name is used as a symbol of a cruel enemy |
| *zakat* | according to the Islamic jurisprudence, the obligatory tax on a Muslim's wealth, which is paid to provide for the poor and destitute |
| *ziarat of Hazrat Ali (RA)* | a religious procession for the Prophet's (PBUH) son-in-law, Ali |
| *Ziaul Haq* | the military dictator who headed Pakistan for eleven years, from 1977 to 1988 |

# 1

## SHIFTING THE FOCUS

I had just finished fourteen months of fieldwork, logging thousands of kilometres on my old Toyota in the process. During that time, I met countless inhabitants of the Shahi Mohalla in Lahore, taped many hours of conversations, engaged in some confrontations with the police, and ended up with four slashed tyres; yet I was still full of unanswered questions. I was desperate to talk to someone who could help me understand how the traditional system of prostitution in Lahore relates to our society. Fortunately, on returning to Islamabad I had a message to call Amjad Shah, who is a senior police officer in Islamabad and a personal friend. He invited me to his house to discuss the progress of my study and my findings. He was also more than a little worried about me and wanted to know if I was okay.

Despite our friendship, I had rarely seen him out of uniform, but here he was wearing a *shalwar kamiz*. His living room was decorated tastefully in a contemporary style. I exchanged greetings with him and his wife, Sadiqa, who was a shadow-being, bringing tea and delicious snacks for guests, persuading them to eat more, then quietly exiting before the discussions began.

As we sat down in the living room, Amjad said, 'I understand that the police have been quite resistant to your research.'

I answered that I had experienced resistance not only from the police, but also from the Ministry of Culture, whose attitude toward my studying the red light district of Lahore was very negative. I mentioned as well another, less direct, kind of resistance—the subtle social disapproval of a middle class woman getting involved with such topics. Hardly anyone encouraged me to continue my research, so strong was the taboo associated with the area and the profession. On the other hand, there was also a scandalous anticipation, as if hoping I might come up with some juicy stories.

I asked him what he thought of the secrecy surrounding the Mohalla, and why it was so difficult to find out anything about that place. I tried several public offices and had tried to contact the police, but apparently no one wanted to have anything to do with research that could uncover anything about the area.

'Why this mystery, creating such a romantic, yet frightening and repulsive image?' I asked.

'You are stepping on many people's toes', he replied. 'I told you that before.'

'No, it's more than that. The reaction is almost instinctive.'

'Instinctive?' he sounded surprised, 'do you mean that people hate prostitution biologically?'

'No, by "almost instinctive" I mean that when something is so deeply socialized, generation after generation, one forgets that it is a socialized value and not natural behaviour. It becomes part of the psyche on a very deep level, acted on without thinking. Most of our gender roles are like that,' I tried to explain.

He became serious and said, 'The place is taboo, so what do you expect? Sure, people are socialized to fear it.'

'Not everyone! It's just the general impression that is maintained. After all, many people from this society like the Mohalla enough to visit it regularly as clients. My point is that society tries its best to hold on to certain myths it has created about the Shahi Mohalla. Through these myths we maintain the mystery, keeping a desirable distance from the Mohalla ourselves while we keep the focus on "those bad people" in the business and, most importantly, protect those whom the prostitutes serve.'

Amjad Shah picked up a pipe from a table next to him and lighted it. He sank back in his chair and asked, 'What myths?'

'Let me use rape as an example', I said, 'this is just an example. I'm not saying that prostitution is rape. Do we agree that society totally condemns rape?'

Amjad nodded, 'Yes, of course!'

'At the same time, however, we often instinctively defend the rapist, by evoking certain myths: It is always the woman's fault. She must have dressed wrong. She must have given the wrong signals. We create myths about the rapists, too. Only crazy people commit rape; they can't be normal. We call it a crime of passion, caused by sexual suppression and frustration. Really, it's now well established that rape has little to do with sex, but is a crime of power. After the act, another set of myths comes into play: Nobody can marry the victim. She becomes *daghi*, stained. Even the term used for rape means losing respect, and it is the woman who suffers and not the rapist. His respect remains fully intact.

'All these myths allow society to keep the woman in the limelight and the abuser in the background, letting him get away with it. We often excuse the rapist in this country. It is part of our heritage to think, "So what? After all, he's young!" We excuse the man while the woman is shamed. She is stigmatised. Even when big political leaders show sympathy and intent to deal with the crime, the woman's head is covered and she is the one on the television news before the whole country, not the rapist.'

'Okay,' Amjad said, 'you're arguing that by focusing on the victim, we are lenient on the abuser. But now make your connection with prostitution. How is the prostitute a victim in the same way as a woman who has been raped?'

'Society uses a similar process. Myths are created about the Shahi Mohalla and red light districts in general, and demystification is totally resisted. The focus is on "those bad people", the prostitutes and their managers. Stories constantly reinforce the idea that they are bad. Another myth is that women who are alone or "without a man" are easy prey for these evil influences and will end up in red light districts. Once there, they can never escape. The larger society will never accept a prostitute in any other role. You've heard all this,' I said, 'it's part of the cultural wisdom we inherit, reinforced in movies, literature and in many other ways, over and over.'

Taking a long deep breath, Amjad answered, 'What if I say that this distance is important. I don't want my daughter to learn too much about that area. This fear at least keeps her away.'

'But what about your son?' I asked. 'Doesn't he need to be scared even more? That's my point. We totally ignore that the people working in prostitution are only part of the phenomenon. The clientele, who are really more important, are not considered. Society protects them. We have to shift the focus onto them now. They are all around us and we don't know them. At the Mohalla, the police protect the customers and harass the prostitutes. I don't mean just the customers who visit between eleven and one at night. I mean the real customers, those who keep prostitution alive. I'll tell you scores of myths about the prostitutes if you tell me just three good ones about the customers!'

Amjad Shah smiled and I continued, 'We have a well known saying that a woman has four potential roles: mother, wife, sister or prostitute. A prostitute who dreams of taking any of the other roles gets nothing but pain. In our culture, being a prostitute has become a completely separate category of existence.'

'There has to be some truth in it,' he replied hesitantly, 'I don't say they can't be absorbed in the society, but...'

'Do they grow on trees?' I interrupted. 'Aren't they also mothers, daughters, sisters?'

'Oh yes, I suppose they are, among themselves,' he said, 'but...'

'We try to portray them as strange beings. But you know better than me how many bright young women from Lahore's educated circles are prostitutes in their spare time? This call-girl phenomenon is spreading and no one knows how widespread it has become. There are no airtight groups. It's a big grey area. I'm studying only traditional prostitution in the Mohalla. Even so, some of the girls who live in Gulberg come to the Mohalla regularly in their cars, unlock their shops, do their traditional dance performance, the *mujra*, for two hours between eleven and one at night and drive back home.'

Amjad kept smoking his pipe and staring into space.

I continued, 'What about the myth that if a woman goes to the Mohalla, the residents would force her into prostitution? Do people know that many women who live in this bazaar have nothing to do with prostitution? Many shopkeepers' families live there. The wives are not prostitutes. Even within the *Kanjar biradri*, daughters-in-law never work, and some daughters of the *Kanjar* household also choose not to go into prostitution.'

'Okay, so if we dispel these myths...then what?' he asked.

'I was going into the reality behind the myths just to prove that they are only myths. My point is that we must recognize that by generating and maintaining the myths and resisting anyone from uncovering the truth, we keep the focus only on the community that provides the prostitution services. We have to include the other side to get a full picture of the issue,' I said.

Raising one eyebrow, Amjad looked at me and asked, 'Which is...?'

'The rest of the society! The focus should be on us! Who do the prostitutes serve? Who has a stake in their activities? What function has society entrusted to them? Do we really want to deal with it? Do we want to know about it? Do we want to start an open debate on it? Do we want to analyse it? Or do we want to continue in denial, blaming those other, mysterious people out there in the Mohalla for being so "bad" and corrupting our men?'

'I'm not sure I buy your argument,' he looked sideways out the window.

'Well, why this secrecy and resistance? Why this fear of the topic? Might we uncover our own contradictions and hypocrisy? Don't tell me that you also think we should continue pretending that prostitution doesn't exist in this country.'

'I'll have to think more about it', he answered.

I raised my voice, 'You tell me. If we are really against prostitution what is the harm in finding out the truth about the business dynamics? Who gets recruited? Who is forced into the profession? Who makes the money? Who provides the protection? Anyone wanting to get rid of this so-called *"nasur"* of our society better start learning more about it. Understanding is a first step in demystifying the prostitutes. Once people find out they are just like us—powerful, helpless, happy, sad, surviving in these hard times, making the best of what they have, loving, manipulating, laughing, praying, honest, competitive, caring, the same as anyone else, then maybe we can begin looking at ourselves, at the larger society.'

Sadiqa, Amjad's wife, intervened, 'Let's go out in the lawn. I've put tea there.'

'You really believe we created them?' he asked, as I was walking outside with his wife.

I turned around and said, 'We can't ignore that historically they fulfilled a specified function in the larger society. There is so much evidence. The *Kanjar* are a large, clan-like occupational "caste". Do you know what that means, Amjad? It means that for generations most women working as traditional prostitutes in places like the Shahi Mohalla have been born into it. From birth they have been socialized to be prostitutes. It is not that they were immoral young women who wanted to do this work or impoverished little girls sold off by their parents.'

His wife took my arm and pulled me towards her. We walked out and sat around the tea table. I began again, 'Like any other occupational group, *Kanjar* by birth were given the occupation of prostitution, the same as barbers, butchers, leather workers and ironsmiths. The old feudal system defined the social hierarchy to ensure that people were available to perform all necessary functions and that those in control could rely on them to provide the services and maintain the status quo. In India, there are many studies that identify castes or ethnic groups who were taught only the family profession—prostitution. People were born into it and they had their own standing in the community like the other specialized groups. How can we fail to look at them in the larger perspective?'

Sadiqa, tired of our conversation, interrupted, 'Stop it, please! Have tea and snacks now and talk about something pleasant.'

I smiled and started talking to her about her family. For the rest of the evening Amjad Shah remained quiet; playing with his moustache and staring into space.

# 2

# THE SHAHI MOHALLA DURING THE DAY...AND NIGHT

I first visited the Shahi Mohalla about eight months before I formally started my research. That trip inspired my study. My boss, Uxi Mufti, the executive director of Lok Virsa (The Institute of Folk and Traditional Heritage) in Islamabad invited me to accompany him and two of his friends, a heart specialist from Islamabad and a businessman from Rawalpindi. All three were serious photographers. My visit to Lahore was primarily for the annual *Basant* Festival, to purchase kites for the Lok Virsa museum. The men wanted to photograph the old city of Lahore, where the festival is held.

Going from one area to another looking for elaborate kites, I was told at one point that we were in the famous Shahi Mohalla. Surprised, I looked around, but felt the same as if I was in any of old Lahore's other bazaars. The narrow streets, the architecture, crowds of pedestrians and children running around among three-wheeled rickshaws, bicycles and horse carts seemed no different from the other bazaars. Nor did the attitude of the men in the bazaar towards me differ from anywhere else. I did notice that every time we stopped in the street to ask for an address or any other information, a crowd of spectators gathered around us within seconds, but this might also have been true in the other bazaars. In general, as a woman, it was as comfortable to walk around these streets as elsewhere in the old city.

That evening my companions talked about going back to the Shahi Mohalla. I asked to go along to see about formally exploring it as a possible area for my research. Everyone agreed, and the four of us returned to the bazaar.

The environment of the Shahi Mohalla at night was quite different from what we saw during the day. It was more crowded, and there were mostly men in the streets. It was alive, with well-lit shops and little boys running around selling flowers and *paan*. Like everyone else, we started out on foot. The 20 ft wide streets were big enough for all the pedestrians. A few cars occasionally cruised the streets, but the heavy afternoon traffic was gone. I noticed that the ground floor rooms of the buildings were, oddly, about 3-4 ft above street level, and directly approachable by a short flight of steps. Sometimes the steps led to a platform or a short sidewalk running in front of a row of such houses.

As we strolled down the streets we saw well-dressed women in these rooms, looking as if they were sitting in their living rooms, without the front walls, however. These rooms had wide open doors, covered either by a sheer curtain of cloth or woven bamboo. As they were well lighted, the rooms' interiors could be easily seen. Most women sat on the floor in the middle of their room, and a few sat on sofas. In some rooms, musicians were lined up behind the women. Most of the women wore *shalwar kamiz* made of silk. Women in one 'shop' were much more exotically dressed in long gowns and Middle Eastern headgear—golden caps hung with strands of beads. They looked like they'd walked off a movie set.

Higher up, heavily made-up women wearing bright clothes bent over their balconies. Their shops were on the next floor of the buildings and they would peep out, smile, and point at men strolling on the street, trying to get their attention before disappearing back into their rooms.

These rooms, on both floors, were like shop display windows with living merchandise. The customers took their time, looking carefully into each window. The names of the area went around in my mind, *Bazaar-e-Husn* (the market of beauty), and *Heera Mandi* (the market of diamonds). It really was a market, with the product fully displayed and the customers wandering about deciding what to buy.

Small boys and a few men moved about in the crowd providing change in one, five and ten rupee notes. They provided this service so the customers could shower money on the dancers—an old traditional way to show appreciation for a dance or a song.

I recognized that the rooms were, in fact, *kotha*, from their depiction in so many South Asian films. In films, a customer often mounts a flight of stairs into such a room to watch a dance performance. The word *kotha* literally means the upper storey. In Punjabi, it can also refer to the rooftop, a multipurpose living space, or even simply a mud house.

We were in town for the *Basant* Festival and I probably appeared somewhat dressed up. Many men on the street apparently assumed I was a local woman who had left her room to walk around. The customers scanned me from head to toe, but no one touched me or tried to harass me. All three of my male companions walked close to me, protectively. After a while I felt quite comfortable and experienced a sensation of openness that is hard to explain.

We selected a room where two women were sitting. I was attracted to them because of their *ghungroo*. This meant that they were dancers, not just singers. Interested in dance myself, I wanted to see a dance performance. As we entered the room, the two women stood up and greeted us in a very hospitable manner. A young boy quickly shut the large, folding doors behind us. My friends told me that the practice is to entertain one customer (or one 'party') at a time to avoid any conflict between the customers during the performance.

The room was carpeted, with a *chandni* spread out on the carpet and tube pillows on the sides. Three musicians, playing the *tabla*, harmonium and *dholak* were seated inside, along with an older woman and a small boy of about twelve. The room was about 12 x 15 ft in size.

Uxi Mufti satisfied the curiosity of those in the room about seeing a woman with the customers by saying that I had come

Covered balconies of the Shahi Mohalla buildings

Quiet *kothas*, closed doors, ready to be transformed at night

1

The transformation of Shahi Mohalla at night attracts pleasure seekers

The *affis* time begins: all dressed up in *shalwar* and *kamiz,* waiting for the customers.

Providing small bills for customers, this local boy earns a reasonable commission

Selling flower garlands is one of the several supporting jobs that a *kotha* generates

3

Brightly lit balconies, with dancers inviting customers up their *kothas*

Restaurants are open all night to serve the customers of this *bazaar*

4

from the United States and wanted to see the dancing. After we sat down we were offered tea which we refused. We were asked what we wanted to hear—'*Ki suno ge?*' One of my companions replied, 'Anything in Punjabi'. The women began to sing a Punjabi song and danced to the music played by the musicians.

Their voices were coarse and they sang a Punjabi film song quite crudely. The music was loud and both dancers made a lot of noise with their *ghungroo*. They danced in the typical film style, with overt sexual gestures. Both dancers focused on one member of the audience at a time. They stared straight into his eyes and made seductive gestures that were obviously devoid of any feeling. The dancers kept at it until they got *vail* from the person. Then they switched to another. They noticed that when they came near me and focused their gestures on me, the others all gave them *vail* on my behalf. Astute professionals that they were, they repeated this manoeuvre again and again to get as much money as possible in the shortest possible time. I realized this was part of their art. After all, other potential customers were out on the street and their time was precious. In a very proficient manner, they quickly dried up our resources and managed to move us out smoothly.

We had made a tactical mistake by sending the little boy for change after we sat down. This let our hosts know how much money we planned to spend on them. We had only changed five hundred rupees and we did not seem to be regular customers who would seek other services after the performance. Thus, after we had given away a little over five hundred rupees, the dancers said they had received some guests in the other room and really had to go and said good-bye. When I said I wanted to talk to them, they told me their names and said they would tell me whatever I wanted to know if I visited them during the day, not during their 'office hours'. The government allows them to perform only from eleven to one at night, so these are called their 'office hours' and the *kotha* is referred to as an *affis* (office). They did not want to waste time on people who were not real customers, but just tourists.

I immediately decided to explore this phenomenon and look into the lives of these women who form such a contradictory, unacceptable, and yet such a permanent part of our society. I designed a proposal for a descriptive study of the Shahi Mohalla, for exploring different aspects of the area. The Shahi Mohalla has become something of a myth for the rest of our society, and represents an extreme example of women as a commodity whose role is to provide pleasure for men. However, I wanted to conduct my study objectively, without any negative bias or pre-judged moral stance.

My interest in this area stems from two aspects of my own background and training. I wanted to learn about the cultural side, to document the musical traditions and the relationship of the area with the performing arts of our society. I also wanted to use a feminist perspective to help understand the women who worked as prostitutes and in the related business. With these intentions I submitted my research proposal to my institute.

Before I could really get started, I ran straight into a bureaucratic brick wall that I did not even know existed.

# 3

# A PH.D. GIRL IN THE RED LIGHT AREA

Of all the adverse reactions I experienced and all the hurdles people placed before me while I was conducting my research, one day stands out most clearly. The Secretary of the Ministry of Culture, about to dismiss me from my job with the Government of Pakistan, had summoned me to defend myself. The Ministry had learned of my study of Lahore's red light district, the infamous Shahi Mohalla, and the senior bureaucrats were furious. I couldn't believe that my seemingly benign research topic had so shaken the government bureaucracy, but apparently they could not tolerate a female government officer going to such a tabooed area, especially if she intended to write about it. They must have feared possible political repercussions. I never imagined the magnitude of the reaction and had no idea that any senior officials could have a stake in my study.

I got out of the official car Lok Virsa had provided and looked at the tall buildings around me. I was in the Secretariat in Islamabad, the nerve centre of the Government of Pakistan located in a quiet corner of the city that most Pakistanis never see. I had been working for over a year at Lok Virsa, an agency attached to the Ministry of Culture. I lived and worked in Islamabad, but had not been to this area before. I entered one of the buildings with a huge stack of files in my hands and a tote bag full of documents on my shoulder. I asked the security guard whether I was in the right ministry. Looking curiously at my load of papers, he nodded and told me the elevator was out of order and that I'd have to take the stairs. A smile flickered under his heavy black moustache. Mounting the stairs, flanked by cold, bare marble walls, I became increasingly uncomfortable. I was angry and disappointed, but somehow, still believed that I could explain the situation to the Secretary.

I was a Deputy Director for Research at Lok Virsa, an institute that documents Pakistan's traditional culture—the material artifacts, musical traditions, tales, legends and other aspects of folklore. A few months earlier I had submitted two research proposals as part of my section's annual work plan. I proposed exploring Pakistan's traditional performing arts and particularly its connection with women's roles in Pakistani society as this has always intrigued me.

The first proposal was related to traditional semi-nomadic theatre groups that travelled from village to village providing entertainment to the local populations and specifically the role of women in Folk Theatre. I also wanted to explore the origins of the singers and musicians Lok Virsa takes such great pains to record. Thus, my second study proposed to describe the performing arts of Lahore's Shahi Mohalla, home to many of the popular performing artists of Pakistan.

Until recent times the South Asian notion of red light districts has been somewhat different from most other countries. The arts of music, song and dance are closely entwined with the profession of prostitution. These areas have deep roots in South Asia's traditional culture. Over the centuries, they have enjoyed a well-defined position in society; equally renowned for their arts as well as for sexual services. Throughout the region, these areas have been the most fertile sources for producing new performing artists.

Both these proposals were scrutinized by my colleagues and Lok Virsa's executive director. The director recalled that it was he who had first taken me to the Shahi Mohalla a few months earlier. After asking me several questions about my research methods, the sample frame and time period, he concluded that the study would be a good addition to the Institute's knowledge base and encouraged me to submit a formal research proposal.

However, a few weeks after submitting my proposal, my immediate supervisor informed me that out of our entire proposed work plan, the Ministry had rejected only my Shahi Mohalla proposal. I was very surprised. Although new in the Institute, I'd been told that the Ministry didn't interfere with Lok Virsa's programmes, and that the executive director was solely responsible for designing and carrying out the programmes. No one in the Institute could, or would, officially answer my questions about why my proposal had been rejected. I only heard a few remarks made jokingly about its rejection during tea breaks.

Many of my colleagues—all men—took their breaks at a nearby *khokha*, surrounded by large trees and lush green foliage. This was often the most creative time of our day when, amid roars of laughter, new ideas for video productions and research projects were developed and discussed, performances for archival documentation were planned, and partnerships were established. It was in those informal sessions that I learned my study had been rejected because it hit too close to home. The bureaucrats were nervous. 'Why?' I asked, innocently, 'When artists from the Mohalla come to Lok Virsa they are praised to the sky.'

At the time, Lok Virsa was video recording a series entitled 'The Great Masters in Pakistani Music'. I was very pleased to be a part of this work, which involved in-depth interviews of the musicians, as it provided invaluable information about their art, training, performance, family background and many other significant aspects of their lives. Through these interviews, I learned that most of the master musicians were, in one way or another, linked to the Shahi Mohalla. I wanted to contribute to what we were learning by further researching the area and their interaction with other performers living there.

Lok Virsa typically organizes a lavish evening event for each singer and musician who is to be recorded. Often the artists produce impressive performances during these sessions and are decked with garlands and given tributes for their contribution to Pakistani music. I had attended many of these sessions long before I joined the Institute. Now, the mention of the Shahi Mohalla, where most of these artists were born or groomed, seemingly scared the bureaucrats. I argued with my friends and colleagues about this sanctimonious attitude. Why could not the place that produced these artists be acknowledged? The social taboos associated with the area made some sense since people generally connected the Mohalla with prostitution more than with music. But I persisted, how can a cultural institute that works to preserve the heritage of all Pakistani artists and promotes traditional music refuse to acknowledge that the country's Shahi Mohallas are also fertile grounds for producing musicians and singers? Did they fear I would uncover secret links between the Mohalla and the State? Refusing to submit to the hypocrisy, I decided to pursue the research on my own, without Institute funding or support.

The Ministry had approved my research proposal for the study of Folk Theatre so I began my research in Lahore, about 300 kilometres from Islamabad. I told my director that while working there, I would also begin making contacts and identifying some informants for my study on the Mohalla. I told him I planned to do that research later, on a strictly personal basis.

I set off on a short trip to set the stage for my study of women in Folk Theatre. While identifying my key theatre informants, I found that many of them also had close links to the Shahi Mohalla and I visited some of them there. One day, soon after returning from Lahore, a group of reporters from the popular English language newspaper, *Pakistan Observer*, appeared in my office. They had heard about my most recent expedition to the Shahi Mohalla and were quite intrigued by the topic. They asked me questions and I answered happily, not knowing that being open and straightforward was the last thing one should do with the press when working in a bureaucracy. Everything should be said in such a roundabout way so that it not only sounds meaningless, but also does not backfire on you. Moreover, I didn't know that government workers were not supposed to even talk to journalists directly. I should have first informed a senior colleague. As soon as I saw how excited the journalists were with the subject, I told them the study of the Mohalla was not an official Lok Virsa project, but something I was doing on my own. They quickly agreed to interview me in my personal capacity, and satisfied, I continued the interview as a professional researcher.

The next day, I was at home when my father came in looking intently at a newspaper he was carrying in his hand. He walked up to me with a puzzled look and asked, 'Is this you, my daughter?' Glancing at the paper I saw a big picture of myself on the front page under the banner headline: 'Ph.D. Girl in Red Light Area'. I was shocked by this kind of attention. My father looked again and again at the picture, his eyes widening each time. I laughed sheepishly and nodded, 'It seems that way.' He opened the paper and there I was again, in different poses captioned with highlighted quotes. The article covered an entire page. No reader could possibly miss it.

I quickly ran to my mother thinking I should tell her myself before she got the shock of her life. After I told my parents about the journalists coming to my office, they were satisfied, or at least I wanted to think so. Being quite liberal, they had come to expect impetuous things from me.

During a long talk with my parents later that evening I expressed my feelings about the Institute's hypocrisy. Although they both agreed on the importance of studying the Mohalla since most people knew about it only through myths and legends, they were at the same time concerned with how I would do it. Not only had they internalized the myth that any woman going there could be kidnapped and forced into prostitution, they were also afraid of the organized crime linked to the area. Little did they know that the greatest reaction against my going there would come not from pimps or gangsters, who are already labelled 'bad people', but from Pakistani society's 'good people', specifically the 'civilized and cultured' people in our national bureaucracy.

Before I had a chance to return to Lahore to continue data collection for the traditional theatre study, I learned that the newspaper article had created hell in the corridors of the

bureaucracy. To my dismay, the director threw the entire blame
on me. Many parallel political issues were revolving within the
Institute. I had recently returned from the USA after eight years
of university education; this was my first real job and my initial
encounter with the national bureaucracy. I had no clue about the
political implications of my actions. I knew only that I was
continuing my work on a personal basis and that no one had
told me to stop.

Not understanding the situation and obsessed by what
I thought of as groundbreaking work, I left for my second trip
to research folk theatre. I had to meet many theatre artists in
Lahore on this two week trip and needed to travel out of the city
to some of the Punjab's most remote villages, following a few
of the surviving folk theatre companies as they journeyed from
place to place. Typical folk theatre performances used to begin
at nine in the evening and continue until six in the morning.
Performed at *mela* and *mandi*, these were a major attraction for
people coming from neighbouring villages. Since they went on
all night, they were convenient places for people to stay before
heading back to their villages.

During this research trip, I also found that the theatre
companies hired women from the Shahi Mohalla because of the
perennial dearth of woman performers. As theatre audiences
had declined in recent years, the companies tried to attract
customers by using dancers from different red light districts to
perform during breaks in the plays.

When I returned to Islamabad I heard that my interest in
studying Lahore's Shahi Mohalla had led my superiors to
formally charge me with gross misconduct. A detailed case had
been fabricated so they could fire me, and I was accused of
using government resources on a research project that it had not
approved. I was very surprised since I had official approvals for
both the trips in my files. Some senior government officers had
apparently read the *Pakistan Observer* article and blamed the
Secretary of the Cultural Ministry for such a major blunder.
Later in my research I discovered that many politicians and
senior government officials have strong links with the Mohalla's

**Interlude** with AMBER MAJEED

# Dr Fouzia – Making waves at Lok Virsa

the rural areas.

These women need education more than anything else to break away from the social shackles that bind them to a life of drudgery and servience.

I thought the Allama Iqbal University was doing a tremendous job taking education to the doorstep of women in villages.

...tificate from a university, open up career op... for these girls. ...however, needs to ...icularly in de... ...ricula for new

...at my masters ...help me pre... illustrations ...e pertinent

...wishful ...of work ...liking. ...when I ...termas

bling through the corridor of power. The commotion only died down with the earth-shaking Ojheri camp disaster.

It must have taken more courage than that to have ventured into the dark alleys of the Shahi Mohalla.

...young girl taking lessons from Ustad Goga.

forced by their husbands or ...hers to take up this profes... for economic reasons.
...who's to blame? ...would be difficult to blame.

...you faced any ...in talking to

...lly. When I was in ...I did a lot of ...work with rape ...other area where I ...a lot of experi... ...working on cases ...violence.
...that a polite ...saying "wife.

...it is more than ...and more often ...abuse.
...veloped a very ...., where the ...in touch with ...notline and we ...by beepers.
...and counsellor ...o the victim's ...e husband would ...the precinct. A ...be brought to the ...in 48 hours, and ...uld be looked after ...usellor.

...was your role? ...a report on how ...uld improve their ...., And the most ...thing was that the ...ations of the report ...into practice right

...vas very heartening to ...th the police and see.

Can't the girls break away from the mohalla?

Social and cultural pressures are such that girls born into the profession stay in it. Mostly, it is the mothers who are keen for them to follow in their footsteps.

Other girls are often

Not much. ...used to me doi... And they are mo... standing, having ...and confidence in

What else doing these da...
I am doing re... Lok Theatre, which coming a dying trac...

I am also worl... biography of Bali J... the most famous Lo... ers in our country, ...me like a daughter ...helped me by briefin... Lok traditions.

In all, it is ...ous work that ye... undertaking. Wh... ...our greatest fear?

Girls have been ...to vanish without a trac... ...the mohalla. The sur... thing is that one has le... fear from the *badmas*... the bad guys – than fron... cops.

My greatest fear is th... I were to disappear one d... there could be no one acco... able.

We are certain th... our readers, who will ...eagerly following you... progress, will not allo... that to happen so eas... ily.

I sure by hope so. In any ...case, I am determined to carry ...on with my work.

We wish you luck, ...and do keep us posted. ...Thank you. Have a nice ...day.

**CRAFT IS KNOWLEDGE**

# h.D. girl in red light area

AMBER & FARHANA

...JA SAEED, who is doing ...ch in Lahore's infamous ...i Mohalla, has found a ...d of brutal cops, mafia ...e gangs and eight-year-old ...formers.

Dr Fouzia has just come ...ck to Islamabad after spend... ...20 days of preliminary in... ...rviews with the residentes ...and transients of Lahore's red ...light area as a part of a year... ...long programme to study the ..."exploitation of women in our ...society."

The Mohalla, which is ...made up of seven different ...bazars, is permitted by ...authorities to open from 11 ...m to 1 p.m. for dancing and ...singing.

"I have just broken through ...the crust," she says. "It will ...ske me about a year to com... ...plete the study which I then ...intend to publish".

Dr Fouzia is deputy director ...of research working under Dr ...adam Nayyar of the Lok Virsa ...Institute in Islamabad.

She is doing research work ...in the Shahi Mohalla on her ...own time and initiative" with ...on involvement of the Lok ...Virsa institute", even though ..."he mohalla is very much part ...of our cultural heritage.

Ninety per cent of our ..."musicians and 99 per cent of ..."ur actresses and TV perform... ...ors can trace their origins back ...o the mohalla," says Dr ...Fouzia.

When asked the names of

all the performers who started their careers from the mohalla, I was told it would be simpler to list those without any ties to this culturally fertile dis-trict," she says.

"And they could name only three," she adds with a know-ing smile but not naming names.

Dr Fouzia says she has found the people of the mo-halla to be very human with deep concerns for the welfare of each other.

"It is the cops who have an inhuman face," she adds.

"Horror stories of police brutality abound," she says. "Girls have less to fear from the pimps and panderers who manage their day-to-day af-fairs.

"I am currently investigat-ing one particularly griz... report of how a girl nabbed by the cops watching TV at her h... the mohalla," the say...

"The cops grab... stripped her naked her and paraded the teeming ba... to the police... They ar... one and ... person, any girl

living in the mohalla, includ-ing naikas (madames), gaikas (female signers), hejras (eunuches) and what she calls the 'management'.

"Prostitution is very much part of life in the mohalla probab... not survive witho... says.

"Often it is husbands of force them to ing, main... reasons", ...

Poverty ... exert thei... ways. "S... for as ... she ...

up ch...

sd Andila practises singing with Ustad Gulzar while her 13-year-old sister watches on.

An overview of the main *bazaar* of the Shahi Mohalla

A typical building houses more than seven families, with shops at the street level

Street cafes with outdoor kitchens

A fruit vendor

8

Streets of the Mohalla

9

Stable for white horses which are used for drawing decorated chariots for special customers

The main *bazaar* of the Shahi Mohalla with street side restaurants

Restaurant specializing in lamb curry

Personal parking spots for the residents

12

business but, at that time, I had no idea of this connection. The Secretary, Khawaja Shahid Hussain, in turn, blamed Uxi Mufti who quickly presented my head as an offering to the gods of the bureaucracy. I had been working in the Institute for only a year and a half and was considered quite dispensable.

However, firing a government employee without following proper procedures is not so easy. In order to get rid of me, fictitious letters were placed in my personnel files. The standard procedure is for a new employee to be on six months probation before being confirmed. Two letters were forged to show that my probation period had been extended twice, amounting to a total of eighteen months. The executive director could thus claim that, after a year and a half, I was still on probation and did not require an inquiry or the usual procedure before being fired.

This manipulation really opened my eyes. 'Welcome to the real world,' I said to myself, but part of me did not believe that such things could happen. I clung to the hope that no one could get away with such shoddy tricks, especially in the government! I thought that the misunderstanding would be rectified once the senior officers learned I was actually conducting another, approved study. I was still blissfully unaware that there were, in fact, no misunderstandings, but only lies, and fabrications. All this because mention of the Shahi Mohalla had rocked the boat and everyone in the chain of command feared losing their jobs.

My executive director could easily have given me a termination letter based on the fictitious letters placed in my file but, like a true bureaucrat, he wanted to cover his flanks. Therefore, he set up my meeting with the Secretary. It was just a token meeting, as I learned later, because the decision had already been taken. I was charged with using Lok Virsa resources on a study that the Ministry had disapproved, and thus my employment should be terminated. In fact, the modest 5000 rupees travel advance that I spent on travelling to villages for the Folk Theatre study had been deducted from my salary, without any notice, immediately after I returned from Lahore, but this was beside the point!

With all these thoughts swirling through my brain, I walked
up the stairs to the Secretary's office determined to explain the
entire matter to him. I brought with me field notes, photographs,
and audiotapes of interviews with theatre actors, managers and
directors from throughout the Punjab, as well as parts of my
draft analysis. The enormous pile was difficult to carry up the
stairs. After three flights I finally reached the Secretary's door.
Opening it, I found myself in a small and untidy anteroom,
crowded with clerks and the Secretary's personal assistant. I was
told to sit and wait. I waited so long that I began losing hope of
even a token meeting. The walls of that cluttered room held
only a calendar, a clock and some memos on a notice board.
Looking at them so many times made me feel sick. Having
people wait is another way for a bureaucrat to put them in their
proper place.

Over an hour later I was finally called in. The huge office
had an air of importance about it. At the farthest end was an
imposing desk with an elaborate chair behind it. The main
purpose of such a large desk must be to create a distance
between the Secretary and the person across from him. I was
surprised to see two other people in the room. They also had
some files, and the Secretary was deeply engaged in a
conversation with one of them, arguing about some financial
approval. The visitor responded by continuously repeating, 'Yes
sir. Yes sir. Yes sir...'

Giving me a brief look, the Secretary said sharply, 'Sit down,
*bibi*.'

I told myself as I sat down that I would be very frank, open
and oblivious to the other people if they stayed in the room.
I put the pile of documents on the Secretary's desk, along with
a bundle of photographs I had taken in the field with the
audiotapes on top of the pile. He finally turned towards me with
a questioning 'Yes?' I began quickly, 'I am a professional and
not a bureaucrat. I would like my work to speak for itself.'
I told him I could show him the work I did in Lahore and that
I intended to write a book on women in Folk Theatre. No one
had told him anything about my theatre study. He had heard

only that I went to study the Shahi Mohalla against the executive
director's instructions. I showed him the approvals of my travel
for this tour on the government files, and the approval of the
advance I received for the work on Folk Theatre. He was
confused, but since it was only a token meeting, he did not
really want to listen to me.

He was surprised by what I had brought, but he showed
complete disinterest in discovering the real issue. He was abrupt,
rude and interrupted me after every other sentence and then he
abruptly asked me to leave. When I asked if I should leave my
work for him to look at, he responded quickly, 'No, no, take it
away.'

Walking down the stairs I knew that he did not care about the
truth, whether or not I was on probation, whether or not the
government had approved my theatre study, or whether or not
my supervisor knew what I was doing. It didn't make a
difference. He wasn't interested in what I had to say. He and
my boss had already agreed to fire me. It was all connected to
the same fear that crops up whenever the Shahi Mohalla is
mentioned. Under no circumstances did they want to be
associated, even remotely, with a work that could threaten their
jobs by making their political masters unhappy.

Shortly after meeting the Secretary, I learned that orders for
my termination had been prepared. I did then what I thought
I would never do in my life. Win or lose, I had always fought
my own battles. Nevertheless, confronted with the gross
falsifications that were used in my dismissal, I didn't hesitate to
ask some of my contacts to approach the Secretary directly.
I made no attempt to use any bureaucratic connections, as these
would have been completely useless. Rather I contacted friends
who were well connected in Pakistan's high cultural circles.
I told them I wanted to stay in Lok Virsa, but that I had no
intention of abandoning my private study of the Shahi Mohalla.
They understood and agreed to help. My friends simply called
the Secretary and said he could expect absolutely no assistance
from them, their families or their friends if I lost my job.

What happened next was anti-climatic. All the noise and furious manipulations stopped abruptly and there was silence. I continued to go to my office and continued to obtain approvals for my fieldwork. My book, *Women in Folk Theatre*, was published the following year—a good deal for Lok Virsa, which paid not a penny for the research expenses, not even repaying the Rs. 5000 illegally deducted from my salary.

I kept on collecting data on the Shahi Mohalla. My colleagues were very supportive and helpful, but Uxi Mufti hated me for my persistence and continued to harass me by ensnaring me in the Institute's internal politics. Ultimately, two years after my meeting with Khawaja Shahid Hussain, I was entangled in a web of political manoeuvring and sent on forced leave, again on a trumped up charge. By this time, I was seriously disillusioned with Lok Virsa and did not try to have the leave overturned. Two years passed before the case was reviewed, and it was held to be without merit. I was asked to re-join the office. As soon as I heard the news, I formally resigned.

Those two years of forced leave were among the most productive in my life. I worked with a small group of women to create Bedari, a community organization that deals with issues related to violence against women. Together we established the first crisis centre in Pakistan devoted to dealing with women's personal crises. During this period, I made my living as an expert consultant on women's issues for all the major international development organizations in Pakistan. And of course, I continued to visit the Shahi Mohalla every chance I got.

# 4

# MY FIRST CONTACT IN
# THE MOHALLA

Finally, after the furore created by my proposed study of the infamous Shahi Mohalla miraculously disappeared, I went to Lahore with the intention of actually starting my research. Lahore, like many other old South Asian cities, has expanded from its compact origins, creating sprawling modern suburbs in the process; but the ancient core has survived. Lahore's history since 1000 AD is fully documented, and several references to a town on the same site date back to 150 AD. Old Lahore was situated on the River Ravi, which has now changed its course slightly. A thick masonry wall, built by Emperor Akbar (1552-1605) and surrounded by a moat, enclosed the old city. Its thirteen gates were closed in the evenings to protect the residents.

Although the British destroyed the gates, tore down the wall, and filled the moat in the nineteenth century, Lahore's residents retained the old infrastructure in their minds, and passed it down from generation to generation. Even today, references to the inner city's gates are common. Lahoris who live in the 'walled' city still give an address through the name of the gate and then the name of the bazaar, or neighbourhood. Any more detail is not needed, as anyone living in the area could give directions to the specific person's home being sought. In this part of the city, people know their neighbours very well.

I had arranged to stay with relatives who lived on the Mall in the centre of modern Lahore. As soon as I arrived I wanted to visit the Mohalla. Until then I had been taken to the Mohalla by others, first, by Uxi Mufti and, later, by theatre artists to meet specific performers for my other study, so I did not yet have a clear geographical picture of the area in my mind. It had seemed to me like a maze of narrow streets at the time. Now that I was going to drive myself, I had to ask my aunt how to get there. Using the traditional reference points, she told me the Mohalla is located at the mouth of the Taxalli Gate, right next to the grand Shahi Qilla, the Royal Fort, modern Lahore's most imposing landmark. After passing through the gate, I should ask someone the whereabouts of the Mohalla. These directions seemed odd to someone used to the rectilinear address systems of Islamabad and Minneapolis, but I ventured out, happy to be there after so much resistance and ready to begin my work.

Shahi Mohalla and Heera Mandi are the most common names for this red light district. Because of its location by the Mughal Royal Fort, Shahi Mohalla means the Royal Neighbourhood. Heera Mandi means diamond market, but some people say it takes its name from a deputy of Ranjit Singh who was called Heera. The original district was a collage of fourteen bazaars, with Shahi Mohalla and Heera Mandi being the specific names of only two of them, but these names became so popular that the whole area came to be referred to in this way. The area is referred to in poetry as, Bazaare Husn, the market of beauty. The other twelve bazaars of the area are: Kucha Shabaz Khan, Main Bazaar, Lerge Mandi, Hyderi Street, Fort Road, Newan Chetram Road, Ucha Chetram Road, Koocha Sabz Peer, Bazaar Sheikhupurian, Bazaar Thana Tibbi, Gadi Mohalla and Tibbi Gali. Musical performances combined with prostitution are practiced in only six of these bazaars at present.

The approach to the Taxalli Gate was crowded with cars, horse-drawn *tongas*, ox and donkey carts, wagons, motorcycles and bicycles. I saw this hustle and bustle through a cloud of dust. The road split into two and I chose the one going straight into the old city. It gradually became narrower, hemmed in on both sides with tall buildings close to one another with balconies visually separating the floors. Although the upper floors of the buildings were mainly residential, retail shops, mostly selling shoes, filled the ground floors. The area looked like a marketplace, and the road was filled with cars and motorcycles competing with countless pedestrians. My car inched forward as the traffic became increasingly congested.

I was happy to be driving and not dependent on public transport. I had also used my car for my Folk Theatre research, chasing down nomadic entertainment groups in the middle of the night throughout rural Punjab. I called my white Toyota Corolla, 'Rani'. Essential to my existence, she was like a dear partner in many of my adventures. In my car I felt confident and secure.

I approached an intersection where a cinema hall had huge, painted cut outs of film actresses hanging in its facade. I rolled down my window and asked a man passing by whether I was in the Shahi Mohalla.

'Where do you want to go?' was his reply. This counter-questioning style was familiar to me. In the old city whenever you ask a question or an address, people quiz you first. A high priority is placed on gathering information orally and knowing about everything that is going on.

'I want to go to Shahida Perveen's house,' I answered, impatiently.

He looked at me and then at my car and asked, 'Where have you come from?'

By this time, the honking of the traffic that had backed up behind me made it difficult to hear him clearly. I looked back in panic and asked firmly, 'is this Shahi Mohalla or not?' He motioned me to keep going straight.

Shahida Perveen was my first and, at that time, only contact in the entertainment community of the Mohalla. She is one of the most seasoned classical singers of our times and is well respected by Pakistan's cultured elite. I had met her at Lok Virsa when she came for a concert and video recording. We had talked at length about where she lived and about her musical training. She was hesitant at that time to talk about the Mohalla itself, but I had told her that some day I would visit her at her home, and she had invited me to come.

I drove straight down the road. After the intersection I passed
through a similar bazaar, with restaurants, video shops, dairy
shops and *paan* vendors. The buildings on both sides were tall
with prominent balconies, reminding me of many scenes in
Pakistani and Indian movies. A peculiar thing I noticed were
the strings of laundry tied across the street, high enough not to
disturb the traffic. On it were hung many multi-coloured towels.
I also saw shops with big garage-like doors in front. The doors
were closed, and the shops looked abandoned, but I remembered
these shops from my first visit to the Mohalla. Every night of
the year, these 'shops' transform into luminous performance
halls for the 'ladies of the night'—the cause of Shahi Mohalla's
notoriety.

I finally reached a large intersection, called Naugaza or 'Nine-
yard' Chowk. Stories speak of a nine-yard long grave located
here, and some people still believe that our ancestors were much
taller than we are today. This grave was supposed to be of a
holy person, and no one knows when it was demolished. No
shrine or any other landmark exists, but the intersection is named
after this mythical grave. There was a market of musical
instruments with the ware displayed outside the shops in front
of me now. Three big restaurants were located on the right, with
their kitchens spilling out into the road. The raw material, mostly
chicken and beef, hung out in front of the restaurants. Big
cooking stoves and platforms of cooked and uncooked food
gave the intersection a special look.

I inquired about Shahida's house twice. The first time a young
man told me to continue to the next intersection and ask again.
Once there, I asked a fat old man clad only in a *dhoti*, with no
*kurta*. He had me park my car and follow him on foot into a
narrow street with a sign on the corner reading Hyderi Street.
Shahida lived just down the way.

I entered her house through the already open door, and saw a
barefoot, ten-year-old boy with mussed hair wearing a *shalwar
kamiz*. Confirming that it was the right house, I asked for
Shahida and was invited in. A short narrow passage led to a
dark well-like courtyard in the centre of a several-storied

building. In front of me across the courtyard was a row of small rooms, but the child asked me to sit in a well-lit room just to my left. This room was about 15 ft square and was furnished with a sofa set and a *chandni* on the floor. A harmonium and *tabla* were placed on one side. Noises coming through the wall indicated that this entrance, which had a large white wooden gate, opened onto the street, and I could tell that it was a typical *kotha*.

Shahida entered and greeted me affectionately and offered refreshments. She seemed to think I had come to book her for a concert, so I immediately began to talk about my research. I explained my objectives and, in my earnest desire not to scare her off, quickly said that I had no moralistic desire to gather information about the evils of prostitution or to be judgmental about the people. I only wanted to understand how the people in this Mohalla live, interact, deal with their customers and promote their music.

I wanted Shahida as a key informant, but no such luck! Despite my best professional manner, she steadfastly refused to admit anything about prostitution. I told her I had no intention of studying her life, but needed her assistance to help understand the sub-culture. She said her mother had abandoned prostitution to focus solely on singing. Shahida followed that path and maintained her status as a singer. She said she remained in the Mohalla because the house was family property and she didn't want to sell it. I told her I wanted to come back and spend time around her house until I could establish other contacts. Unwilling to be an informant, she was happy to be my hostess and introduce me to other people who might be more forthcoming.

I visited her often over the next several days and each time she introduced me to a few more people. One day, I asked to go to the toilet and Shahida had a young girl take me outside, across a dark courtyard that smelled of urine. On my way across, I saw a naked child standing and urinating into a small open drain flowing through the courtyard. The girl led me up a set of narrow wooden steps, which didn't seem like the regular steps up to the next floor. The steps ended at a door leading directly into a room. When I entered I couldn't believe my eyes. The medium sized room had panels of mirrors on the walls and ceiling and boasted a huge, carved, gothic-style wooden bed as well as a television, video player and refrigerator. Fully carpeted, the room was quite modern, but oddly enough was covered in dust so thick it appeared not to have been used in a long while. The washroom attached to this beautiful bedroom was fully tiled and had a modern, maroon coloured commode; but spider webs and dust everywhere. Surely an interesting tale lurked behind this, but Shahida never revealed it.

One night I went to Shahida's around 10 o'clock, planning to stay and observe the Mohalla's evening activities. I was sitting with Shahida when two young girls came in and Shahida explained that she allowed them to use the room in the evenings as a *kotha*. I asked whether she charged rent and she gave a long explanation of how since she hardly earned any money from her serious singing she needed to take a share of their earnings just to make ends meet. She didn't describe the details of the arrangement, but I later learned there is a specific system of distributing all income from the musical performances among the musicians, dancing girls and the one who provides the space. Knowing Shahida's resistance to talking about anything related to prostitution, I left it at that.

The next day Shahida introduced me to Shakira, a heavy-set woman in her late forties. Shakira invited me to her house, where she plied me with long stories about her family's piety. She apologized that I couldn't meet any of her daughters because they were reading the Quran and she didn't want to disturb them. She claimed she gave much more *niaz* at the shrine than anyone else in her extended family did; she had offered two *deg* of food at the shrine of Data Sahib just the previous week. Shakira worked hard to convince me that her family, who belonged to the Shia sect of Islam and mourned each year for the entire forty days of *Muharram*, would never go into prostitution and were only performing artists.

Although this session was unproductive as far as building rapport and trust went, it was valuable nonetheless since

I learned that the reluctance to admit that prostitution exists in the Mohalla extends beyond well-known artists like Shahida. In addition, the apparent need to maintain a religious façade seemed to spring from a desire to counter the stigma attached to their sub-culture by the larger Pakistani society.

The practice of providing sexual services through a system of complex traditions and rituals had previously been an open secret. Music and dance were always a part of it and the entire system was well supported by the elite. When prostitution became illegal after Pakistan achieved independence, however, the courtesans were suddenly told that they could legally work only as musical entertainers. Although everyone knew that their other work continued unabated, the women began to hide this aspect of their profession. In the past a distinction was clearly made between common prostitutes in brothels such as those in all South Asian port cities, and those who worked in a more cultural context, closely associated with the performing arts. The courtesan's relationships were considered more respectable since they were very particular about their customers and, at times, maintained long-term relationships as mistresses with certain individuals. Now, however, all sex workers are lumped together into a single, degenerate class.

To my knowledge, the only comparable examples outside South Asia are the Japanese Geishas. Well trained in painting, music and singing, the Geishas were also available to men for long or short-term relationships. Backed by a long tradition, a certain standard of customers was maintained. A Geisha committed to one client, called *danna*, as a long-term mistress would not see others. Likewise, in the South Asian tradition, a *tawaif*, or a courtesan, with one long-term client was bound to provide services and maintain a relationship with that man only. Indiscriminate use of the word 'prostitute' for anyone involved in providing sexual services for men, be she a prostitute off the street, or a mistress with a long-term relationship, is a recent phenomenon. South Asian languages clearly distinguish a definite hierarchy in the wide range of terms used to define different types of sex workers, from courtesans to streetwalkers.

I had initially felt that two weeks with my first contacts would be sufficient time to build rapport, and that the data would then start flowing in. Here I was, long after the time limit I had set for myself had passed, still faced with a wall of resistance I could not break through.

When I started my research, I also contacted some other female dancers and singers in the Mohalla whom I had met through my work at Lok Virsa. I tried to build a rapport with them but they resisted talking about their professional lives because of the social taboo associated with prostitution. I was an 'outsider' and older household members, especially the women, did not trust me and would not allow me a chance to talk to the young dancers. They were well aware of the extremely precarious situation the prostitution business faced. Since prostitution is officially illegal, they would open themselves and their community to severe risk by admitting their involvement in the business to a stranger. In addition to these legitimate concerns, I believe that most of all they feared losing control over the young women by allowing them to be exposed to someone like me. This was very threatening to them because, as I learned later, their entire existence depends upon the continued development and control of young prostitutes.

After all the commotion my proposal had created, I was delighted to be doing the study on my own, and was determined to continue until I could answer the questions I had in my mind. After unsuccessfully pursuing Shahida Perveen and some other singers and dancers, however, I decided I needed a new strategy for data collection.

# 5

## AN ALTERNATE ROAD INTO THE SHAHI MOHALLA
### The Musicians

Finding an entry point into a community is a crucial step for any researcher. My first approach to the Shahi Mohalla directly through singers and dancers met with resistance, so I decided to try another strategy. I would use the community of musicians—a distinct part of the sub-culture—as an alternative route.

All professional musicians in the Mohalla are male. Their basic role is to provide music in the *kothas* for the dancing girls. Most play stringed or percussion instruments, but some also work as composers, singers and, most importantly, instructors. With no direct link with prostitution as such, they nonetheless work very closely with the prostitutes.

The majority of Mohalla musicians belong to the *Mirasi* occupational caste. Musicians who are not *Mirasi* either pretend to be or at least adopt similar behaviour and values. The term *Mirasi* derives from *miras*, simply meaning lineage. In the old feudal system, this group was closely attached to the landlord class, and the members were responsible for keeping track of the larger families' lineages as well as providing entertainment at weddings and other celebrations. Specific *Mirasi* families were attached to different landlords and were compensated according to the status and wealth of their feudal lord.

I contacted some friends at Lok Virsa for a few references for musicians living in the Mohalla. My first contact among the musicians was an *ustad* named Mohammed Sadiq. I had met him before briefly in the context of my research work on women in folk theatre. I did not have his address, but having his name was sufficient. No address was necessary since in this close-knit community people knew each other well.

When I returned to the Mohalla, I asked a shopkeeper how to find *Ustad* Sadiq's *baithak* and he sent a small boy from his shop to guide me. The boy took me to the Mohalla's Main Bazaar. A small alley from the Main Bazaar road led to the entrance of Sadiq's residence. I knocked on the door, and an unshaven young man of about nineteen, clad in wrinkled *shalwar kamiz*, opened the door. I asked for *Ustad* Sadiq. Seemingly bewildered by such an unusual visitor, he went in, yelling, '*ustad, ustad*, there is a woman at the door asking for you'. Through a half-opened door I could see Sadiq in the second room. He was wearing only a *shalwar*, so he took a shirt from behind the door of the room, and put it on as he came out. A dark man of medium height with a thin moustache, Sadiq wore *surma* in his eyes, and there was an oily shine in his hair.

To get myself inside his *baithak*—a small two-room unit in a large residential building—I briefly introduced the purpose of my study. I entered the *deorhi*, an antechamber, through a low wooden door. Tin suitcases, boxes and folded bedding were stacked on one side of this small room, and the rest served as a passage to the second room. I noticed a water tap, a stack of dishes and a small stove in one corner of this passage, indicating that it also served as a kitchen. Such economy of space fascinated me.

Matting and sheets of cloth covered the floor of the inner room. The upper parts of all the walls were decorated with coloured posters of actresses and coloured newspaper pictures of singers and attractive, large-breasted, women. A big nail, hammered into one corner of the room, appeared to serve as his dressing room. This nail proudly supported a small mirror and a little pouch, elaborate enough for an *ustad's* needs. Another nail, hammered into the adjacent corner, served as his clothes closet. A harmonium sat in another corner next to a pile of bedding.

As we sat on the floor of what seemed to be the main living area, I introduced myself to Sadiq, who was very courteous and immediately made me feel welcome. My work with Lok Virsa helped a lot. All artists know of the Institute and regard its work highly. The reference from a mutual friend was also very useful.

Three other men were present in Sadiq's *baithak*; his partner, Riaz, who was staying with him at that time, was introduced to me in an elaborate manner. The other two were introduced in a casual way and I understood that they were his students. Listening to the heavily accented Punjabi, typical of the *andrun sheher*, the old city of Lahore, was very refreshing. Sadiq seemed quite comfortable in my presence. I noticed that he was constantly swearing. I could understand some of the more common Punjabi profanities, like mother fucker and sister fucker, but not others. (I resisted my temptation to take out my note pad and start writing these down as valuable data and politely went on with simple conversation necessary for getting acquainted with the group.) In Punjabi, swearing at others does not necessarily mean that you are upset with them and, for Sadiq, this was merely a natural mode of address.

My strategy of using the musicians as an entry point to the culture of the Mohalla worked well. My initiation into their circle was smooth and the information started to flow easily. First, I found out more about the musician community. Later, this link opened up to me the larger system of the dancers and prostitutes.

I started visiting *Ustad* Sadiq and some other musicians regularly. One day when I reached Sadiq's *baithak* I found that he had invited about fifteen other young musicians for me to interview. I thanked them for taking time out for me, but told them that I wanted to see them again in their own *baithaks*, visiting and spending time with them as they carried on with their routine work. Some told me they didn't have their own *baithaks* and that they stayed at different friends' places. Others, who considered themselves residents, gave me an open invitation to visit.

I wanted basic information about their work and their families. Most of them stayed in the Mohalla hoping to jump-start their careers. They said that being around other supportive professionals was very beneficial. Many talent scouts from the television and film industries come to the Mohalla and the musicians wanted to exploit such opportunities.

One young man said, 'I accompany singers on the *tabla*. We follow the music composed by an *ustad*. The *ustad* needs lyrics from a poet, and also other musicians for *sangat*. Alone, I am nothing. I can only perform when all these people work together.'

I asked him how he made his living. He answered, 'Sometimes I am hired by the radio or by agents for a private concert. It is very unpredictable, but we artists are used to that. We don't know what is coming for us tomorrow. I am very new in the Shahi Mohalla. I used to live in a similar Mohalla of Sialkot and have many friends there, all musicians. I am the only one of my group who has come to Lahore looking for better opportunities.'

'Has it been better for you financially?' I asked.

'Yes', he replied, 'Even if I don't get much work, Lahore pays better! Thanks to *Pah* Sadiq, I played at a private concert just yesterday and earned a thousand rupees.'

I questioned further, 'How do you know who needs your services?'

Sadiq explained, 'That is why we have to be here in the Mohalla. People contact someone, anyone they know, and that person passes on the message to others or puts together a group himself.'

'And keeps the whole commission as well!' Riaz added, laughing.

'What about the competition,' I asked, 'don't you feel that whoever is contacted would prefer keeping the business himself rather than passing on the message?'

Sadiq laughed and said, 'A week ago I got a call that a family wanted to arrange a musical programme—no dancing, just singing. They wanted a female singer and two musicians.

I suggested that they needed at least three musicians, *peiti*, *tabla* and *nal*. Then I contacted Chanda for singing, my friend Abdul for *tabla* and Riaz for *nal*. I was on the *peiti*, I mean harmonium. I also sang a few songs. It helps to be able to quickly contact other colleagues and make a group according to what the customer wants.'

I asked about the multi-coloured towels hanging in the streets where they lived. Amused by my question, they said the towels belong to the *hamam* quite common in this area. They explained that living space in the Mohalla is scarce and that a small *baithak* can be quite expensive. Thus, they rely on the traditional system of public baths, which have small bathing rooms and modest facilities. Many barbers work with them, providing customers with shaves, haircuts and head massages. The service is for men of poor economic backgrounds and is a daily need so the charges are nominal, but high enough to make it an attractive business.

*Ustad* Sadiq himself moved into the area in the early 1980s. In his childhood he worked as an errand boy to the great masters, and considered it his good fortune to have had a chance to learn from them. He couldn't be admitted to his village school after fifth grade, but since he had an ear for music a great musician, Sakhi Dhol Wala, had taken him in at a young age, with the permission of his father. Sadiq did all the chores for this *ustad* and his companions, a group of musicians who performed at local festivals. Sadiq got their food, washed their clothes, ran around after their instruments, replaced the tobacco in their *huqas*, brought them water or tea and, at night, massaged his *ustad's* head and legs.

Sadiq never got much attention from his *ustad* and received little structured training. He learned about music by being around the musicians. He listened to their talk about *ragas* and watched them play their instruments and sing. Typically, when *ustads* in that era took students from outside their families, they used them as errand boys. This was the same as other common apprenticeships like tailoring or bicycle repair, where little children taken in to train in a specialized skill served their teachers for years as servants and only learned the basics on the side.

Sadiq remembered that after a performance, sometime in the middle of the night, when the whole group was tired and finally lay down on their *charpais* in the tents, they would ask Sadiq, who was about ten at that time, to sing for them. At times he was their entertainment. His *ustad* did take him seriously and some times rewarded him with one rupee.

Although Sadiq belonged to a *Mirasi* family, his father did not adopt music as his profession, but took care of a fruit orchard in a small Punjab village. Sadiq's brother became a wrestler, another unusual profession for a *Mirasi*. Only Sadiq chose music. Even as a child he knew that he would become a musician. After leaving his *ustad's* group, Sadiq became a formal student of Jamil Shah Sahib, worked with several traditional theatre companies, and eventually decided to settle in the Mohalla, where, in his view, his profession was centred. Everyone in the field had links to this place.

Sadiq left his family, wife and children, in Okara, a town near Lahore. At that time the landlady of his building was looking for a good *ustad* for her daughter, Laila. She agreed to rent him a two-room unit in her building in the Mohalla if he would take her daughter as a student. The arrangement was mutually beneficial, rent was agreed on and Sadiq moved in. He visited his family often, although his schedule was dictated by the work available to him. As an *ustad* to a dancing girl, he was to ensure the musical arrangements for her evening performances. So Ustad Sadiq, along with some other colleagues, provided the music for Laila's dance performances at her *kotha*.

Sadiq was an excellent informant and I spent about two weeks talking to musicians in the area. In a way, he was my *ustad*, guiding my journey in this forbidden land. One day he told me he had called Laila and Chanda, his two senior students, for a lesson. As he had been very busy the last two weeks with a sudden increase in requests to arrange performances, his landlady was complaining that he was spending too much time organizing music shows and too little with her daughter.

Soon after I arrived, a tall, dark and very slim young woman walked into Sadiq's *baithak*. I was surprised because she looked very different from the other women I had seen there. At first, I took her for someone's mistress, a higher class of prostitute. She seemed mature and well taken care of. Her long black hair was brushed back nicely, flowing over her shoulders. She walked with a rhythm. Intriguingly, she walked straight into the *baithak*, without knocking at the door or saying anything, and sat down on the floor. She looked stunning.

*Ustad* Sadiq looked at her and said, '*Aa gai oon!* (You have come!).' He introduced her to me in an elaborate manner. She was apparently one of his best students, one he frequently used as a singer in the shows he organized. A junior musician sitting close by and listening to the elaborate praise, decided to tease her and said to Sadiq, '*kuch kaht karo, bot ucha pucha dita e* (Cut it down a bit, you've gone too far).' There was laughter in the room. The woman also laughed and lovingly yelled at the boy in a deep, hoarse voice. When she opened her mouth to speak, I saw that her teeth were orange from eating *paan*. Her voice was loud and her retort was just a long string of profanity that ended in a hard slap on his back. I was shocked. This was Chanda!

She turned to me and said, 'Don't listen to this bastard. Tell me what brings you here.'

Sadiq jumped in with an equally elaborate introduction for me and my work. We started talking to each other. She told me about her house and her family and said she would enjoy talking to me since she gets tired of her routine work. She confided in me that even though she had only finished high school and didn't go to college, she liked to read and occasionally bought herself books. She asked me to visit her and I promised I would. As I got to know her, I discovered her exceptionally bright mind and generous heart. The many dimensions of her personality never failed to surprise me. She could be childish and a crazy lover, a very responsible and assertively mature woman, an insightful and curious person and, often, totally absorbed in enjoying her skill at hooking a customer.

Sadiq began her music lesson. He was very upset at Laila for being late. Every once in a while he would stop the music and

grumble about her, cursing his landlady, Kaisera, for having
bothered him so much about not being serious with Laila's
lessons. Now it was her daughter who was proving she was not
a serious student. He sent a small child upstairs to ask, as he put
it, 'if the royal queen might come down.'

Eventually, Laila came down from the back entrance of the
building. She was a short, cute young woman, a little overweight. Sadiq looked at her angrily, which made her laugh. She
laughed for a long time and did not really listen to his
complaints. At the end of this scolding session she said in a
naughty and seductive manner, 'you look very angry today *ustad
ji*.' Sadiq was even more upset by her non-serious attitude. He
looked at me and said, 'this is my bright student, Laila Kaisera.
I thought she would be a good contact for you in the community
of dancers, but only if you can handle her.'

I told them to continue with the music class, and said I'd
slip away in the middle without disturbing them. I promised
Laila that I would visit her within the week.

# 6

## THE STORIES BEGIN

The next day I made my first visit to Laila's house. I used the entrance from the main road that led directly to their portion of the building. The old wooden entrance door was somewhat hidden between a laundry and a milk shop, close to the main intersection of the Naugaza Chowk, where restaurants dominate the business. This door led to a narrow, dark curved staircase, with high steps and a sharp spiral. It was shortly after noon but I could see hardly anything and had to feel each step with my feet. Another door stood at the top of the staircase. Only a little light shining through some cracks prevented me from bumping into it. I knocked at least three times at reasonable intervals before someone answered. A young woman's voice called, 'who is it?' A difficult question. She wouldn't understand if I said, 'Fouzia', so I answered, 'Laila's friend'. That did it. The door opened and I stepped into the world of a family that has for generations been in the business of prostitution. Later, as I came to know them better, I learned of the complex relationships and power dynamics that make up the structure of this sub-culture.

I found myself in front of a little girl of about six who was swaying from side-to-side to some unknown rhythm. She looked at me with curiosity and continued to sway. I said I was a friend of Laila's and had come to see her. She told me to sit on the living room sofa while she ran through another doorway covered with a ragged black cotton curtain, possibly the entrance to the rest of the house. As I moved to the sofa I noticed that the staircase continued up through another doorway right next to the main entrance door.

The room was carpeted and held a western style sofa and chairs. I saw wooden arches along one wall that led to a long narrow covered balcony, looking down onto the main street. The arches were covered with *chics*, 'just like in the movies', I thought. 'This must be where they stand in the evening, all dressed up, attracting customers.' I figured that the 'living room' was probably the *kotha*. It looked more western than in the films and it was smaller than the spacious *kothas* in movie sets. I told my mind to lay off. As a researcher I hadn't come to reinforce any preconceived ideas, but to learn what this life was all about. I told myself strictly to keep an open mind and not to start interpreting things until I had sufficient relevant data.

I also found the walls intriguing. A large mirror hung at an angle on the wall opposite the entrance door. Photographs were displayed on the walls, and two big black and white portraits of women caught my attention. They resembled actresses from the 1950s wearing net *dupattas* and the typical hairstyle and make-up of that era.

After five more minutes an older, sharp-featured woman came out of the door, wearing a modest cotton *shalwar kamiz* with a muslin *dupatta* covering her head. She had on a gold nose pin. Fair complexioned, she had a face which showed experience. She greeted me politely and I introduced myself. She had clearly been briefed about me before she came into the living room. She said Laila had told her about me. After a few pleasantries, she told me that mornings were a challenge for Laila and she was still getting up. 'Morning?' I wondered. It was nearly one in the afternoon.

I enjoyed this woman's Punjabi accent and replied in my best Punjabi. Although I could hear a trace of an East Punjabi accent she said she had lived in Lahore all her life. I did not think it proper to push for information about her past at this point so I switched the topic to her children. She told me she had a daughter and a son. The son was married with two daughters and two sons of his own. I asked if her son lived with them.

'Yes,' she replied, 'my son lives with me. He travels quite a bit for his business, but my daughter-in-law and my grand-children are here all the time.'

I was asking only those questions that people generally ask in the old city when meeting for the first time. I did not want to jump into a research mode just yet. At one point, I felt she was satisfied with the information she had given about herself and wanted to talk about me.

I had already given her the basics about myself, that I lived in Islamabad, worked at Lok Virsa and wanted to write about this area, and was staying with my uncle in Lahore. She looked at me from top to bottom, raised her eyebrows and said, 'How do you know *Pah* Sadiq?'

'We have common friends,' I replied confidently.

I mentioned some well-known musicians and singers, all men from the *Mirasi* ethnic group. She smiled and nodded as if satisfied by my references and said, 'You are our guest and like a daughter to me. Tell us, now, what can we do to help.' I was delighted to hear this because I had thought it would be very difficult for me to get into their network. Little did I know that I should not have considered this invitation as a green signal. She knew quite well how to deal with intruders like me, who thought they could dash in, find out whatever there was that could be easily learned about the area and dash out again to write about it.

Laila entered the room, dressed up in a dark blue, and tightly fitted *shalwar kamiz* made of flat crepe. Her complexion was not as light as her mother's. Laila was short with large features, and a little plump. Her prominent mouth was accentuated by light orange lipstick and her face was dusted with light makeup, whitish powder, and some eyeliner. Coming forward and hugging me, she said, 'I told my mother that my friend would visit me soon.'

I tried my best to maintain a non-threatening, friendly stance, and in general my appearance is not overpowering. Laila's mother looked at her and said, 'She is a Lahori. Did you see the *khusa* she is wearing on her feet?' This comment was important for me, because it told me what she had noticed.

Laila looked at me and said, 'Yes, the other day at *Pah* Sadiq's I noticed she didn't look like someone from Islamabad.'

I asked what women from Islamabad looked like?

Her mother answered quickly, '*Git pit git pit kardian ne* (They do 'git pit git pit'—slang that expresses the sound of spoken English).'

I laughed.

Laila said, 'Yes, she's right, you speak very good Punjabi.' She came closer to me and said to her mother, 'Ami I love her hair, look how long and beautiful it is.' I was happy I hadn't done anything to offend them. I thought they were gradually accepting me.

While we continued with our general talk, the researcher in me was very active and noticed each word they spoke, their accent, their gestures and their eye movements. I noticed that the two children, a six-year-old girl and a younger boy of about four or five, were wandering around as if they had little to do. Occasionally, the grandmother would send them on small errands. She asked the little girl to get tea from the market, not a big challenge since she had only to go down the stairs and yell to the tea stall boy, 'Four teas, upstairs, quickly!'

The tea boy brought the tea and later took the glasses back. I told my hosts politely many times that I did not take tea, but they ordered some for me anyway. I had to sit with a glass of hot tea, full of cream, steaming in front of me. Over the years, I often wished I had developed a taste for tea. This is often my first hurdle in research when I am trying to make friends with a new group. I always have to get around it creatively. In villages when I decline tea offered by my hosts, they immediately think I don't want to drink from their cup, an old prejudice carried over from when people used to distinguish between the cups of different religious or ethnic groups. To avoid such mis-understandings, I always asked for a glass of water. That usually worked, assuring people that I did not consider them inferior to me. However, it opened me to the risk of drinking muddy water at times, with 'things' swimming in it. Tea, at least, is boiled water. Such is the price I have paid for not drinking tea and yet choosing to practice field research.

I said to Laila, 'Since you are my friend, you will drink this tea for me. Please get me a glass of cold water, I am feeling hot in this weather today.'

To my embarrassment, they got me a 7-Up. In Lahore, guests are not served plain water, only soft drinks. I survived the hospitality session and said, 'You can treat me as your guest only today, but not later.' Looking at Laila's mother I continued, 'you called me a daughter so I want to be treated like one and not as a guest.' She seemed pleased with what I said.

I started talking about music and asked Laila what kind of music she liked.

Her eyes brightened. 'Indian film songs', she replied.

She had not named a single major *ustad* from her area, no famous Pakistani singer or poet. When she mentioned the songs she liked, she also knew the lyrics and the name of the film it was from, but never referred to the composer or the poet. My experience was that people familiar with the art of music or who work in the field, always acknowledge at least the composer when mentioning a song, or the poet when mentioning a *ghazal*. My short experience with the musicians of the Mohalla had confirmed this. They always mentioned the name of the poet before singing a *ghazal* even if it came from a film. Without being judgmental, Laila's descriptions of her favourite songs reflected her knowledge and her relationship with music.

I asked how she felt about the big artists who came from this Mohalla.

'Oh! I want to be like them, 'she replied.

'Like who?' I asked. 'Give me an example.'

'Like Reema (a famous film actress)! She is such a good dancer and has reached the height of popularity. But it is not only talent you know, we need contacts also.'

This answer clearly revealed her focus. Acting, not music as such, interested her.

The first meeting went so well that I was invited to return, which I often did.

One day, when talking to Kaisera about the Mohalla's business, she told me, 'We do not do *bura kam* (bad work, implying 'prostitution'). My father was a man of high prestige. People in other districts knew him well. He loved both of us a lot.'

'Both of you?' I asked.

'Yes, my sister and I, both of us,' replied Laila's mother carelessly.

'Is she older or younger than you?'

She glanced at me as if she did not want me to try to get more information than what she was offering. Looking away, she said casually, 'older', and quickly continued with her story.

'He brought us up well. We were both beautiful and civilized and knew how to talk and sit. People used to talk about how well we were brought up. We never did any *bura kam*. My father was very tall and handsome. He wore a huge turban, because he was a Pathan. He used to wear a dark green *kurta*. He was a very handsome man.'

'It seems you were very close to him.'

A smile came over her face, as if she were drowning in memories buried deep down inside. She did not answer.

Giving her space to play with her memories, I remained quiet for a while. Then I said, 'What about your children, have you raised them in the same way?'

A strange expression of disgust came across her face and she said loudly, 'No! Times have changed, demands have changed, girls have changed, everything has changed!'

Seeking an opportunity for more information, I jumped in with an open-ended question, 'What do you mean?'

She gave me a look that seemed to say, 'If you think you can make me talk, forget it'. Instead, she smiled and sweetly asked what I would like to drink.

Aware of both my impatience and her internal struggle between speaking and maintaining a façade, I answered that I didn't want to be treated like a guest. This was my third visit to their house and they had been very hospitable.

Laila had just entered the room and immediately started pestering me about what I wanted to drink, so I said, 'A coke will be fine.'

She laughed, 'So you are a *paindu*'. She had enjoyed my response and was making a friendly invitation for more interaction by joking with me.

'How is that?' I asked.

Throwing herself back in a sofa chair and giving me a naughty look from the corner of her eyes, she said with a heavy Punjabi accent, '*Paindus* drink Coca Cola. The more classy people drink Sprite or 7-Up.'

I laughed with her, 'You're right, I am a *paindu*. I enjoy it. You know I drink milk at home. Here I asked for a coke to look a little modern.'

We both laughed, but her mother did not enjoy the joke as much. She did not want Laila to become too friendly with me. She wanted to maintain a façade and was hesitant to share information about their family profession.

'Laila, go in and finish what I had asked you to do,' Kaisera said with a grim look on her face. She clearly wanted Laila to leave my company. Perhaps she wanted to tell me more stories, to convince me that her family had nothing to do with prostitution.

Laila looked at me laughingly and winked, making sure that her mother didn't see. With a serious face she asked, 'What work, mother?'

She was playing dumb to tease her, but her mother gave her a stern look and said, 'Don't you remember what I told you this morning.'

Laila, making an innocent face, said childishly, 'No-ooo.'

Kaisera took a cushion from close by and threw it at Laila. This was a good way to jolt Laila's memory back and she left the room laughing. As she lifted the curtain of the door to go into the other part of the house, she looked back and winked at me again.

While Laila saw something exciting in me and wanted an independent relationship, I knew the older woman wanted to

keep me at a distance from her daughter. Clearly, my role at
that point was not to argue or try to prove that I knew her
family was involved in prostitution. I wanted to maintain a
friendly stance so that she could begin to trust me. So I gave her
my full attention and continued with simple questions about her
background and that of the people living in the area.

Laila's mother began her story again, 'I have no idea what
people in this bazaar do. I haven't put my foot out of my
building in years. Children, and my stupid servant, bring
whatever I need to the house. I have no social life.' She
continued, 'I have also told my daughters not to indulge in
*burai*.'

'How do you live,' I asked naively.

With a great deal of pride, she replied, 'I live off the rent
from this building.' Then she spoke again of her father, saying
he had left her this property.

A knock at the door announced the entrance of a servant
called 'Bhuba'. He was a short, seemingly retarded young man
in an old and dirty *shalwar kamiz*. His head tilted to one side
and he seemed to have a speech impediment. I could scarcely
understand him but the others had no such problem. He was a
strange character in the house.

Laila cleverly took his arrival as an excuse to return to the
living room. Pretending to have come to open the door, she
quickly snatched the coke bottle from his hand and handed it to
me. I smiled and took it. Hanging on to my smile and not
looking at her mother, she sat down next to me.

Speaking to me in English, she said, 'I can speak English,
you know. I went to college for two years. I know good English.
You can test me.'

I praised her, not sure whether she was showing off her
abilities, sharing something exciting or letting me know that her
mother does not understand English and that we could have a
secret language. I didn't start talking to her in English though,
and only praised her education.

Looking for an excuse to send Laila back out, her mother
asked her to send Bhuba for breakfast. Throughout much of old

Lahore, breakfast is not cooked at home but bought from the
market, where many special freshly cooked breakfast dishes are
available. Laila responded like a spoilt five-year-old, 'I don't
know what to get, you do it,' she said, making a face and
playing with a corner of her *dupatta*. With Laila acting up,
Kaisera rose and went inside, probably to get money and Bhuba
followed her.

Laila and I exchanged looks. I had wanted to ask her
something for a while and hadn't found an opportunity to do so.
Perhaps I should have waited until I was certain of our rapport,
but I felt she had indicated her willingness to talk to me several
times. I took her hand in mine and turned it to look at the ten or
twelve lines across her wrist that I had noticed the first time
I came to her house. I had thought about these marks every
night. While they did not seem like blade marks left from a
suicide attempt, their location and direction indicated something
similar. I guessed she must have made a half-baked attempt at
suicide.

'What happened, Laila?'

She said, 'I'll tell you, but I can't speak here. I'll have to
meet you alone.'

'Why not here?' I asked

'They'll never let me meet with you again if they find out
I'm telling you things that they don't want you to know,' was
her answer.

'Do you think we can meet alone?' I asked.

'No. They won't let me out of their sight for a minute. Didn't
you see how she doesn't even let me sit with you for long.' She
imitated her mother: 'Go in and do what I told you in the
morning. Huh! In the morning? I had just woken up!'

Her mother came back to the room talking to Bhuba. She
looked at me and asked, 'What would you like for breakfast?'

I laughed, 'This is past my lunch time, and I ate early today.'
It was about two in the afternoon, but Kaisera said that was no
excuse and that I should be careful from now on not to eat
before coming to visit.

Laila broke in, 'You said you drink milk at home. Our market has the best milk in the whole world. It's famous for it, made with almonds and pistachios. It is very sweet.'

Her mother retorted, 'And what do you know about the world?'

Laila was quick to respond to the insult, 'Plenty! I went to college and we studied about the world.'

The mother jerked her head, 'Sure, in college they taught you about the milk of Shahi Mohalla.'

Laila said sarcastically, 'You know a lot about the world, you've been everywhere, right? What do you know about what they taught me in college'. Quickly turning back to me, as if she did not want her mother to answer back and continue with this argument, she said, 'Try it, Fouzia.'

Tension was growing between them so I agreed to try some of Shahi Mohalla's cold milk. Asking Bhuba for two glasses, one for each of us, Laila turned to me, 'I was a good student. I could have gone for a Bachelors, but Mother said two years of college is enough so I did FA'. After a pause, eyes sparkling, Laila rose from her seat and walked over to her mother across the room.

In an excited voice she said, '*Ami*, Fouzia has offered us a drive in her car.' Kaisera became confused, as it was the last thing on her mind and she couldn't think of an excuse quickly enough to decline politely. Giving her no chance to respond, Laila continued, 'Oh! The weather is so nice and we haven't been out for so long.'

Without waiting for an answer, she turned towards me, 'It's so difficult to come back when we go out. Rickshaw drivers have a thousand questions when we say we are going to the Shahi Mohalla. They give us such bad looks. Nobody respects us. I try to get off in another *mohalla* close by and walk home.'

Kaisera couldn't stand such frankness from Laila. She asked, 'What are you talking about?' Trying to stay calm she continued, 'I never go out so I really don't know of these problems.' Laila regressed into her stubborn five-year-old tone, pushing her mother to go out with me. Since she was focusing all her energy on getting her mother to agree, I joined in, 'Yes, that would be very nice.'

I couldn't understand why Laila kept saying 'we.' It didn't seem like an attempt to be alone with me, but without any prior notice, I just played along and finally, Laila had persuaded her mother that she, her mother, her young niece and I would go to the Lawrence Gardens.

It took two hours to get everyone ready. Watching them coming in and out of the living room with their preparations was interesting. They kept yelling at each other to look for the things they could not find.

I looked around the room and thought I could spend many more days just absorbing it all. The two large black and white portraits really intrigued me. They looked like old actresses, with puffed hairstyles and fancy clothes. Their eyes seemed to hold mysteries and secrets and I had a strong urge to know their stories.

Kaisera was ready first and she came and sat with me. She said this had never happened in her family before; they never went out with anybody. 'The system is that everything you want comes to the house. Going to the hospital is the only exception. All the shops are nearby and even the tailor makes house calls. 'I send my grandchildren out,' she said, they can run down the steps and get anything we want.' I told her how happy I was because she was allowing her family to go out with me.

As we walked down the stairs, everyone in the market turned to look. They couldn't understand where I could be taking everyone. Kaisera wore a white *chaddar* over her dress. Laila had a very tight fitted purple *shalwar kamiz* with a low neckline. Unsure whether or not to hide her cleavage, she sometimes covered it with her *dupatta* and sometimes pulled the *dupatta* back, throwing it around her neck, revealing her front. She would take deep breaths and push her breasts forward as if showing them off. When we sat in the car, Laila made sure she sat in front so that everybody saw her as we drove through the bazaar. She wanted everyone to know she was going in a car. As we drove towards the Taxalli Gate, she kept looking around to see who was fortunate enough to witness her riding with her friend in a white Toyota. She felt sorry for those who missed this significant event. I felt like I was driving a Rolls Royce.

We parked at the Lawrence Gardens parking area and walked towards the nearest *khokha* for cold drinks. The gardens are one of Lahore's oldest recreation areas, and had been well maintained during both the Mughal and the colonial periods. The size of the old trees can be frightening to children. Bats with wingspans of over 2 ft inhabit some of them. The Gardens have many open areas with cement benches, a big hill covered with grass and flowers, smaller gardens, beautiful walkways, and space for an open-air theatre.

Laila's first request was for soft drinks and ice cream. I immediately obliged, quite happy since I had been visiting the family for only a week and already they had come out with me. This was progress. We finished the first round of drinks and asked a young boy from the *khokha* to get us ice cream. Laila enthusiastically said to her mother, 'Since it's such a nice day, let's walk around the hill.'

Kaisera looked surprised and said, 'You know my health condition. I can't walk.'

Putting her mother in a situation where she couldn't stop us from going, Laila quickly replied, 'Oh, that's too bad. Why don't you sit here then and we will take a round of the hill and come back.' Once she made sure that her mother was comfortably seated on a bench, we left.

Kaisera called us as we were leaving and told Laila to take her niece along. Laila looked at me as if to say, 'Well, after all, she's my mother. She had to think of something to keep me from having a moment alone with you. But, rid of the old lady, taking care of a six-year-old won't be too difficult.'

As soon as we got out of her mother's sight, Laila told her niece to walk faster, a little ahead of us. She came close to me and said. 'Did you see how difficult it was to steal a moment from these people? They watch me like a hawk.'

I asked whom she meant by 'They' and she answered, 'My mother and my elder brother.'

I hadn't met this elder brother yet. She said he was out of town at the moment.

'I really wanted to study more, but they think if a girl studies too much she gets out of control,' she continued.

'Then why did they send you to school in the first place?' I asked.

She explained that the customers like educated women. A little bit of English helps in getting better customers. 'But they want to make sure we do not fall in love with our studies. They want us to go to school, but not take it too seriously and then quit as soon as we become adult.'

'Adult?'

'When we start work, you know usually fourteen, fifteen or so. I am considered to be a late starter because I stayed in school so long.'

I was intrigued. This was the first time I had learned something about the business of prostitution from someone directly involved in it.

Laila was very excited about coming to the garden. The beautiful big trees and interesting people distracted her. She was constantly commenting on women's clothes and wanted to know what women were wearing these days. She confessed that she got her guidance on clothing and make-up from the movies.

I asked about the scratches on her wrists.

'My brother and mother fight a lot. They fight with me too. They're looking for a man for my *shadi* and when they do not find a suitable person they fight with me as if I am not doing my job well.'

I asked what she meant.

'When I have customers for my dancing in the evening they think I don't excite them enough for them to put up a big price for my *shadi*. I don't like their control. They push me too much. They say we give you food, clothing, a video player to watch films on and you don't do what you're supposed to. Isn't it terrible to have your own family say that? They should provide me food in any case, shouldn't they?'

I was a little confused about the *shadi*. I knew about *nath utarwai*, the ritual when a dancing girl gets her first customer. The term literally means taking off the nose ring but *nath* actually refers to virginity, highly priced in this sex market. This concept of *shadi* was unclear to me, being the term the mainstream society uses for marriage.

I hesitated to say that I thought prostitutes did not marry, so I asked, 'What do they expect from a man who wants to marry you?'

She looked at me surprised, and said, 'Money!'

I thought I should phrase the question differently, and asked, 'Is this *shadi* like a regular shadi'?

'Yes.'

I was still not satisfied. 'After the *shadi*, do you go with that man?'

This I knew for sure could not happen, but I asked anyway, because I wanted to know how she was using the word *shadi*.

Slurping the last of the ice cream from her cup she said, 'No, the man lives with us at times.'

'At times?'

'Yes, when girls aren't lucky, the husband leaves and they go back to the business.'

Now I had some basic information to use with other informants.

I asked, 'What exactly happened when you tried to kill yourself?'

'The usual fight', she said. 'They were blaming me for not letting the family have a decent living and a reasonable future, for not thinking of my younger sisters and brothers, whose future depends on me. They were going on about how much they do for me and how I don't do my duty to them in return. They expect me to be eager to attract customers and earn good money for the family. I got very angry that day. I was eating a cantaloupe with a fork and tried cutting my wrist with it. I bled a lot. They had to take me to a hospital.'

'What was their reaction?' I empathized.

'They left me alone for a few days, but then started again. They can't blame me for bad business. Everyone in the Mohalla is having a hard time.'

Neither of us realized how fast the time flew by. We had gone round the hill and saw Laila's mother on the bench in the distance. She seemed restless and stood up in anticipation as she saw us walking towards her. As we came near she looked intensely at our faces. I felt she was trying to see whether we had discussed her family or had only made small talk.

We got in my car and drove away. I had been to the Gardens many times before, but this walk would forever remain engraved in my memory.

# 7

# THE UNBREAKABLE LINK OF OIL AND WATER

One morning I arrived at Sadiq's *baithak* just when his partner, Riaz, was about to begin a lesson. He asked me to stay to meet his students. Riaz was not yet a senior musician, and so his students were young children between two and eight years old.

His students started trickling in around 4 o'clock. First, came a two-year-old girl. Riaz said she was always the first to arrive, and the last one to leave. 'If all my students were like her,' he quipped, 'I'd soon be rich!' This little barefoot girl, dressed in pyjamas and a light sweater, had short hair with bangs and a permanent smile on her face. She spoke with a childish lisp. Riaz enjoyed listening to her little sentences. Other students came in soon after—a total of eight girls and one boy.

Riaz took out his harmonium and began singing a song about a bird. Some of the students sang with him, but the others just stared curiously at me. Riaz stopped to allow me to talk to them a little so they would get used to having me around. I didn't want to disturb the class.

After a while, he said he would start the dancing lesson. I thought it was because of me that he wasn't being very serious about teaching that day. But later, Sadiq told me that neither the teacher nor his students were very serious about the instructions. Riaz's payment was quite modest so the lessons never became very rigorous. He said that families who are serious about music get well-known masters to teach their girls. They pay well and the *ustads* teach very seriously.

The dancing began. Riaz played a *lehria* on his harmonium, and one of Sadiq's students played the *tabla*. As the students started to dance, I felt certain that most of those over five years old were copying dance steps picked up from watching Indian films. Riaz and the *tabla* player really wanted me to see this two-year old girl. They laughed with enjoyment as they encouraged her. Neither my presence nor Riaz's laughter bothered this little dancer. She was fully involved, in perfect sync with the beat, and very original with her dance steps.

The musicians' sub-culture is a distinctive feature of the Mohalla. In general, the musicians rarely live with their families, but, like *Ustad* Sadiq, maintain a *baithak* in the Mohalla and visit their families regularly at homes elsewhere. A clear set of traditions guides them in their personal, social and professional relations with the dancer community. Many *Mirasi* told me they live among the prostitutes 'like oil and water'. This phrase seemed part of their oral tradition and was used frequently to explain to the new generation the distance they should maintain.

Initially, I spent a lot of time at *Ustad* Sadiq's *baithak*, using it as my daily centre of operations. Then I started paying regular visits to the *baithaks* of *Ustad* Gaman and Allah Bakhsh. I became acquainted with many musicians who frequented these three *baithaks* and visited them often, arriving late in the morning, about 11 o'clock, which in fact, was quite early for them. Coming in just as they were waking up, I could meet whoever stayed the night in that small room. It took only five minutes to turn the *baithak* into a music room. Most of the musicians could play several different instruments. Often I saw that they would readily take whichever one their host handed them and just start playing.

One day while visiting *Ustad* Gaman, I met someone new who had just arrived from a distant village with a reference from one of Sadiq's colleagues. He was introduced to me in the typical manner. Introductions are an opportunity for a host to show hospitality to a guest. The man was described as one of Pakistan's promising young poets who write *dhamal* (folk songs or ballads). People always lavished praise on their guest artists, even if they had yet to produce their first work. Both the artist and the person making the introduction, love these flowery preliminaries

The poet took out his notebook and recited poetry for us. Some of the musicians went out to arrange for some breakfast. *Ustad* Gaman and the others sat with me in a circle on the rug and listened. Instruments were brought out and four musicians took up harmonium, *nal*, *dholak* and a *chimta*. First, *Ustad* Gaman played the harmonium and sang a song he had composed from the young poet's verses the night before. The musicians made changes as they went along. They praised each other on every *murki* (vibrato), and the poet at every punch line of the verses. Then they chose another *dhamal* and began composing a tune for it.

I found the process fascinating. The composer gave instructions to each musician. Often he instructed them to change instruments to give a different touch to the *dhamal*. Once he asked someone to fetch a musician from a neighbouring street who played the flute. The flute player had been asleep, so it took him a while to arrive, but his flute added a beautiful touch to the composition. The poet was very motivated and added two more couplets to his *dhamal*.

This continued until the breakfast of tea and *nihari* (lamb curry) arrived. This was not their usual breakfast, but had been arranged as a special treat for me. Only a few of the more senior *baithak* residents ate with me, while others just drank their usual tea. I was treated in this manner only occasionally, when the host was happy for some reason. This time *Ustad* Gaman had had a very successful stage show in Okara two nights before. He had led a troupe of four dancing girls and six of the musicians now present.

The music workshop continued with breaks of *jugat baazi*, slapstick jokes about people in the community. The composition of three songs was completed, including the one begun the night before. The composer decided to call his student Chanda in the evening to try out one of the songs. The other two songs he would sing himself. He told me he was planning to bring out his own album of *dhamals*. He also disclosed that he was using most of the 'boys' staying with him in a musical stage show for a wedding in a neighbouring town the following week. He had already received some money in advance and was expecting to make more from it.

In the past, the Shahi Mohalla was known for the high quality of its classical music, melodious singing voices and beautiful compositions. The musicians were the trainers and many young *Kanjar* girls learned their lessons well. As I spent more time in the area I learned that a growing number of girls no longer take their music training seriously. The lax attitudes of both students and teachers during their lessons made this evident, but it was also painfully noticeable in their performances. Only a few *ustads* actually teach classical singing to their students, and these few also compose *geet* and *ghazals* for their best students. These teachers usually push their students to become professional singers, first for radio and television and, eventually, for the film industry. Young performers aiming to be truly classical recording artists are almost non-existent.

The demand from the customer dictates the level and the quality of performance. Some families still try to keep up with their classical *ragas* and *ghazals*, but most have switched to film songs because the customers rarely request anything else.

The average number of customers a *kotha* typically entertains in a year has dropped by almost half since the 1970s. Most of them are just struggling to survive. They have no time to nurture good music. If people demand Punjabi film songs, the *kotha* management will not invest in maintaining high quality classical performers. Customers are less discriminating about music and are usually pleased with whatever is performed. The typical customer today is also much poorer than the patrons of even the recent past. Few can afford to enter extended, exclusive relationships with individual dancing girls. In the past, these relationships created a security shield allowing a woman to focus on her music. Now they focus more on extracting money from each fleeting visitor. I clearly observed that people who were trying to continue the tradition of classical music struggled for work while those who responded to society's highly commercialised demands were doing comparatively better.

Dance training is as important as singing lessons for these girls. Dance is not only a significant part of the Mohalla's regular evening performances, but is also a key to success in potential future film careers. Being a good dancer is equally, if not more important than being a good actress. In South Asia, acting and dance are inseparable, especially for women. Each film has about six songs, many of them are group dances. Women who are serious about pursuing a film career stress their dance training. The most famous film dancers of our time, Ishrat Chaudhry, Meena Chaudhry, Zamarrud and Alia, all came from such Mohalla families.

In the past, classical dancing was considered a more serious pursuit. *Kathak* was popular during the Mughal period. Dancers were trained by renowned teachers and were well rewarded by their patrons. However, in the red light districts and their counterparts in the royal courts, dancing for its own sake was not common. The dancer was trained to dance to the words of songs she would sing. The *bhao* or movement accentuated the poetry. The dancer would also sing a *ghazal* in a sitting position, while her hands moved in the dance form and facial expressions conveyed her interpretation of the words. These hand movements are still very common among professional singers.

The quality of dance in the Mohalla has declined over the past few decades. Dance styles now are mostly copied from Indian or Pakistani films. The dress and make-up of the Mohalla dancers are careful imitations of their favourite stars. They might even wear coloured contact lenses to make themselves look more like a certain actress. The dancers of today try to make as much noise with their *ghungroo* as possible. The dance moves are crudely seductive and perform a highly complex function with the body and the eye movements controlling the customer. While a girl may learn basic dance moves from her dance master, she learns their appropriate use in controlling customers by observing older dancers and listening to her manager. Some dance masters are even being replaced by video films, from

*Ustad* Tafu, a prominent *tabla* player and composer

13

*Ustad* Mohammad Sadiq on harmonium and *Ustad* Goga on tabla are training a young pupil

In addition to a music teacher, a dancing girl requires a teacher for learning dance

14

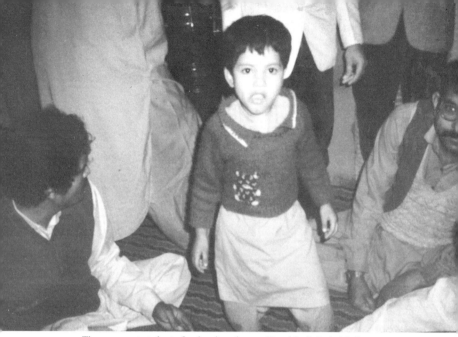

The youngest student of a dancing class at *Ustad* Sadiq's *baithak*

The dancer learns to use her ankle bells with the rhythm of the *tabla*

*Ustad* Mohammad Sadiq's
first published cassette

*Ustad* Sadiq with his pupils

A group of budding artists working together in a musicians' *baithak*

16

which the actions are copied and performed at night during the *mujra*. However, social pressure still requires engaging a proper *ustad* for training in singing.

The government's attitude towards the Mohalla has been a major factor in its decline. Constant harassment of the residents, clients and community leaders of the area, by the police and the local administration adversely affects their business. The stigmatisation of this community also discourages the residents from attempting to make their name as musicians. In the early 80s, Pakistan radio and television authorities were verbally instructed to enforce a ban on hiring artists from the Shahi Mohalla, thus demoralising the whole community.

Haji Altaf Hussain, commonly known as Tafu, a prominent exponent of the *tabla*, is one of the Shahi Mohalla's most respected *ustads*. Tafu is a serious musician who is deeply concerned about the decline in the quality of music in the Mohalla. He links this dilemma directly to the government's harassment, through the police. He feels that laws like Hudood that regulate extra-marital sex, including both rape and adultery, are implemented selectively in the Mohalla more to aggravate certain people than to provide a general control mechanism for society. These laws are commonly used to lock up residents of the Mohalla. It is open knowledge that prostitution is practiced here, but the police use these laws selectively either to extort money or to harass specific individuals at the request of high level politicians.

Tafu describes the application of the law as, '*Sui te thaga howe tad o law lagda e. Je sui nu phar lain te thaga bazar wich phire, tad nain lagda*' (When the needle is threaded the law is applicable, when the needle is put aside and the thread roams the bazaar, it is not applicable). His point is that the law is only applicable when a man and woman are caught together committing adultery, but the police often pick a woman from her house and a man from the street and book them both under Hudood. He claims that most of the cases are trumped up, and cites this as the main hurdle that has forced many *ustads* and serious musicians to leave the area.

Tafu thinks that the government should either completely shut down the music, including radio, television and film, or let the music flourish so that women need not focus on prostitution so much. In his opinion the society is getting 'free diamonds' in the form of trained artists without spending any money on them and it shouldn't create a fuss. He believes that if society and the government gave their support to music, good artists would return to the Mohalla making the main focus beautiful music and creativity.

Tafu and his extended family live in two adjacent *havelis* in the Mohalla. Over the years he has tried to maintain a standard of high quality music there and is himself one of the most popular *tabla* players in films. He has played extensively with Madam Noor Jehan, Pakistan's most popular and respected female singer. Nevertheless, he feels obligated to promote interaction between younger musicians and the great *ustads* and is very concerned about the economic well-being of the great masters who are still living. Even though some are thriving because their children have succeeded in music or another business, none have many requests for concerts. Tafu wants to establish a system where some *ustads* could be supported to accept and train selected students, and has played a key role in arranging fundraisers through the Artist's Association.

Tafu and his brothers are incomparable musicians who rule the music scene in the Pakistani film studios. Every year, the family challenges any musician to come and compete with them. They organize a big gathering in the Ali Park, between the Lahore Fort and the Shahi Mohalla. Several musicians play the *tabla* before the Tafu brothers begin to display their art. No one dares challenge them. Not only because they are the best *tabla* players, but also because of the respect they command in the bazaar.

Artists from the Mohalla generally feel they are not appreciated in their own country. Support from other artists, both inside and outside of the community, provides them recognition and appreciation for their art. Approval from the older *ustads* means a lot to the serious young singers and musicians. It is on this limited support and scarce economic opportunities that some serious music still survives.

Tafu, though a star performer, is also an *ustad*. Because he succeeded through hard work, he only takes students who will work just as hard and is very strict regarding daily morning practice. He maintains a regular schedule of several hours of practice early in the morning and makes sure that his brothers and all his students do the same.

A *Kanjar* girl child hears the music of *tabla* and *ghungroo* from the day of her birth and must begin her formal music training well before her non-*Kanjar* friends start going to school. Each performing girl must have an *ustad* of some level, usually a *Mirasi* male, but occasionally a man from another family with strong musical traditions. The musicians, of course, perpetuate the idea that no performer has any future without a proper teacher. *Be-ustadi*, i.e., without a teacher is both a negative epithet and a swear word within the sub-culture of the musicians and dancing girls.

I met a thirteen-year-old girl and her father when they came to a *baithak* I was visiting. The musicians sitting in the room constantly joked about the girl not having an *ustad*. The father argued that his daughter could sing and would do all right. The musicians laughed at his arguments, and finally he admitted he lacked the money to afford an *ustad*. The others rejected this excuse immediately because of the range of instructors available. This social pressure to have an *ustad* seemed to reflect the unspoken belief that prostitution as a profession had to remain linked with music and dancing in order to survive in its traditional form. The musicians also use this pressure to ensure their own place and standing in the community, as well as a source of steady income.

The ceremony where an *ustad* is accepting a student can be quite elaborate. The *ustad* receives new clothes and sweets are distributed. A sum of money, depending on the family's presumed status, is given to the *ustad*, and a fixed monthly remuneration established. The gifts given not only reflect the family's personal preferences, but also reflect their wealth and the social status in the community. The *ustad* and his close friends and relatives, usually *Mirasi*, make known these gifts to other residents, thus reinforcing the donor's social status and enhancing the *ustad's* potential earnings. *Kanjar* families usually have to keep the *Mirasi* happy, as they can quite easily damage anyone's social image. In this way, the musicians maintain a subtle level of influence over the prostitutes.

Wealthier families request the *ustad* to come to their home to give the lessons, but usually the students go to the *ustad's baithak*. The students are required to go every day for at least a couple of hours, but many students, and some *ustads*, are relaxed about this.

The benefits of having an *ustad* go beyond merely learning music. He becomes the performer's main link to the music network. He not only brings musicians to play at the *kotha* every evening, but is also responsible for the development of his student's careers. He enables her to perform in stage shows, usually organized by senior musicians and prepares her by teaching her a variety of songs and makes her art presentable. He guides her on what to sing in front of which audience. Ultimately, he acts as an agent and introduces his better students to composers in radio, television and the film industry. If the *ustad* manages to push a student to a level where she becomes famous, his status as a musician and as a teacher also rises. He earns fame and more income by remaining with her and continuing to be her agent.

Sadiq had several students, but his heart was not in teaching. While he taught and accompanied his students in their *kotha* performances, he spent considerable time looking for work outside the Mohalla. He told me his income from performing at Laila's *kotha* hardly covered his *baithak* expenses, leaving nothing for his family. The income was higher previously; now, he could not rely on it to sustain him. He had turned increasingly to organising entertainment programmes for people outside the Mohalla as a source of income to support his family.

These shows are a strange mixture of old traditional theatre plays, television stage shows and the traditional dance performance of prostitutes, the *mujras*. The traditional theatre, which featured live stage plays lasting at least eight hours, included songs and dances during the breaks. Earlier, songs were included to give the actors a rest and for the stage workers to change the sets. Singers gained more popularity when radio was introduced into rural areas and the breaks in the theatre performances expanded while the length of the plays contracted. Eventually, just before the collapse of the traditional theatre as a recognizable art form, actors had to spend hours waiting for a popular singer to finish a set of songs.

The current form of rural theatre is now called a 'Variety Show' and features dancing girls dressed in flashy frilly western dresses and singers, mostly men, interspersed with comedy skits. The dancers, mostly from Shahi Mohalla, perform a modernized *mujra*, while the singers and musicians, typically *Mirasi*, sing popular Urdu and Punjabi songs. Pakistani television has contributed to this trend by producing their own hotchpotch brand of musical entertainment. A typical televised stage show has a few songs and some guests to joke with the master of ceremonies, himself usually a comedian, or a would-be one.

Rural middle class society accepts these 'Variety Shows' although the environment surrounding them is similar to a *mujra*. Men in the audience throw money at the dancers throughout the performance and often end up contacting the dancers for sexual services after the performance. Although some landlords and businessmen continue to request traditional *mujras*, many have switched to the 'Variety Show' alternative because modern society attaches social stigma to the word *mujra*. Replacing the Urdu 'mujra' with the English 'Variety Show' has lessened its disrepute. The 'Variety Show' format gives the traditional *mujra* a modern look by changing the dancers' costumes from *shalwar kamiz* to western dress and by adding a music synthesizer or a modern drum set. These changes may make people think they are not really attending a *mujra*. One should not to be confused as to why men attend 'Variety Shows'. However, they cannot be compared with other kinds of musical gatherings, like concerts and *mehfils* that are attended purely for the purpose of enjoying music.

Over a period of several months, I continuously observed three organizers of Variety Shows. The invitations received for the shows were from small businessmen, and not big landlords. These were men who felt a need to show off their wealth to their relatives. Almost all of these shows were performed for large audiences when a family was celebrating a major event. Usually these were weddings, but occasionally a man would celebrate his son's birth in this manner.

One difference between a *mujra* and a 'Variety Show' is quite clear; *mujras* are organized by the managers of the dancing girls, while the organization of a Variety Show is largely done by musicians. I later learnt that this makes a difference in the dynamics between the dancers and the audience. In a traditional *mujra* the entire focus is on making connections for sexual services. The organizers of a 'Variety Show' focus on the overall entertainment value of the performance, hoping for repeat requests.

Sadiq told me that he hopes to earn enough money from these shows to set up a recording studio where he can produce audiocassettes. This was his dream; and in his mind he had started working out the details of his plan.

## VIEWS

*Shoaib Hashmi, an educator and a prominent figure in the Pakistani cultural scene*

I had a very interesting discussion with Shoaib Hashmi, hoping for a good perspective on what Pakistani liberals think about the Mohalla.

Shoaib started off by saying, 'I hear you have been going around making *pangas* with the police. We need you, and your parents also surely want you to live. What are you up to, girl?'

As it was very difficult to be serious with him I laughed, and replied, 'you know I've been studying the Shahi Mohalla for quite some time now. I want to know what you think, specifically about the Mohalla, but also about the whole phenomenon of prostitution. Can you start off by giving me some historical perspective?'

He answered, 'Prostitution is considered to be the oldest profession in the world. What we know for sure is mostly from the times of Mughals when almost all the kings were great patrons of music and art and supported a huge number of performers, many of whom were also prostitutes. These artists used to live around the royal settlements, and were in their service, like employees with fixed salaries.

'Art requires some kind of patronage to develop, unless, of course, the society is aware enough to support it through the market. In our country, very few institutions hire performers or support artists at all. The Mohalla has produced this country's best singers and musicians, and I look at them with respect. Those people have sustained our art. Shahi Mohalla has nurtured the performing arts.

'This kind of prostitution must be understood within its context. These were places where the nobility would send their children to be groomed, to learn the manners associated with sitting through a *mehfil*, appreciating classical music, poetry, good wine, and beautiful women. It was all part of their education.'

'Things are very different now', I smiled.

'Yes,' he laughed, 'they are! I don't think many businessmen go there to learn manners anymore. But what's the harm? Society lets off a little steam there, helping it to maintain peace and a sort of moral balance in general. People go of their own free will. Most of those in the business are also doing it of their own will. I say if there is a place for young men to get their frustrations out, let them.'

'What do you think about forced prostitution?' I asked.

He answered loudly, 'Obviously that should be prohibited, but most of what is happening in the Shahi Mohalla, I believe, is the carrying on of the family occupation. Don't you agree? These people have been socialized into it by their families.'

Agreeing, I said, 'The element of force is, however, growing day by day. But to get back to your point, are you saying that we should not be too strict about prostitution? As long as people are not forced into it and indulge in it of their own will, on both sides, we should, in a way, ignore it.'

'Yes,' he replied, a little hesitantly, 'this can be considered an outlet of the society. Besides our society places so many restrictions on creativity, we should let this place nurture musicians and singers.'

I asked him politely, 'Do you think only men get frustrated? What about women? If you think this is an outlet and should be ignored, shouldn't there be a bazaar of men where women could go?'

Shoaib looked at me seriously and after a pause said, 'You have me there! This I never thought of. Yes, I was being liberal for men and opposed to these obnoxious restrictions that the government imposes, which is frankly harassment of the community, as well as their clients, but no, I did not think of this angle. Yes, I suppose that perhaps there should be one for women!'

I concluded, 'I'm not saying women need such a bazaar, but I just wanted you to realize how socialized we are when we view this phenomenon from only one angle.'

Mr Mehmud Kanjar, an influential political personality of the Shahi Mohalla

17

The police throw their weight, under the pretext of strict control over performance
timings of the dancers

No matter how involved she may seem in her dance, the dancer is fully aware of her customers

Holding her *dupatta*, the dancer sings to her customer, while musicians accompany her singing on their instruments

Rewarding the seductive moves of a dancer by showering money

# 8

## MEETING THE GREATEST PIMP
## OF OUR TIMES

For several weeks I had been pestering Sadiq to get me an appointment with Mehmud Kanjar, whom everyone referred to as Mudha Kanjar. A well-respected personality in the Mohalla, he was considered the key spokesman for the area. I was getting impatient to meet him because I knew he would give me an invaluable perspective. Finally, some other artists I knew in the Mohalla gave me his telephone number and I called his house from Islamabad. A woman answered. I introduced myself and told her the reason for my call. She told me to call the next day around 1 p.m. since Mudha Kanjar was out most of the day after that time. Like others in the Mohalla his day started around noon so one in the afternoon was about eight in the morning our time.

When I called the next day Mudha Kanjar was at home. He was charming and respectful and when I asked him for time for an interview so I could make plans to come to Lahore he was happily surprised that my trip would be determined by his availability. We arranged a time for me to meet him at his house on Friday.

The following Thursday, getting ready to leave my office a little earlier than usual in order to reach Lahore before nightfall, I mentioned my appointment to a colleague, Arif. His jaw dropped. 'Do you know who he is?' he asked, in an odd voice.

Casually, packing my briefcase, I answered, 'Yes, he is a big leader of the Mohalla, and I guess he has been in politics as well.'

Arif slapped his forehead and screamed as if he were truly frightened, 'He is the biggest pimp of our times! He is one of the most powerful men in the Mohalla and has links with leaders of big organised crime gangs. You don't know who you are dealing with!'

Tired of everyone worrying about my visits to Shahi Mohalla, I said, 'Give me a break! I'm just going to interview the man!' I sat on my chair and started to write a note for another colleague.

Arif stood staring down at me and asked, 'Are you taking someone along?'

'Like a bodyguard? No, I'm going alone.'

Arif shouted with frustration and fear, 'Do you know the risks you're taking? They could involve you in something and you wouldn't even know about it. You are crazy to go alone. My God! I don't understand how you roam around there by yourself in any case, but meeting with this guy, Fouzia, you're making yourself really very vulnerable.'

I finished scribbling my note and stood up, 'Nobody has chased my car or even uttered an offensive remark to me in the Mohalla. I'm afraid I can't say the same about this liberal city of Islamabad. I need a bodyguard when I'm NOT in the Mohalla. People chase me for fun on the Grand Trunk Road when I'm driving to Lahore. Why? Just because I'm a woman travelling alone. I hear lewd remarks all the time in other markets in Lahore, but, even though the Mohalla is very crowded, no one there has ever touched me or offended me.' With that, I picked up my briefcase and my car keys, and left the office.

Later that evening, in Lahore, I sat with a few musicians who knew Mehmud Kanjar. Two of them had abandoned music. Afzal sold shawls on the street and Iqbal had started a video shop. To prepare for my interview the next day, I asked as many questions as I could about the political scene in the Mohalla and its relationship to the nation's politics, and specifically about Mehmud Kanjar's position in the area.

The musician who was still struggling to survive in his profession said, 'Mudha Kanjar is very well known here. He roams the Mohalla like a lion on the plains. Even people who have never been to the bazaar know his name.'

Iqbal continued, 'When the police arrest our people and put them behind bars to harass them, people run to him for help, and he always gets people out of jail.'

Afzal added, 'Mudha has never ditched us. He has always stood up for us, no matter how strict the government.'

I had already talked to other people about Mudha Kanjar. Most considered him a spokesman for the Mohalla. They said he was the manager of several brothels. There were mixed opinions about his role in the community. People feared him but at the same time they thought of him as a hero, a great leader.

The next day I found his house, a modest looking place with a simple wooden door, on a narrow street, away from the main bazaar. When I knocked, a young man came out. He seemed to be a servant and I told him who I was. He asked me to wait, but didn't invite me inside the house. Almost immediately, Mehmud Kanjar appeared. A tall, fair complexioned man in a starched *halwar kamiz*, he had a powerful appearance. His grey hair and thick grey moustache gave him a very impressive look. After greeting me he said, 'Let's go to the house of our treasurer, Zamurad. We can sit there and talk.'

We walked through some streets to the main bazaar road, an area quite familiar to me by now. He stopped at a house and announced that this was the *haveli* where we would sit. The entrance was grandiose, a huge, ornately carved wooden door with stucco designs on the side and a heavy frieze on the top. The door opened, and we went up a flight of steps and entered a living room on the second floor. The staircase continued up. A young girl of about eleven ushered us into the room, which was partially furnished in the western style, with a sofa, and partly in the typical eastern style, with floor seating. Tube pillows lined one side of the room.

Mehmud and I sat on the opposite ends of the sofa. A harmonium lay to one side and various ornaments and photographs decorated the walls. The girl came back with two bottles of 7-Up. She was dressed in a very modest *shalwar kamiz* and had a curious smile on her face, as though she enjoyed showing us in and serving us drinks. Something interesting was happening in her day.

Mehmud clearly did not want to start the formal interview just yet. He made polite conversation while we waited for Zamurad. It seemed as though he wanted me to talk to them together to get both points of view. He felt she had a unique perspective on the Mohalla's standing in our society and the current issues the people were facing. I made my position clear as well. First, that I wasn't wearing any moralistic hat, so they didn't have to prove their chastity to me. Secondly, I wanted to let him know I had a basic understanding of the system in the Mohalla so they wouldn't think I was a naive outsider and tell me fairy tales. I spoke informally, using specific jargon typical of the sub-culture, and talked about recent events in the area. I asked whether 'Mian Sallu's' political office was still in the City Cinema. 'Sallu' is the nickname of Yousuf Salauddin, a political figure of the Mohalla who owns many properties there. I asked whether the *pagri* of Tibbi Thana was still the highest. This referred to the bribe a policeman must pay for a post in the Mohalla. The commander of the Tibbi Thana, the Mohalla's Police Station, is the most expensive post in Lahore. Men competing for it offer hundreds of thousands of rupees in bribes. Once in position, they harass the inhabitants to quickly recoup their investment and make a profit before being transferred again.

Zamurad came in. She was in her early forties and a bit heavy, exquisitely dressed, well made-up and very attractive. I could not help but notice the big diamond rings on both her hands. Mehmud introduced me as someone from Islamabad writing about the Mohalla.

I began by asking about the history of the Mohalla and how long it had been in its present form. Mehmud sat upright and began, 'I am sixty-seven years old. Long ago the bazaar used to be in Purani Anarkali, then it shifted to Lohari Mandi. Chowk Chakla in Lohari still retains its name. A famous courtesan Shamsa Begum, who later became a famous singer had her *kotha* there. The set-up then moved to Landa bazaar and from there to Moti bazaar. It moved to this area about a hundred years ago. When I was born there were gaslights, but no electricity. The Tibbi Thana had Banyan trees nearby and no one went there during the day.'

When I asked about the organisation which he heads, Anjuman-e-Fankaran-e-Lahore (Association of the Artists of Lahore), Mehmud's eyes lit up. This was his pet topic. 'This organisation was formed in response to the suppression we faced from the administration over the years. It's main objective is to protect all the Shahi Mohalla's performing artists. We take care of our community. The organisation has twenty-nine people in the executive body. They represent different families, but all are from our *biradri* (the Kanjar community).'

Fixing her *dupatta* and bangles, Zamurad added casually, 'When the system doesn't provide protection, people have to do it themselves.'

Mehmud, with a strong tone of complaint in his voice, continued loudly, 'Both the society outside and the administration within the Mohalla consider us to be bad people. If one of our girls sings somewhere, they consider her a prostitute, but when Tahira Syed or Gulshan Ara Syed sing, they are not abused, although they learned the art from us.'

I interrupted politely to ask whether the organisation was limited to Lahore's Shahi Mohalla, or whether it was larger than that.

Mehmud looked at me proudly, and said, 'The organisation represents performing artists from all over Punjab—Sargodha, Okara, Pattoki, Rawalpindi, Lyallpur, Lalamusa. Wherever our people are working, we keep in touch with them. But, we do not represent musicians.'

Curious, I broke in, 'You don't consider them artists?'

'No, no ...', Mehmud raised his hand to explain, 'Musicians are different. We cannot represent them. They have their own ethnic group and their own work. Their organisation is Ittehad-e-Musikaran (Unity of Musicians). They are the teachers and the trainers. Our girls are not born artists, and must be taught.

To us teachers are respectable, just like a father, but in the eyes
of others in the society even they have lost their value.'

I let the issue go as I thought I could learn from the musicians
why musicians and dancers are considered different when it
comes to fighting government discrimination.

'You were in politics, weren't you?' I asked Mehmud.

'Yes,' he replied. 'In 1979, I became the councillor. In 1983,
they divided our area into three wards, so that one councillor
could not represent the whole area. At present, Tibbi area, Shahi
Mohalla and Heera Mandi are separate electorates. I have always
worked for our people. In 1979, a convention was held under
General Sawar Khan. All the councillors were bringing up issues
from their areas. When I stood up, people objected. They said
I was from Heera Mandi and my area should be closed down.
General Sawar told the audience of councillors that if they
wanted to shut the place down so badly, they should 'own' our
women and men. He asked those who were willing to marry the
prostitutes to raise their hands, and when no one did, he said
'Until we marry all their girls, and give our girls to their sons,
we will not transform the society. If we cannot do it now, we
should wait until the whole society is reformed. Then Heera
Mandi won't be needed anymore.'

Sinking back into the sofa, he continued, 'Since Ayub Khan's
time*, we've been participating in politics, working actively
and participating fully, but people consider us untouchables. If
you look at the people this area has produced, you'd be
surprised. We have produced senior government officials,
advocates, and some military officers. Being in the mainstream
they can't openly disclose their association with us and can't
fight for us. A few people like Iqbal Hussain, a teacher at the
National College of Arts, have the courage to declare their
origins in our area.'

'We inhabit altogether about fourteen to fifteen bazaars; we
could build a wall around it and declare it a state. The population

---

* Field Marshal Mohammad Ayub Khan was Pakistan's first military ruler
during the 1960s.

is about four or five hundred thousand with about 200,000 voters. Don't you think we should have our own representative? The rooms used for the singing business alone number around 400-500. Many more families than that live in this area. Why doesn't the society accept us? Look at our contribution in the field of cricket and hockey. We gave them so many good players.'

'But when it comes to voting,' he said angrily, 'they keep asking the names of our fathers. It is not good to embarrass people. We say if we start putting down the correct names of the fathers on the National Identity Cards we will be in trouble. We should be allowed to put our maternal grandfather's or uncle's, or our brother's names on our ID cards rather than this insistence that we give out our father's name. What if we don't know his name? What if we do, and he is a big politician or an army general? What will happen to us then?'

'The Art Councils were initiated during Ayub Khan's period,' he continued, 'compare how many artists they have produced against the number we have given to the country. Actually, many of the artists working in the art councils also come from our area. We provide performers to the whole country. The musicians are ours, the dancers are ours, the songs are ours and the teachers are ours. The tragedy is that we cannot openly take the credit for it.'

We were interrupted by the food and tea, a significant part of life in the Mohalla. The same young girl, accompanied by a male servant this time, brought *kheer* for the guests. Conversation stopped while Zamurad bent forward to fix the cover on the centre table before the food was put down. She looked at me and said, 'This is a speciality of this area.'

'And my favourite dessert!' I exclaimed. Both Zamurad and Mehmud smiled.

I noticed that Zamurad had hardly spoken. I wanted her to join the conversation. I knew she had married outside the Mohalla and outside her clan, so I asked her about that.

Zamurad sighed and said, 'I was married for twenty-five years, but to tell you the truth my husband's family didn't accept

me, not for a single day. I experienced constant hostility from
his family as well as his friends.' Her voice broke. She cleared
her throat and asked for a glass of water, and Mehmud took
over.

'Yes, take Zamurad's example,' he said, 'she was married to
Mian Sahib. He forced everyone to accept her as his wife.
Nevertheless, society does not accept a woman from this area,
and now that he has died his family is afraid that she will get a
share of the property, so they have forced her and her daughter
to leave. They won't accept any woman from this area even if
she marries one of their men. They only accept, and even then
only to a certain extent, a woman who is successful in the film
industry. They respect her and let her sit with them, but always
condemn a woman who has been taken directly from our
profession.'

'I broke every link with the Mohalla when I left,' said
Zamurad sadly.

'Was coming back your own choice?' I asked.

She answered, 'As long as Mian Sahib was alive he stood by
me. His family always thought he made a mistake and they
pushed me out the day he died. I had no other choice, but to
return to my family.'

Mehmud bent forward. Putting his elbows on his knees, he
said, 'Now she is here. Where else could she go? Her daughter
is in a hostel, and she lives here. This does not mean that she
indulges in prostitution. She just lives with her family. Her
financial conditions pushed her to work in the films for a while.
She had to survive.'

I looked around the room and noticed there were no
photographs of Zamurad on the walls. Maybe they were removed
when she left twenty-five years ago. Mehmud started talking to
Zamurad about some activities that he would co-ordinate with
her in the evening. I think he did not want her to get emotional.

Mehmud looked at me and said, 'we are openly discriminated
against in every way. Just think, we have only a limited area, a
few of the inner city bazaars, in which we can conduct our
business and only a limited time each day, from eleven in the

evening to one in the morning. We tried talking to the politicians, but it was of no use. For eleven years, during Ziaul Haq's martial law, we suffered continuously. Even after that, no one cared about us. They made excuses not to meet with us. They only come at election time. Some of the politicians are in the drug business. On the one hand, they perform Haj and, on the other, when they get our women pregnant, they make them abort their babies. What can we do with these people? The bureaucrats are strange. They don't even consider us human. We aren't sure if we live in our own country, Pakistan, or in Israel. They put a crown of gold on the head of one girl and call her *Malika-e-Taranum* or *Malika-e-Ghazal*, and our other girls they call *gashtian*.'

Mehmud continued describing the oppression they face, 'Why have they restricted us to performing only from eleven to one at night. We agree that one o'clock is late, so why can't we start at eight or nine in the evening? They do not even let us rehearse in the evenings. We are forced to close our business for the month of *Ramazan* for fasting. Tell me any business that can afford to close all of *Ramazan*. During the month of *Muharram* they force us to close for more than thirteen days for mourning. All over Pakistan, businesses close only for the ninth and tenth of *Muharram*. Even the Shia continue their business, though they mourn. We have a hard time to fight for our rights.'

Zamurad raised her eyebrows and said, 'And *Basant*?' Perhaps she just wanted to remind Mehmud. She was not saying much, but listening carefully, as if to make sure Mehmud covered the significant issues. Mehmud, on the other hand, enjoyed making speeches. His political career was very evident in how he spoke. I could imagine him being in a big audience making a loud speech, pausing for emphasis at the right moments.

Mehmud quickly responded, asking, 'What should I say about *Basant*, the kite flying festival? That has become controversial for everyone, but even religious occasions, like *Shab-e-Barat* and *Meraj Sharif*, are difficult to celebrate. When our girls go to the shrine of our Sufi saint Data Sahib to say the morning prayers, the police and the civil administrators harass them. They say they have other intentions.'

'We did not suffer like this under Ayub Khan. People say that this bazaar was closed in Ayub's time, but it isn't true. He only closed the Tibbi Gali area, where women indulged in prostitution with no connection to singing or dancing. I think he made a mistake because 400 or 500 women left that bazaar and established themselves all over the city. When people raised an uproar about that some residents were allowed to return. The place is still closed, but not the business.'

'Ayub Khan never shut the singing down. How could he? He was a Pathan and Pathans are among our biggest customers. They invite us to sing on festive occasions. We provided the entertainment for the wedding of Ayub Khan's children. The beautician who did the make-up of both his daughter and his son's bride, was our girl, Rebecca. Was it bad that we went to do a 'function' at his house? No, it was acceptable because he had social and political status, but it is not all right when we go elsewhere. Are they pushing us away now because their own girls have started to appear on television, so their girls get to sing instead of ours? They say we are a threat to their values, but when daughters of big military officers and other big shots sing on television in a western style, its okay. When these girls sing are they promoting *chadar aur chardiwari*? Don't they accept money for their work?'

'From 1978 to 1988, we supported General Ziaul Haq in whatever way we could. Despite that, his people were very harsh with us, and tried in every way to suppress us. We suffered a great deal during Ziaul Haq's martial law. Ziaul Haq made statements on television like, 'My faith will not be shattered by listening to *Malika-e-Taranum* Noor Jehan!' Such statements, cynically impugning the dignity of our greatest artist, hurt us very much. All the actresses and singers who reached the heights of popularity in the film world are from us but are also respectable. Our girls are religious; they are sensitive. Some of our girls who do not get into this business are properly married. They are brought up in seclusion. We have our own ways and tradition. We educate and train them. No one should put us down without understanding our system. We were hoping that democracy would bring us some freedom and an opportunity to exercise our rights as citizens of this country. No regime has proved to be any better than the others for us. We will see what the future holds.'

'About ten to fifteen days ago the head of the police station, recently appointed here, called me at eleven o'clock at night. He asked me to sit down and said his senior officers have an objection against me. They don't want me to roam around the bazaar at night. I told them it's my area, and I am the people's leader. My sisters and daughters are here, and although none of my family members do business in this area, these are my people. 'Why shouldn't I go out?' I asked. Nobody had ever objected before. I told him that he was concerned only because we had won the election twice and this time the Inspector General Police must have his own candidate in mind. It's all a political game. They were trying to pressure us, but it won't work.'

Sympathetically, I told Mehmud that I had been hearing a lot about this kind of intense discrimination. 'What specifically is your organisation demanding from the government?' I asked.

Gulping down the *kheer*, he answered, 'We want the laws to be as in the 1970s. We had protection then. We could perform freely in our homes as artists.' He put his plate on the table, looked directly at me, 'We have an order, passed by the High Court in 1978, permitting us to conduct our business from ten thirty to one o'clock at night, but now we cannot open before eleven. We used to be able to inform the police whenever we took our girls for performances in other places. This protected them from any accident or mishap with the host party. We want that back. These days, on top of all the government restrictions, the police are even worse. They abuse the law and use those restrictions to make money out of us. But they will never succeed in suppressing us.'

He continued, 'Sending our girls out on jobs to perform for weddings, birthday parties or other functions is rarely possible now. We are always afraid the police might use some excuse to arrest them. They have no security. The police have check posts, where they investigate the relationship between any man and woman travelling together. They claim the girl is lying if she says she is with her *ustad* or her brother. They ask, 'Does your kind have brothers, too?' We protest this discrimination. We pay *zakat*, *ushr* and willingly give any kind of donation of food, clothes and money. We pay tax on the property we own here. We pay for electricity, water and other facilities at commercial rates. At those times we are Muslims and Pakistanis, but when it comes to our rights it seems we are considered to be neither.'

Mehmud's voice became louder and louder. He seemed happy to have an audience for what he wanted to say to the authorities. He went on, 'We don't want to go out and beg people to have mercy on us. We want to work for our people. You may not realize it, but here we are worse than prisoners. Prisoners, at least, can move around in their own area, but if our girls come out in the bazaar the police become suspicious and harass them. They cannot even pass through the market in peace. If we 'knock the door of the law' and get lawyers to protect us, the police accuse us of making false charges. Meanwhile, they continue to make false charges about carrying guns, using heroin, gambling, or whatever they feel like. Once the police put me in jail. The whole Mohalla came out in protest. The police said they would not let me go because I was behind everything here. A member of the Provincial Assembly intervened and I was released. But what is the use? The politicians get us locked up and then they get us out to keep us obligated to them.'

'Let me tell you what happened. It was the night between the 7th and 8th of May, and was the 20th and 21st day of the month of *Ramazan*. We were planning to go to the police station to ask about the check post at the entrance of our area. The administration is very strange; they make police check posts right on the roads. We were planning to take out a *ziarat* for Hazrat Ali (RA) and had worked out the route and were planning to inform the police about it. You have to work out different routes for the women and the men. I had called a meeting and we were obtaining contributions for the arrangements. This was for the *iftar* of 21st *Ramazan*. Just imagine they charged me with gambling. I am the leader of our people and a member of the Shia sect. I am also the secretary of the Shia organisation. We were holding their contributions in our hands and were giving it to our boys to arrange to distribute *tabaruk* among people at specific spots. The police raided and grabbed us, dragged us to the police station and started beating us. That was the reason that the whole fight took place. People reacted and demanded an open court for this case. They wanted a neutral person from outside to decide whether the accusations were right or wrong. How can a man, who is so active in Hazrat Ali's (RA) ziarat every year, gamble during Ramazan?'

'We took the legal course of action. The administration that was supposed to respond to our appeal suppressed us all the more. They pressured us as much as they could, but, little did they know, we cannot be suppressed. How can society be so cruel to us? We have given them art, music, and poetry and look what they give us.'

When we finished both Zamurad and Mehmud sent me off with prayers and wished me luck in completing my work and wanted me to come see them often. I made plans to visit some of the *kothas* in the area the next weekend with Mehmud.

I returned to Islamabad and to my work and happened to meet Arif. He asked, 'So, you've returned. Did you see him?'

I smiled, 'I drank with him, ate with him, had a good talk with him and am planning to see him again. I couldn't ask for more.' I was walking fast, late for a morning meeting, and Arif rushed to keep up with me.

He looked confused, 'so…so how was it?' he stammered.

I said, 'The best part was the kheer. I loved it!'

On that note, I went into my meeting.

# VIEWS

## A government civil servant

'I wanted to talk to a government official about the steps the government was taking to curb prostitution in Shahi Mohalla. The man I met obviously supported the efforts fully. Sitting stiffly behind his large and imposing desk, he looked at me, and asked, contemptuously, 'do you think we can deal with these people kindly? Do you think any civil attempt would make them give up their profession? Not at all! These pimps are so shrewd they can manipulate us all. We have to be strict with them. The only way to make them stop is to attack their source of income. We limit their hours of operation, only let them sing and dance and nothing else, no hanky-panky. Legally they can only sing and dance, but we all know what happens there. So, if they are, as you say, 'harassed', it is because of what they do.'

'What about the fact that prostitution is spreading all over Lahore since people feel police extortion in the Mohalla is too much and they are safer taking their business elsewhere. Some people say the harsh behaviour of the police in the Mohalla is just a show for the public.'

'You don't believe all these opposition lies, do you? We're strict with them and will continue to be strict because that is the only way to deal with these sinful people.'

'Why are the police not strict with the visitors who come after the official hours, all those high flying politicians and senior officials?' I asked.

'No one goes there after one o'clock!' He said.

'I saw them myself,' I said calmly.

'Nonsense! Those must be the residents. You know they are up the whole night, it's their lifestyle,' he said angrily.

'Do you think you can eradicate prostitution like this, or in any way, for that matter?' I asked.

'Of course!' he answered, 'at least we must try. We cannot say, like the activists do, that prostitutes should be treated with dignity and that they are women being humiliated by the police.' He laughed loudly, 'we will humiliate them; we will crush them; they are the scum of this society. We are an Islamic society. We should not tolerate this.'

'*I understand your approach,*' *I said,* '*although I don't agree that you can eliminate prostitution like that. What I do not understand are the double standards. In your raids why don't you catch the influential people who are there? Anyway, don't the police collect bhatta from those houses? And tell me why the pagri of the Tibbi Thana is the highest anywhere? People must be making some good money there, right? The story is full of contradictions.*'

'*It's all hearsay,*' *he answered, looking annoyed,* '*there is no pagri for that police station and no contradictions. It's easy to attack people here because they're all in one place. We can't attack prostitutes spread all over the city.*'

'*Don't you realize that the stricter you are with people in the Mohalla the faster prostitution spreads elsewhere? I've been told it's easier for sex workers outside the Mohalla. Another thing is that the kind of prostitution that's spreading is far more dangerous than what you have in the Mohalla. There, at least the women are born into a clan with some sense of responsibility for their livelihood. The new trend outside the Mohalla involves forced prostitution, with pimps setting up new brothels in every part of the city, and the women being dumped in the gutters as soon as they lose their beauty.*'

*He concluded,* '*We will follow them and crush them wherever they go. I think we are making their lives so difficult that they're leaving their business and running away.*'

# 9

# NEW YEAR'S EVE

I had abandoned my friends in Islamabad to keep working in Lahore on my research. I wanted to be in the Shahi Mohalla every weekend and whatever other time I could take away from my office.

New Year's celebrations are not a traditional part of Pakistan's culture, the solar year being followed only for convenience. For celebrations and other critical occasions, the lunar year is used. Unfortunately, the lunar year starts with a month of mourning so the Islamic year makes no room for celebrating the New Year either. Since Islamabad is more westernised than the rest of Pakistan, New Year's Eve does hold an attraction for people there, especially the young.

I was staying at my uncle's house in Lahore. Schools and colleges were closed for the winter break so I had many cousins around. Sara, a friend from Islamabad, called to say she was in Lahore and she and her American husband would like to go to the Mohalla with me on New Year's Eve. Sara was born in Pakistan, but brought up elsewhere. She looks Pakistani, but her behaviour is not traditional. Some of my cousins overheard my conversation with her and began nagging me to take them along, too.

Young Pakistani women, even those in college, can be quite childish about insisting on getting what they want. I couldn't blame them for wanting to go to the Mohalla. Society has created such a mystery about the place that anyone would be intrigued by it. These were three young girls of about the same age. Two were seniors in college and one, Faiza, was doing her masters'. They wanted any opportunity for fun. Other than studies and wearing colourful clothes, their life was quite monotonous. Nothing seemed as thrilling as a trip to the Mohalla. They desperately wanted to be a part of this adventure.

Sadia pleaded, 'Please, please, please, take us there, I have read many *afsane* about these women. I really want to go and meet one.'

I told them, 'They are just like us, you know! Like any woman in the old city of Lahore!'

Samina said, 'We have to see at least one with our own eyes. Once a friend of mine drove through that area and she saw....'

Sadia was astonished, 'Alone?' she exclaimed.

'No, stupid', said Samina, 'her brother and his friends were going and she went along.'

'How lucky! My brother would kill me before he would take me there,' said Sadia.

I said, 'So, why do you want me to take you, so I'll get in trouble?'

Samina answered, 'No one will know, I promise. You know, this friend of mine told me that they saw bright lights and women all dressed up in rooms and musicians sitting around.' Sadia and Faiza were listening with their eyes wide open.

'Did she visit a *kotha*?' I asked.

'Are you kidding?' her eyes popped, 'God, no!' Samina shrieked, 'They were all terrified. They drove through the bazaar and came back. They didn't even stop to eat. Actually, their plan was to go to the *Phaja paie wala* and eat *paie*. They really just wanted to see the *kothas*, but they were so scared that they didn't dare stop anywhere.'

Sadia asked curiously, 'Do her parents know?'

Samina laughed cynically, 'Sadia, how stupid! Parents can't know things like that. They would have killed them. No one is supposed to go there. They kidnap girls and force them to become prostitutes. Haven't you seen that in the movies?'

'Please!' I interrupted, 'if you think we'll go to the *kothas* you see in movies, just forget about it. What you see on film isn't what you'll find there. The movies are the filmmakers' fantasies where they try to re-create the times of the Mughals, when rich people had big *havelies*. One *kotha* shown in a film can fit twenty real *kothas* from the Mohalla. They're very small rooms really. The dancers are quite simple compared to what you see in films, absolutely no *pishwaz* and gorgeous dresses and jewellery like the movies show. The women are noisy and rowdy and not sophisticated like Rekha, Meena Kumari, and Rani (famous actresses who have played courtesans). They make so much noise with their *ghungroos* that you can hardly hear the singing. Many of them have hoarse voices. Few sing well. The pretty ones, good dancers or singers, are taken out of there by film producers right away, so what you see are the leftovers.'

I noticed how I had disappointed these excited young women. Looking at their long faces, I said, 'I'm so sorry, but this is what has become of the Mohalla. The customers have no taste in music. All they want is vulgar sex, so the entertainment is geared to very obvious and shoddy gestures. No subtle romance. You've probably changed your minds about going there now.'

'No!' came the single, shrill note from the whole group. They all started talking at once, 'We want to go. Please take us. We'll never have this opportunity again in our lives. Don't be so cruel.'

On and on they raved about it. Sara and her husband arrived and they started lobbying with her. I told them that I would take them only if they got permission from their parents, but of course they couldn't do that. Instead, they guilt tripped me for being unreasonable, and said I should believe in women's empowerment and shouldn't think that adult women like themselves needed permission from their parents to go out for an evening. Finally, I gave in.

Since I was taking such a chance I thought I should call Mohsin, a young, male, cousin of mine to come along. I figured I might need someone mature to handle so many guests. He came right over, without telling his parents where he was going either. He was about thirty years old and very level-headed. I also called Laila, to warn her of the invasion.

We left in two cars. We parked in my regular spot in the Mohalla and as usual asked the shopkeeper nearby to watch our cars. The three young women were very ambivalent about how to behave. In times of confusion like this, the standard behaviour for young Pakistani middle class women is to giggle: In addition, they all decided to cover their faces, suddenly realizing they would be in big trouble if they were seen here by anyone who knew their parents, their friends, their future husbands or future in-laws. In their self-induced panic they clung to each other, covered their heads and faces with their *dupattas*, and giggled.

I began walking towards Laila's house and realized that nobody was following me, not Sara, Mohsin or Sara's husband. I turned around and all I saw were three bundles standing by my car. I couldn't believe the fear they had of this place, or the terror they had of being seen here. I shouted at them, 'Act normal! People will notice you more if you walk around like mummies.' They loosened their *dupattas* a little, but kept their faces covered and quickly followed me. I could hear the three girls whispering, each blaming the other for bringing them there.

The Americanized Sara, on the other hand, was so intrigued by everything that she kept saying 'hi' to everyone. People looked at her in astonishment. I pulled her close to me and told her she needn't be so friendly with people on the street. 'They don't see women, other than prostitutes, in the bazaar at night so they are surprised by us. People are trying to guess whether or not we are prostitutes.' Her husband was also acting like a tourist, and being white, was attracting a lot of attention, which he returned with big smiles and nods. Mohsin was the only normal one. I looked back and saw him walking behind the three girls. I muttered to myself, 'Thank you, Mohsin, I do need help with this group tonight.'

A few days later Mohsin told me that when he was following me on the street behind the young women, his legs were trembling. He had never been to the Mohalla before and was fretting, 'What am I doing here, and why did I listen to Fouzia, who is nothing but trouble.' He actually thought that he was putting his future on the line. Listening to him tell me this later, I couldn't believe it and had a good laugh.

Once we reached Laila's *kotha* everyone relaxed. The environment struck them since it's really like a living room in any house. The dancer and the musicians were the only difference. I noticed my cousins' mouths were open with astonishment, and they were starring at Laila as though she was an object.

I laughed and said, 'Laila, why don't you talk to my friends while I visit your mother.' Kaisera wasn't well. I went to the balcony, while Laila enjoyed the attention. She loved showing off, so she went into her English routine. The girls were amazed and kept touching her and talking to her as if she had just come from Mars.

Sara was doing her best to speak to the musicians in Urdu. Thinking she was my friend and they shouldn't make fun of her, they tried their best, but could not really understand what she was saying in her American accent. One of the musicians came towards me and yelled, 'Dr Sahiba, they are calling you here.' When I turned and looked at him, he asked in a low voice, '*Ae wlati kuktri kithun liandi e* (Where did you find this western chicken)?' I told him to shut up.

I turned to my guests and found Sara sitting on the floor by the musicians trying to ask them about music. Her husband, with a big smile on his face, was roaming around the room in his cowboy boots, while everyone else had taken their shoes off. He was looking at the photographs on the walls. The three girls were sitting very closely around Laila on a sofa, touching her hair and hands and looking at her with frozen smiles. I couldn't help laughing. The way they were looking at Laila reminded me of how she looked at me when I first came to her house. She had also touched my hair and examined me from head to toe.

Laila began singing. She always opened a *mujra* with the same song. A long *alaap* with her *dupatta* draped over her head, covering her face. Gradually, she lifted it to display her beauty to the audience. The song was a famous Indian film tune, *Ghar aiya mera pardesi*. The balance of instruments and the singer's voice is very different at these gatherings than in television recordings, or even live performances on stage. These singers don't use microphones, and almost compete with the musical instruments rather than supporting each other. On top of that, they use their *ghungroo* almost like noisy rhythm instruments rather than using them gracefully to show the skill of the dancer's footwork.

My guests thoroughly enjoyed the performance. I had asked Bhuba, the servant, to change a thousand rupees and he got me ten stacks of one-rupee notes, which I distributed among my friends. I showed them how to throw money at the performer—to take a stack of bills and come close to the dancer, then throw them one by one, very quickly, so the rupees shower over the dancer. I also showed them another way of giving money where you put a one or ten rupee note on a friend's head. The dancer dances in front of that person, giving him or her full attention, and then bends forward to take the note. Men sometimes have fun and place the note on someone's face, meaning they want the dancer to seduce the other person. She comes, dances in front of him and takes the note, pinching his cheek sharply.

The group had fun with the money and so did Laila. This was a nice 'homey' environment, as they had become friends with her. In addition, since we were the only people in the audience everyone felt very comfortable. After the first song, Laila asked what we would like to hear. Sara immediately asked for a pure classical piece. Laila looked at me, and I intervened, saying that they could ask for Urdu and Punjabi film songs and *ghazals.*

I went close to Sara and whispered, 'Not many classical singers are left here.'

Surprised, she asked, in her American twang, 'But why?'

'Because no one requests classical anymore. Even the few classical singers find it difficult to survive. Other than Shahida, no women really sing classical songs professionally,' I answered.

My three cousins engaged in a vigorous consultation before finally making their request. Faiza was pushed forward to asked for '*Sone dia kangna*', a popular Punjabi song. Laila was delighted with the request and started off in full vigour. The girls enjoyed her singing and sang along in low voices.

It was then that I noticed that two boys about seven years old had come in and were sitting in a corner of the room. I had never seen them before and had no idea why they were there, since they had neither flowers to sell nor small bills to provide change to the customers. I thought that maybe they came from the tea stall.

Laila's mother came into the living room and met all my friends. My three cousins had a big whispering conference, exchanging glances and giggling. They tried to ask me something by nodding their head towards Laila's mother, but I totally ignored them. I was embarrassed that they thought Kaisera Begum would not notice their excitement. In fact, she had a high fever and soon went back inside the house.

After she left, Faiza came and whispered in my ear, 'Was she the *naika*, the Madam of this *kotha*?'

I looked at her face. She seemed about to die with excitement. The mother of the prostitute—so often seen in the movies. The one who makes and breaks the deals with both hero and villain. The hero always has to kidnap the innocent dancing girl before she becomes a prostitute, or before the *naika* makes a deal for her daughter's first customer. After the hero's family disowns him for wanting to marry a prostitute, he runs away from his family as well, marries his dancing girl and lives in hiding in a small town. Then the *naika* appears out of nowhere, accompanied by pimps and servants, and takes the girl back. In more dramatic movies she appears when the dancing girl, the heroine, gives birth to her first child, who happens to be a girl, to claim the baby girl and take her away to the bazaar. The hero has to come back for more kidnapping. He fights the whole bazaar to take his daughter, his 'honour', back from the 'vicious people' of the Mohalla. For the movie going South Asians, the *naika* personifies the profession of prostitution. She fascinates them, and represents the pinnacle of the corrupting power and manipulation they have come to associate with prostitution.

Looking at Faiza, with her mouth open in astonishment, I laughed and answered, 'Yes, Faiza, she is the *naika*.'

After a while, hospitality began with soft drinks, milk and *kheer*, so everyone sat around the tea table in front of the sofa. Most people opted for milk as they found it fascinating to drink sweet milk with almonds from big glasses wrapped in thin paper with the name of the shop printed in bold red letters on it.

Laila's oldest niece, Yasmin, came out, adding another thrill to the *mehfil*. She was not dressed up, and hardly wore make-up, but looked quite charming. Yasmin is not very talkative so she sat quietly in a corner chair and observed everyone. Laila, on the other hand, was all over the room, joking with me, pushing everyone to eat more, laughing with the musicians, switching to English from time to time.

After a while I asked everyone if they wanted to go to another *kotha*, but they all said no. They were happy at Laila's and the three young women didn't want to go out in the bazaar again until we left for home. Once inside, seeing how close these people were to me, they felt comfortable. So, we continued with Laila as she sang more for us. After another half-hour we concluded our session and begged permission to leave. Laila called her mother. We thanked her and said good-bye.

I had many things to carry: some papers, a tote bag and a purse. I picked everything up and we all headed toward our cars. My cousins repeated the same drama of wrapping themselves fully before appearing on the street. We were not so far from the car, but many people turned around and looked at the mummies walking past. As I approached the car, I realized that I had left my car keys on the table in Laila's house. I asked Mohsin to go back to get them, and told him exactly where I had put them. I told Sara and her husband they need not wait for us, but they said they would stay a little. Mohsin came back saying that the keys weren't there. I didn't feel comfortable leaving everybody on the street to go look for the keys myself, especially the girls. I also didn't want to take everyone back in because it was almost one o'clock and I didn't want them in a *kotha* after the performing time was over. Since *Ustad* Sadiq's *baithak* was right around the corner, I suggested that we go there. They could wait there, while Mohsin and I ran back to

look for the keys. I left all my friends in Sadiq and Riaz's hands
and took off for Laila's *kotha*.

The number of police cars suddenly increased, and I realized
it must be 1 a.m. Mohsin confirmed the time and seemed
nervous. I said, 'We'd better leave quickly. I do not want to
stay here after one, not with all these people. The police really
become vicious then.' We both went up to Laila's living room
and looked everywhere. I went through my purse, tote bag, and
everything else that I was carrying, several times. I knew I had
put my keys on the side table right after I came in the room, but
they were not to be found. Mohsin suggested we go back to the
car and that he would try to open it without keys.

We came down and were going towards the car when we
noticed an uproar by the *baithak* where I had left everyone.
I rushed there. A police inspector was coming out of there with
some other policemen. Sadiq came out with him and said, 'They
are her guests.'

The inspector looked at me and said cynically, 'So, Dr *Sahiba*
is here.' He raised one eyebrow and looked at me with a crooked
smile, 'are these your guests?'

I quickly answered, 'Yes, we were leaving, but I seem to
have lost my car keys. We will arrange something soon and
leave.'

He said, raising his voice, 'Tell your friends the time for
visitors is over. I do not want to hear any music.'

'Of course, I understand,' I said, not fully comprehending
what he meant. I intentionally did not take them back to Laila's
*kotha* because it was close to one o'clock and the police rule
begins after that. They look for opportunities to arrest people.
After all, they need some action, to make money.

Mohsin and I rushed in and found everyone extremely calm
and Sara learning *kathak* dance steps from the musician there.
I could not believe my eyes. She was in the middle of the room
in a basic *kathak* dance pose and talking to the musician telling
him to give her the beat. The musician was trying his best to
understand her Urdu. Everyone else was watching as if they
were in a big theatre watching Birju Maharaj, the famous dancer.

'Stop this right now', I said. 'Don't you know that we have a problem? The time for visitors is over? I looked at Sara angrily and said, 'You are practicing dance in this area. Do you know what you are doing?'

She shrugged her shoulders and said, 'Just showing him what I learned in my dance class in Islamabad. I wondered if he could teach me some new steps right now.'

'It was the *tabla* music that attracted the police. We'll do something about the car, why don't you two go.' I asked my cousins to go with them, while Mohsin and I fixed my car. Faced with the choice of leaving quickly or staying for an uncertain length of time, the girls still wanted to cling on to me. I thought that if some of them went, I would have less of a burden. Clearly, none of them knew they were playing with fire. The police are the most brutal people in the Mohalla.

Sara and her husband left. We went to the car with my musician friends to try opening it without the keys. It was quite dark. As soon as we reached the car, Mohsin shouted and pointed to the tires. He couldn't speak. All four tires had been slashed. I realized that the disappearance of my car keys was not coincidental. Mohsin and I looked at each other. We could smell trouble.

Mohsin has technical skills so he started working on the car lock. The three girls huddled together. They dragged a nearby wooden bench to the car and sat close to one another. Their faces were now covered only with the loose overhang of their *dupattas*. Unaware of the danger we were in, they were using this opportunity to look at every passer-by, quite confidently. No one could see their faces, but they could see everyone.

The police jeeps had their lights flashing, and from time to time, would sound their sirens. They were showing off for us more than for anyone else still around. A vehicle passed every five or ten minutes and asked what the problem was. Mohsin had succeeded in opening the car door and now was working on the steering to see if he could get the car started. Whenever I left my cousins to be with Sadiq or Mohsin trying to find the right tools, they grabbed the opportunity to tell the police what had happened. I kept telling them not to say anything and to let me handle things. I was worried about them talking to the police. When these young women are in a group they easily slip into a frivolous mood. They were talking to the policemen as if they were boys on campus, giggling, and asking for help, and the police were enjoying this quite a bit. I lost my cool and told them I didn't want them sitting there. I took them back to the *baithak* and said, 'you're not leaving here till I say so. I have enough trouble on my hands already.' I asked Faiza, who was a little older than the others and generally more mature, to come with me. I thought she could help me, and also wanted to separate the girls. Young college students in Pakistan, men or women, seem to regress when they are in groups.

We went to see how Mohsin and *Ustad* Sadiq were doing. They had opened the trunk and had taken two tires off. Mohsin told me he would take a taxi to get three tires fixed, and would replace one with the spare in the trunk. I became a little less tense. A stream of police cars kept coming by, asking the same questions, and getting the same answers. No one offered to help. They only smiled strangely and left. The musicians were superb at giving us support. It was very cold, and they had given the young women blankets to cover themselves. The two men stayed with Mohsin and brought tea for him from time to time.

Faiza and I went to the shopkeeper. He had shrugged his shoulders earlier when I asked him who slashed my tires. 'There are so many police around, how could anyone slash tires like that and get away with it?' I asked.

'Unless, of course, they are friends of the police,' commented Faiza.

He said, 'Dr *Sahiba*, we saw them do it, but we couldn't do anything. How can we dare stop the police themselves.'

I was shocked. I suspected that the police might have encouraged or given protection to the person who did it, but this was too much. Faiza and I looked at each other in astonishment. I was very angry.

I tried to convince Faiza we should all take a taxi and go home, letting the local people look after the car until morning. Faiza was very nervous about this. She said it was out of the question to arrive in a taxi at home at three in the morning, and would lead to very bad rumours about them. Going and coming in one's own car is a different thing, even if someone saw us arriving home late at night. No one would be willing to go home in a taxi at such an hour. 'Good girls don't do that,' she explained seriously. Nothing scared these young women more than their parents, not even these brutal police.

Mohsin finally brought two *rickshaws* from the main road, and took the three tires to be repaired. Where we were, all such shops were closed, and taxis were not available, so he said he'd have to take them towards the main highway where shops are open all night. Riaz stayed with the car. *Ustad* Sadiq, the girls and I came back to the *baithak*.

The police cars had tapered off. It was now about three o'clock, and the Mohalla looked very different than it did either during the day when it functions as an ordinary bazaar or late at night when it's open for its other customers. A mysterious wind was blowing through it. The place was dark, but not at all dead. Very much alive, the streets were quite busy. The people seemed different from those I saw at other times. I had never stayed later than 1 a.m., so I took the opportunity to experience the atmosphere.

Many musicians had told me the Mohalla changed totally after the ordinary visitors go home. This was the time for the real customers, the more committed and the more powerful. These visitors, mostly political people, were men who treated the police like dogs. Cars kept coming and going. The streets were not as crowded with pedestrians as they were between 11 and 1 a.m., but there were plenty of big, expensive cars on the streets. These visitors were not selecting their dancers at random; they clearly knew where they were going. They were more or less permanent customers of specific women.

We waited for Mohsin for about an hour, surprised at how long it took him to get the tires fixed. I went out every few

minutes to observe the changes on the street. Faiza and I decided
to call my uncle's house, thinking we would get Faiza's brother
on the telephone because he studies all night. We went to a
modest, traditional restaurant on the main bazaar road. Their
telephone was not working so they sent us to a *paan* shop
across the street. Just as we went out we saw a big procession
coming towards us. We quickly slipped back inside the
restaurant. It had no door, just a wide passage lined with tables
and chairs.

About twenty people were walking towards us. We couldn't
tell whether they were singing or crying, but they were definitely
very drunk. They could have been coming from either a party or
a fight, perhaps both. One fair, well-groomed but extremely
drunk man, with blood on his off-white silk *kurta*, was talking
very loudly, swearing at someone. The others seemed to be
following this leader. Faiza held on to my arm, squeezing it
tightly as the group rumbled past us and continued towards the
*haveli* of Yousuf Salauddin.

After making sure that they were gone, we came out and
called home. To our great relief, Faiza's brother picked up the
telephone on the first bell. We told him we were stuck in the
Mohalla. He complained about not being included in such an
exciting plan, but said that in case either of his parents woke up
he would cover for us. We said we'd call again before leaving
so he could open the gate of the house for us, without waking
his parents.

I asked the shopkeeper about the uproar and he answered,
'At this *peher*, these things happen in the Mohalla. Nothing
new for us, so we don't even bother asking about it. These
important people get drunk and fight for one reason or another;
if they don't find a reason, they fight anyway.'

I liked his use of the word *peher*, from the old division of
time. A full day has eight *pehers*: four in the daytime and four
at night, each *peher* is three to four hours long. In the Mohalla,
each *peher* has a very different feeling. The morning is like
morning anywhere in old Lahore. People crowd the restaurants
to take out food for breakfast but those involved in prostitution

and music are fast asleep. The performers wake up in the second *peher*, and come out around noon to get their breakfast and queue at the public baths. The third *peher* is for music practice and going to the market to buy shoes, musical instruments or whatever one needs. At the last *peher* of the day it's time to prepare for the glamorous night. Describing hourly changes of activity in any village or city is not difficult, but in the Mohalla, the changes occur throughout the entire night as well, each *peher* bringing out deeper and deeper secrets.

I learned later that senior politicians dominate the 'after-hours' Mohalla. Major political decisions are discussed and deals struck in these *kothas*, long before their public announcements. It's a place where the powerful relax. Planning meetings at favourite *kothas* are convenient and provide a most confidential environment.

These highly influential people come to the bazaar after two o'clock when the police have forced the riffraff out. Their time begins then, and the police give them full protection. Harassment is out of the question for them. The police can play out their little harassment dramas only with common customers who lack the power of retribution. These important men listen to the music and enjoy themselves, scheduling their meetings after 4 a.m. so their colleagues are sufficiently relaxed to discuss important matters of state. The artists of this area, musicians as well as dancers, have been trained since the Mughal era to keep their customers' business confidential. The entertainers have a long history with statesmen, musicians and dancers playing in the courts and private quarters while important matters were discussed. The girls were often exposed to state secrets while providing intimate services to the royals. Confidentiality is part of their profession. Politicians can discuss their secrets quite comfortably in the presence of musicians and dancers, fully confident that no word will leave the room.

Mohsin was still not back. Moving into the last *peher* of the night, I decided to talk some more to the shopkeepers about these late customers and their activities. The streets were not friendly at all, and a strange crudeness hung in the air, created by the men swaggering by, yelling and swearing drunkenly. I was told that this is when murders take place. Both the important customers and the pimps go a bit crazy at this time.

Mohsin arrived around 4.30 in the morning. The car had radial tires so he had a hard time finding a specialized shop for them. Then he had to wake the repairman and give him a big tip to do the job urgently. We all helped put the tires on and were soon ready to go. Mohsin hot-wired the car to get it started. We thanked our hosts, one of whom had spent nearly the entire night in the cold watching my car. They had smiles on their faces, but said they were ashamed I had so much trouble in their area. I answered that they'd been telling me about police brutality from the day I arrived; now I had my own story to tell.

My car keys appeared as mysteriously as they had vanished. The next afternoon Laila found them lying in the middle of the room. She suspected that someone had entered quietly earlier in the day and left them, probably the same children I saw sitting in the corner of the *kotha* the night before.

# 10

## CHOICES

The next morning when I came into the living room, my aunt and uncle were having breakfast, without a clue about the previous night's disaster. I joined them. Soon Mohsin came in and exchanged greetings. They invited him to have breakfast, which he did. After some family chitchat, he said good bye. After he left, my aunt commented he had visited rather early. 'Perhaps he wanted to stop in on his way to the office,' she muttered to herself. Little did she know that he had been sleeping, for a few hours at least, in her son's room.

My aunt told me about Khanum, an actress she knew who lived near the Shahnoor Studios. Khanum, like most film actresses, came from the Shahi Mohalla. She offered to talk to her friend to arrange a meeting if I thought it would be useful for my study. I knew that after leaving the Mohalla, Khanum was in films for a while and was now someone's mistress. I had started exploring long-term relationships and the concept of *shadi* for these higher level prostitutes, so I readily agreed. Strangely, while I was discovering the dynamics of proposals for the dancing girls by short-term and long-term customers, I confronted a family situation with strong indirect connections to my explorations in the Mohalla.

I was very close to Faiza's family. As young children, my siblings and I had a lot of fun with Faiza and her three brothers. We were all older than my uncle's children, but we had many little adventures together. Faiza was studying for her Master's in Fine Arts at the University. Her eldest brother had gone to England to study, the second one was studying in a medical school in Karachi and the youngest was preparing to go to

England. Faiza was unconcerned about her studies because she knew she would neither be sent abroad nor expected to have a serious career. Fine arts satisfied her creative spark and gave her an opportunity to get away from home and be with her friends. She was, however, a very intelligent young woman, and a creative thinker with good interpersonal communication skills. Effective in her social interactions, she was an excellent organizer. I liked her assertiveness, especially when she organized her own family.

After the holiday guests left, I moved into Faiza's elder brother's room. As he was out of the country, my uncle had told me I should consider that room mine whenever I was in Lahore. My uncle was a jolly person, full of life. He had retired from government service and was now working with a private firm.

One day, I came back from the Mohalla around nine in the evening. By now, my aunt and uncle were used to my unpredictable schedule. That was my condition for staying with them and they had fully accepted it. Faiza seemed in a bad mood. She usually greeted me as soon as I entered her door. But that day she was shuttling in and out of her room, going into the kitchen, then to the neighbours, and then to the courtyard. My aunt, as usual, asked me how my day had gone and I told her how happy I was to be making friends and being accepted at the Mohalla. Then I asked about my uncle and she said, 'He's gone out for a walk. He was very angry.'

I raised my eyebrows and looked at her for more information. Putting her teacup on the side table she laughed in embarrassment and told me they'd had a fight. I asked what happened, and said, 'I see Faiza is also upset.'

She answered, 'Well, we had a family over to see Faiza, and it started from there.'

'Ooooh! I get the picture: A wedding proposal for her. Tell me what happened?' I persisted.

'You know the aunt of the sister-in-law of my old class fellow...?'

'No. How could I? I am surprised you know her.' Relationships get quite complicated over here.

My aunt continued, 'I had asked her to look for someone for Faiza. She has suggested a few other people, but they did not like Faiza.'

'Yes, I know,' I replied resentfully.

'This time she sent over a family who was looking for a wife for their son. Their maternal family came from Ludhiana, a city in East Punjab, India. I liked the mother and the sister. They brought the boy along as well. Your uncle does not like the boys coming with their families to select their bride, but in this case we didn't know beforehand that the boy was coming.'

Just then Faiza came in from the courtyard and heard her mother telling me the story. Without saying anything she came over and sat down on the carpet by my chair.

My aunt continued, 'Faiza brought tea in the living room for them and served snacks.'

'Yes,' Faiza interrupted, 'I was on display. They wanted to see if I could walk and talk.'

'Oh, stop it child, you said enough to your father. It's the tradition. How else will we get you married off,' said my aunt.

Faiza started to sob. Putting her head in my lap she cried, 'I've done that so many times I'm sick and tired of it.'

My aunt looked at me and said, 'Now look here Fouzia *beti*, I didn't make these traditions, and neither did your uncle. Ask her why she blames us for putting her through this. It's the way it's done. People come, they see her, and then we don't hear from them again. It's not our fault. I've told her not to go out in the sun. It's not good for her complexion. I wouldn't mind if she quit that college. She is so busy with her assignments. She stays up late at night painting, and gets dark circles under her eyes. At her age, she shouldn't stay up so late. She should rest, stay away from the sun and take care of her complexion. Shouldn't she do that, *beti*?'

'She's still studying,' I said, 'why are you so worried about her marriage?'

'This is her age, *beti*,' answered my aunt, 'if it passes, we won't be able to get anyone. This is the time when we have more choice. If we wait, the choice is very limited, and after that you are left with divorced men or widowers.'

'Whose choice are we talking about, may I know?' said Faiza sobbing. She looked at me and said, 'They say I am too dark.'

I felt so terrible I didn't even know how to react. This had long been an issue in her family. As soon as Faiza graduated, her parents started seeking a good proposal. A girl's parents only seek a proposal indirectly, asking friends and relatives to talk about their daughter to people with sons who are looking for a bride. The boy's family has the privilege of actively looking around, and visiting families of different girls, making their selection, before they finally send a formal proposal.

My aunt was very clear that Faiza was continuing her studies only because she was waiting. The day a boy and his family accepted her, they would make her leave school and get married. That was the priority, and considering her a child who did not appreciate the tradition, the family would not listen to her.

In general, the parents of young girls worry about getting a good proposal for their daughters, but they are often quite helpless about who will choose her. Physical beauty and the financial ability of the girl's family to give sufficient dowry matter a great deal. For the boy's family, seeking a bride is fun, and sisters and other close relatives join the selection committee comprising of the boy and his mother and go out shopping for a bride.

That night I kept thinking about Faiza. I loved her deeply, and appreciated her talents. With all her abilities she could be an excellent leader, maybe a good businesswoman. What a difficult tradition she was confronting, simply focusing her whole attention on being selected by a boy. Her future, her social status and identity would, from then on be defined by him.

I tried to discuss the matter with my aunt the next day. Given Faiza's talent, I asked why she worried so much about her marriage. Her answer was typical, she wanted to see her daughter in a socially safe position with her future secured. She did not want her to 'miss the bus', as she put it, and be left alone. My aunt declared that Faiza's future was with a husband and children.

I chatted with my aunt and uncle every morning since we all got up early. They both had interesting stories to share. My aunt especially was very engaging and gave detailed descriptions of people and situations. That morning my aunt told me that she had arranged to meet Khanum. Although my aunt did not know her, a neighbour of my aunt's neighbour's mother-in-law's sister knew her and my aunt announced, matter-of-factly, 'With such a close link, she is obliged to take us to Khanum's house. After all, Khanum lives in her lane!' I was happy she had already arranged it, and said I'd be back in the late afternoon so we could go together. I asked her to bring Faiza along, wanting to get her mind off her current problem. My aunt is a very jolly person, and when we set off she was making jokes about what we'd find at Khanum's. She told me that a film producer picked her up from the Mohalla and then someone else took her as a mistress.

I drove. First, we went to my aunt's neighbour's mother-in-law's house. She greeted us, served us tea and snacks, and then took us to her sister's house, where we again received full hospitality, as she could not let her sister's daughter-in-law's neighbour leave her house without food. We then went to her neighbour's house, a very kind person who agreed to take us to meet Khanum, but only after we had some tea and snacks. We begged her to skip the hospitality and she finally agreed. I was in a light mood and enjoying it all. Faiza and I kept exchanging looks and smiling at my aunt who sweetly asked about the whole family of every woman we met.

Finally, the neighbour sent her young maid to Khanum's house to announce our visit. Five of us were now going to visit the actress. I had never seen her films and had no idea of her talent. She lived on a narrow street in a lower middle class neighbourhood in a modest looking house opposite the Shahnoor Studios. I was familiar with the area since many theatre artists live there in hopes of landing a part in a film. They hang out near the studios to catch a glimpse of a director, a person who could change their lives forever if he showed an interest in them.

Khanum was tall and fair complexioned, with long black hair and big South Asian eyes. Her manner clearly reflected her background in the Shahi Mohalla. Her voice was hoarse and her mouth stained with betel leaf. She spoke Punjabi in the old city's typical accent. Khanum had asked us into her living area where she was sitting on a *charpai*. There was a strange sense of pride in the way she moved. We had a long conversation. My aunt was quite good at asking questions, and soon learned about all of her connections with other famous actresses. I asked how she got the opportunity to act in films.

'I was not worth the opportunity. It was simply God's gift to me,' she replied, but her tone of voice did not support her humble speech. Gazing into the air she continued, 'One day Khawaja Sahib, a film producer, came to our *kotha* with another man who was one of our regular customers. Khawaja Sahib was not looking for new talent, but just happened to come along with his friend. When things are meant to happen, they just do. He came to our *affis* and said he wanted to hear some songs. My *ustad* had taught me good *ghazals* and I presented my best. He liked it.'

'Did he like the *ghazals* or you?' broke in my aunt.

Khanum laughed, 'Both, actually. He told me to try film work. I kept meeting with him and he kept giving me hope. Many of my friends told me film people exploit you this way, neither paying nor giving you a chance in the films. My mother wouldn't listen to anyone, saying, "Other people are jealous. If God has sent him like an angel to our door we're not going to lose the opportunity." I just followed him around. He'd call me to his studios and I'd sit around all day. My mother came with me most of the time. He took me out at night, and sometimes, he would buy me things. One day he said he had a role for me in a film. My whole family was ecstatic. He and my mother arranged the terms. I don't know much about that. He wanted me to be exclusively his, but my mother disagreed, and said that would harm my career.'

'Why was that?' I asked.

'I think he didn't agree to my mother's terms. He wanted us to re-pay his favour. Actually, I respect him very much, and think he is a very nice person but my mother was more cautious. She said that I would be available whenever he wanted me, but I couldn't be exclusively his, unless, of course, he made a contract. You know, a marriage, with monthly payments and all.'

I wanted to hear more. 'What did he say?'

'He already had two wives,' she continued. 'He couldn't do that and yet he couldn't let go. Then, the film didn't do well. He was very disappointed and told my mother he'd take me to other directors. He introduced me to another friend and my mother pursued that option. Moving around in the industry gets easier after the first film, but if it flops, the doors close quickly. Even though I had a small role and couldn't be blamed for the failure, it made a difference.'

'What roles do you play?' I asked

'I'm a dancer. I did one film about a dancer who is raped and ends up at a *kotha*. In the end, I die. I had two dances in it,' she said proudly.

The neighbour smiled and said excitedly, 'I saw that movie. I've seen all of her movies. Since we're neighbours, so we should go see her work.'

'In another movie I did two night club dances,' continued Khanum. 'In one, Nadeem is singing while I dance. But after that I stopped working.'

'Isn't your career just beginning?' I asked, 'Why have you stopped?'

'Now I live here with *Seth* Rehman Khokhar, and he doesn't want me to work,' she smiled.

I was surprised; the house didn't look like a '*Seth's* house. Usually, rich men keep their mistresses in big houses in posh neighbourhoods. I asked how she met *Seth* Rehman.

'He was a customer,' she replied. 'I didn't stop working at my *affis*. I wasn't sure that my career would take off, so my mother told me to keep working. If you're on television or in movies you get better customers.' She laughed.

Her frankness was delightful, so I continued, 'Well, what made you decide to get married and live outside the Mohalla?'

'My mother decided for me. Running after directors and producers is also difficult. They are also busy and can't always have work for you. *Seth* Rehman came to see my film shootings several times. Then he told my mother he'd rent me a separate house and support me. I don't know what deal he made with my mother, but here I am.'

'Every woman in the Mohalla dreams of going into films,' I said. 'Do they idolize you or talk to you about it?'

'I know my elders are happy and satisfied. My mother says my work in films helped the family. It's good for my sisters, so I'm happy. I liked dancing in front of the camera. It's very different from dancing in our *affis*. I like it when people recognize me and compliment my work. I like going to the Mohalla with my sisters, and mother feeling proud of me. *Seth* Rehman said he might allow me to work in a film if his friends are involved in making it. We'll see.'

'Would you like to make more films?' I asked.

'I'm not sure about acting, but I like dancing. I liked my role as a night club dancer, but, I didn't like sitting around in the directors' offices begging for a small part. Now it might be easier, but I prefer this. *Seth* Rehman approached my mother and offered this arrangement with me and she accepted. He treats me nicely. He bought my mother a diamond ring just the other day, and he gives me things too. My mother wants security for me. She worries about my future.'

'How long will you stay with him?' I asked.

'No one can predict their future. I would like to think I'll be here as long as I live, but who knows? No one knows how long regular marriages will last these days. How can I know how long this arrangement will last?'

Earlier in the conversation, my aunt had told her about my work at the Mohalla, and she was curious about who I knew there. When she asked, I mentioned Kaisera Begum.

She asked, 'Her daughter is Laila?'

'Yes, they live in the main bazaar.'

She said, 'Kaisera and Shamsa were two sisters. I don't really know them, but my mother knows them well. They're looking for a proposal for Laila these days. Her mother is very worried about her. '

'Mothers are always worried, aren't they?' I said with a sigh.

'Yes, it matters who she gets. It determines her status and her nieces' future as well.'

I asked, 'If the customer doesn't want a long-term relationship, what does it matter if he is a big shot or not? Laila would still continue her own business.'

She smiled and answered, 'The status in the *biradri* is also important. Everyone who lives there is in the business; they have to keep their market. The pimps, the *ustads*, the show organizers, are all spectators. If you have a rich customer for your *nath*, your market value goes up and so does your sister's. The whole family gains. You're right, though; it isn't only one customer. Whenever a dancer gets a rich customer, she brags about it, and gains status. Now take Nazma and her sister. That fat politician—what's his name—comes to their *kotha* so often even the police behave with them. When any of their friends have trouble, they ask Nazma to get them favours from the officials. Nazma's mother hardly ever asks for a favour from someone else. It does make a difference. Look at me. God has given me a good future. My sister just had a proposal from a landlord in Multan for her *nath*, a sign of good fortune.'

My aunt asked about the *Seth's* family.

Very casually she replied, 'He has a wife and four grown sons, two of whom are married. *Seth* Sahib has large land holdings, and gets his wealth from there. His family doesn't object. You know these people, they can have what they want. If he wants me, his family can't object. It's part of their tradition.'

Later that night, I couldn't sleep thinking about the importance of marriage for women and the role of men in their lives and social standing. I wondered about this desperate eagerness of mothers to ensure an 'appropriate' marriage for their daughters. I thought about Khanum. Her mother worried about her future and followed all the traditions of her culture to secure a good future for her daughter. Kaisera worried about Laila, just as my aunt was worried about Faiza.

# 11

## THREE DANCERS

It was half past eight in the morning; I had never been in the Mohalla so early before. But I came very early to have a look at the famous breakfast food stalls. People come from far away to buy goat's feet here. Seldom staying to eat, most take the food home for their family and friends. I was walking on the main bazaar road close to the *Phaja*, Lahore's most famous restaurant for goat feet curry, when a small Suzuki pick-up truck stopped behind me. Turning around, I saw Laila standing in the truck. 'What are you doing here?' she screamed, looking happy to see me.

With Pami and Chanda, Laila was just returning from a show in Pattoki. They had gone with a band for a Variety Show at a wedding. It was the *valima* of a mid-level landlord who was involved in provincial politics. He had never run for an elected post, but apparently had served on several campaign committees.

'I thought you were in Pattoki,' I exclaimed. Laila gestured for me to come to her place, so I left the appetizing fragrances of the hot food behind. By the time I reached her house the men had gone, and the three young women were already lying down, exhausted, two on the floor and one on the sofa.

One of Chanda's *ustads* had organized the show with seven musicians, three dancers and a comedian who also acted as the master of ceremonies. They had travelled in the *ustad's* small Suzuki and the girls were grumbling about how crowded it was. When I entered the room I said, 'Oh! You certainly look tired after a good performance!'

Laila, lying on the sofa, raised her hand and said, 'Not such a good performance. But, yes, yes, we are tired.' Chanda and

Pami, another dancing girl from the neighbourhood, were lying on the floor with their overnight bags thrown on one side. I sat on an armchair and asked, 'So, how was it?'

All three started talking at the same time. Laila said, '*Shode* (show off), it was a gathering of *shodas*.' Chanda yelled, 'What do you expect in a performance like this, the more *shode* they are the better it is for us.' Pouting, Pami murmured, 'My feet have blisters.'

'This *kaam chor* has blisters,' Laila explained, 'not from dancing a lot, but from her silly heels.'

Pami sat up, upset. 'What do you know. I danced for eight hours.' Both Chanda and Laila laughed, 'Listen to this, Fouzia, the whole show went on for six hours and she danced for eight hours.' Laila looked at Pami, 'Who were you dancing with that we don't know about?'

'Yes, tell us,' Chanda continued, 'Where were you dancing and with whom. We're dying to know.'

Pami got more upset, and said, 'You're the one who went into the back room with that big Moustache. Laila and I had to work on the stage. I didn't sneak out.'

Laila mimicked her in an exaggerated manner, 'Yes, and she got three *parchian*. Oh! She got three invitations of love and we got none.'

Pami, still stewing angrily, said, 'I don't fall on people's laps to get a customer.'

'Ooooooh! She is so *sharif*. Why don't you leave the business and get married?' chided Chanda.

Pami, continuing to pout, went on, 'No matter what you say, it was a very rowdy crowd.'

Laila laughed so hard she almost fell off the sofa. 'Laila, what is it?' I asked.

She caught her breath and said, 'Fouzia, we were dancing and there was one *shoda* who was jumping around a lot. He wouldn't come out with any money, but he wanted us to be close to him.'

Chanda confirmed, 'Yes, the one in the black shirt. What a filthy guy! He wouldn't take his money out, only tens, huh! And he kept trying to pull us close.'

Laila started laughing again, 'He pinched Pami so hard she still has a bruise.'

Chanda got up and said, 'Really! Is that why Pami is so upset? Come on, that's a compliment! Don't you know what business we're in?'

Chanda fell back on the floor. Laila continued. 'You were in the back room with the big Moustache. Pami and I were on stage. She went off to this corner and the guy took her hand and pulled her off the stage onto his lap. When she came back she showed me her bruised arm. She almost cried.' Pami was pouting and did not bother to say anything.

Chanda said, 'Our host's cousin was pretty cool.'

Laila turned around so she was lying on her stomach. 'Oh!' she said, 'he was so good, but he never looked at me. He was gaga over you Chanda. So when are you meeting him?'

'This evening. He's coming to Lahore. You'll learn the tricks of the trade fast enough. Let's admit it, I've been around longer than you and Pami. You've got to make these men crazy. That's our job. That's what they want us to do, and that's why they invite us and pay us.'

I asked her how she arranged her meeting with this guy. 'He gave me a piece of paper and wrote the date and time on it,' she said. 'My mother never sends me anywhere before fixing the rate, but I'll convince her about this one. I liked him and I think he has more *dum* than our stingy host. We've got to keep looking for those *moti asami*, you know, the guys with deep pockets! Business must go on!'

Laila broke in, 'I also enjoyed that long-haired guy, the one in the golden coloured *kurta*. You know who I mean?'

Pami smiled, 'The local booze really hit him hard. He made a real fool of himself. He was so funny.'

'Fools are the best ones. That's what you don't understand. You two just enjoy it like a show,' Chanda said, looking at

Pami. 'If you had more sense, you would have grabbed him. He was easy.'

Grimly, Pami asked, 'Why didn't you go for him then?'

'I was working on someone else, you silly,' Chanda replied, grinning like a warrior who had just won a battle. 'You know how good I am at identifying rich ones and those with heart. I think I'm pretty good at my job. Perhaps if I'd put my mind to something else, I could have been a big shot myself.' She laughed.

Laila sighed and said, 'Anyway, I had fun. At one point, I was laughing so hard that my stomach hurt. I must say most of the men were expecting more excitement, but weren't open with their wallets. The last show we did was much better.'

'No comparison, Laila,' said Chanda. 'Goldsmiths are the best. Hasn't your mother taught you anything?'

Laila said, 'For you, the whole show was on one side and the guy with the golden *kurta* on the other.'

We all laughed. The loud laughter brought Laila's mother into the room. She did not seem at all pleased. Maybe it was too early in the morning. 'Why are you laughing so vulgarly? Haven't you any manners?' she scolded. 'To think I had to live to see such times when *Kanjarian* came down to this level.'

Everybody hushed up. She looked at the bags thrown to one side and at the women lying around the room. 'Look at this, you're so careless. Chanda and Pami, what are you doing here? Don't you want to go home and rest? Go on! Go on! Go home. Your mothers must be waiting.'

The three girls looked at each other and giggled. Laila made a baby face, 'Ammi, I just invited my friends in for tea. They will go home after that. You go away.'

Laila's mother looked at me. 'Did you see that, Fouzia? No respect for her elders! You can ask these *gashtian* to giggle, laugh, eat and sleep, but they won't learn manners and how to do their own work.'

Laila got up from the sofa and screamed at her, 'What the hell was I doing all night at Pattoki? My feet ache from dancing.

The musicians can change places, the comedian went out and took his breaks, but we were on stage the whole time.'

'Your tongue is too long. When your brother comes I'll fix you,' Kaisera shouted as she left the room.

Laila yelled, 'Bubha! Bubha! Is anyone getting us tea? I'm tired. I want to have a cup of tea and sleep. Is that too much to ask?' She began to cry.

Bubha ran down the steps to the market.

Laila continued to complain as her friends looked at her with sympathy, 'I don't know what they want from me. I try my best. She just doesn't like to see me laugh.' Her mother heard the commotion and came back. She stared at Laila as if she would hit her. Finally, she sat down next to me. She looked at Laila and said, 'It's just my bad luck to have you for a daughter.'

Laila started crying loudly, almost like a child. Her mother said, 'You just don't want to grow up. All you want is entertainment. You didn't go to have a good time. It's your work, and your work supports this family. You should think about your sisters and brothers, but you refuse to take responsibility. You get so wrapped up in enjoying yourself and laughing at people that you don't remember your own *rozi*, your livelihood. That's your problem.' Kaisera also began to cry.

Now I understood why Kaisera kept complaining. It wasn't our noise that woke her up. She had been waiting for Laila and, before she even reached home, Kaisera had already learned how much she had made the night before. This was the bottom line for her and what she learned made her very upset. Her daughter had brought in only what the *ustad* had promised before the show—no extra money. This meant that Laila hadn't been skilful at getting *vail* money from the audience. Thus, the *ustad* wasn't generous and gave her nothing extra. In addition to this, she hadn't brought back any invitations from the customers.

Bubha came back with tea. Kaisera scolded him for not bringing me anything. I timidly refused, but didn't think it was a good time to argue. Bubha ran back for the milk. The silence grew heavy. All I could hear were Laila's sniffles. She quickly gulped her tea and stood up. Rubbing her eyes, she walked towards the inside of the house mumbling, 'I am very sleepy. I am going to sleep.'

Kaisera looked at Chanda and Pami, who were still sipping their tea. 'Okay, okay, finish your tea and go home. Your mothers will be waiting. Bubha can take your bags.'

She looked at Chanda, and asked, 'Chanda you have brains, why don't you put some sense in Laila's head?'

Chanda turned to Kaisera with a strange expression on her face and said, 'Don't tell me anything. I've enough bruises of my own. No matter how much you do, there's never any satisfaction.' I could see hatred in her eyes. Even though she said she was totally involved in her business, I could tell she felt just as entrapped by the management in her own home.

Chanda and Pami finished their tea and went off with Bubha to their respective homes. I also got up and excused myself. Kaisera did not say anything to me, but held my hand and pressed it. I didn't quite understand and started to leave. She pulled me back and with her eyes told me to wait. I didn't move. After the young women left, she said, 'Please stay for a while.'

We sat in the living room, with our feet curled under us on the sofa. She was feeling depressed and wanted someone to talk to. In her mind, there was no better person to hear her woes than I was. I had become a trusted friend and was always there to listen.

She said, 'I do not know what to do with this girl. She's becoming an economic liability and a social embarrassment for me.'

'What is the problem?' I asked.

'Laila watches Indian films all day. She gets up late and hardly goes to rehearse. Then she performs so badly with customers. I agree that our *rozi* has to do with what God graces us with, but we also have responsibilities. We have to work hard. She loves the glamour and her attention is always on being entertained.'

'What do you mean?' I persisted.

'I should marry her off soon, but still don't have a good *rishta*. My son and I are trying our best, but we cannot wait for ever.'

I knew the system well enough to understand that she had to formally arrange for Laila's first customer before she could openly start working. Laila was performing in the evenings in her own home and it was known that dancers accept offers from selective customers, but she couldn't do it openly because she hadn't yet been formally initiated into the profession. This was supposed to happen when her mother arranged her *shadi* with her first customer, the ritual of *nath utarwai*. Taking a high price for her virginity, she could then continue to work with other customers providing sexual services.

I could see the pressure building on her mother. Kaisera said with frustration, 'Laila doesn't help. When she goes out she gets too busy laughing at every funny thing she sees.'

She looked at the big black and white portraits hanging on the wall and said, 'My sister has already given me so much pain. I don't want any more.'

'Is this your sister?' I asked, my eyes wide open. Suddenly, I saw that the other person in the photograph looked like her and said excitedly, 'And this is you. My God, why didn't I see this before?' I had asked several times about those photographs and always got ambivalent answers.

She replied, 'Yes, things were different those days—very different. We used to work hard. We listened to our elders no matter how burdensome it got.'

'What about your sister?' I asked.

Tears came to her eyes and she couldn't speak for a while. Finally, wiping her face with her *dupatta* she said, 'She lives in London. Someday I'll tell you about her. Right now talk to Laila and tell her she'd better listen to me or else she'll be left without any future. It is already late.'

'Me!' I was startled. Pleased that she trusted me so much and wanted to involve me in a family problem, I could not imagine myself convincing Laila to listen to her mother and take her career as a prostitute seriously. I remained quiet.

She continued, 'You're like a sister to her. When a sister doesn't get a good match the family should help. Why don't you look for someone nice in Islamabad.'

I felt like someone had thrown a rock at my head. My eyes widened and I suddenly became aware of what was happening. I didn't know whether to smile, remain serious or leave. Anyway, I decided to hear her out and take care of things right there and then.

She said, 'Your city is full of rich bureaucrats and big businessmen also. I'm sure you can find someone who is interested in Laila. We aren't greedy, but we have our *biradri* and honour to think about. We'll demand only what's appropriate to maintain our family status.'

'How much are we talking about?' I asked.

She wasn't so naive as to give me an amount just like that. 'We'll see,' she replied.

I held her hand and looked straight in her eyes, 'I want to be very honest with you. I like Laila a lot, and you too, and I understand the pressure you are under. I see similar tension in our families when the daughters are not getting a good match and the parents are worried that they will get old, but in this case, I can't help you. I can't even make a false promise. I want you to know that I cannot get involved with these things.'

She was looking straight into my eyes, listening to me very carefully.

I continued, 'I respect you and I know you're trying to protect your daughter from a bad future where she might have to go out on the street and struggle for money to barely survive, but I just can't get involved.'

She lowered her head and after a few seconds she hugged me. 'Pray for me, then,' she said, 'I want peace for my soul.'

# 12

## PAMI'S FAMILY

Pami's mother had been cutting vegetables for the last half-hour, and was getting quite tired of it. Her heavy body felt the heat more than most and she sweated a lot. She was sitting on a *charpai* with a stack of spinach in her hand and a big tray on the floor right by her. She cut the spinach and it fell into the tray. That is how she worked since her weight made it difficult for her to sit on a tiny *piri* in front of the oil stove.

She lived in a small apartment on the ground floor of a tall building. Like most residential dwellings in the inner city, there was an open courtyard in the middle of the building. This was the hub of all activity with three families living in the rooms all around it. Pami's family had taken three rooms—two for living in and one for business. They all opened onto the courtyard rather than the main street. The two other tenants on the ground floor had two rooms each, also opening onto the same courtyard. The one toilet for everyone living on the ground floor was in a corner. The cooking, dish washing, laundry and children's bathing all took place in the courtyard, and it was also the social centre for sitting around and chatting.

Pami's mother liked to sit very close to the door of her main room so she could see who was coming and going in the courtyard. In the late afternoons, she would move her *charpai* outside and sit there doing her housework. When she got tired she would stretch out and nap on the same *charpai*. A dark complexioned woman with large features, she had a round face and large hands. She tied her black, dyed hair tightly in a braid, and usually wore a printed cotton *shalwar kamiz* with an off white muslin *dupatta*. Her clothes were often soiled and wrinkled.

Pami's mother had seven surviving children. Two had died at birth and one when three months old. All three children who died were boys. Now she had five daughters and two sons. Pami was her eldest daughter and, as the *Kanjar* do, her mother took on the name Pami *di ami* (Pami's mother). Her eldest son was two years older than Pami, but since girl children are more important here, a woman is more commonly referred to by a daughter's name.

Her eldest son left home when he was fourteen, seemingly ambivalent about his life. Pami's mother told me that he had been possessed. He grew up doing basic household work, shuttling between the house and the nearby shops all day. He got breakfast, cigarettes and matches for customers and change for their big bills, *paan* for his mother, tea for guests. He had things repaired, bought cassettes for his sisters, changed them if they didn't like the music, took his mother's messages to various musicians and so on. It might not have been what he wanted for his future, but he certainly did not have a dull life. Pami's mother told me he left his family because a spirit made him leave. She rarely talked about him, and only said he could have got together with Shano's boy, Pupoo, and earned some money for himself and his family. Apparently, Pupoo was a medium level pimp who got deals for his sisters and other neighbours.

Pami was the princess of this modest household. As the eldest daughter and primary earner, her mother spoiled her. She had inherited her mother's tendency to put on weight and, at nineteen, was already quite heavy. Of course, by that age, a Shahi Mohalla prostitute is already in the later half of her career. Pami could maybe keep working for another three years, but she needed to start making plans for her future. Two other sisters, at seventeen and fourteen, were in their prime. However, looking at the modest household, it didn't seem that this family had five girls. Pami's mother blamed it on bad luck.

I was in Lahore for ten days this time. On my first afternoon I came to see one of my informants who lived in Pami's building. A student of his told me that he had gone out and would return soon. His house was locked. I had never been locked out before, people were always hanging around inside. I had to plan my next ten days in the Mohalla with him so I decided to wait. Since I had some free time, I thought I could make friends with the neighbours. I had met Pami several times at other people's *kothas*, but had never formally met her family.

Pami's mother and I had a relationship of sorts, but we had never talked much together. As I approached the rooms where Pami lived, I saw her mother sitting on her *charpai* cutting spinach leaves. She had large dark sweat marks around her under-arms. She kept her head down and only raised her eyes to register me, never changing the expression on her face. I felt as if I was moving past a hippopotamus that noticed me, but only moved her eyes to follow me as I walked by. I said hello to the people sitting in the courtyard and headed straight over to greet her. She was forced to lift her head and reply, '*Walaikum salaam*'. I told her that I had come to see her neighbour, but had to wait. Without saying much, she used her big knife to move the spinach leaves spread over her *charpai* and, with the same knife, silently signalled me to sit. I sat right next to her. It was very hot and quite noisy. A boy and a girl were playing in the courtyard. Two other girls sat on another *charpai* in the yard and one girl was washing clothes close by. Pami's mother pulled her *charpai* very close to the door of the room.

I asked about Pami, and she said she was out on a job. I appreciated the frankness, and started telling her about myself a little, to make sure that she wasn't wondering what I was doing there. She raised her hand with the big knife and stopped me.

'Don't I know you?' she said, 'Of course I do. Everybody here knows you.'

I was a little embarrassed and answered, 'Well, I knew you, but wasn't sure whether you knew me or not.'

Swinging the knife in front of my eyes, she asked, 'Don't you call our house from Islamabad?'

I thought I caught a smile on her stern face and answered, 'Yes, and your children have been very helpful in passing on my messages.'

Making another stack of spinach leaves she said, 'Well, I have too many of them. They should be good for something.'

'You have five daughters,' I asked. 'Shouldn't you consider yourself a lucky woman? People around here do *manat* at the shrines so they will have daughters.'

She took a deep breath and said, 'Yes, yes...good fortune is also important. Just having girls is not enough.'

She finished cutting this stack and called one of her daughters in a loud voice. It was as if she had a loudspeaker fixed in her throat. I knew by then that women in the Mohalla often have very loud voices as they sing without microphones, but this was more like the voice of a theatre artist. She told her daughter to take the vegetables and the knife away. I was quite relieved to see the knife go.

The daughter took the vegetables to the stove. This was in the part of the courtyard close to where another daughter was washing clothes. Both girls who had been sitting on the *charpai* together now huddled up in front of the stove. They seemed very close to each other. One was named Rozi and the other Soni.

Pami's mother made another roaring announcement. I could only get half of it, but thought it was an order for the kids to be quiet. There was barely any reduction in the noise level, but one daughter came up to ask me if I would like tea. As usual, I declined and they offered milk instead. Being a Punjabi to the core, I could not refuse.

I asked Pami's mother where her daughters performed. She lived in the back section of a building with an entrance in a very small alley. There was no performing room, and their living space was open to all. There was no privacy. Their two rooms were crowded with people. She answered, 'At anyone's *kotha*. It varies from time to time. These days *dairedaar*, the *kotha* managers, don't want to give a fair share to the dancers. When we tire of one we go to another.'

I asked how the shares were divided, and she looked at me with amusement. Perhaps it was the directness of my question, but she had already been frank with me, considering this was our first formal meeting. I matched her smile and explained, 'I'd really like to know the system.'

'I'll tell you, but not now.'

Surprised, I asked, 'When?'

'After you drink your milk.'

She looked across my shoulder. I turned around and saw her daughter standing there holding two glasses of cold milk. I hadn't noticed her at all. We all laughed. She gave one glass to me and one to her mother, who put it straight to her mouth and in the first breath drank most of it down.

I took my first sip and asked, 'Now?'

She laughed, 'I've heard you are very highly educated. It is funny that you are asking me to educate you.'

'Exactly,' I answered.

She made herself more comfortable in the *charpai* and suggested that I put my legs up to be more comfortable as well. Then she began, 'The evening's take is brought together at the end of the performing hours. All the parties sit together.'

'What parties?' I asked impatiently.

'Wait, let me tell you first.'

'Okay! Okay! I won't interrupt,' I promised.

She continued, 'First the *niaz* should be taken out of the total earnings for the evening. It is usually 25 per cent. This amount can be determined more or less by the parties. Then the rest is divided into two halves. One half goes to the dancers and one to the *ustads*, but the *dairedaar* gets a share in each. That is her right. Understand?'

'Almost! The *dairedaar* is the person who manages the place, right?' I asked.

She replied, 'Yes'.

She put her hands in front of her stomach and began making extensive use of them. She put them together as if she was holding water in them and said, 'Out of sixteen *annas*, say we decide to take two *annas* out for *niaz*. Now the other fourteen *annas* will be divided into two.' She separated her hands. One part goes to the *ustads* and one goes to the dancers. The *dairedaar* gets one from both.'

I interrupted her, 'Please explain how the *dairedaar's* share is determined. If hundred rupees go to *ustads* and hundred to the dancers, what will the *dairedaar* get.'

She replied, 'If there are three dancers, there will be four shares of the hundred rupees—One for each dancer and one for the *dairedaar*. The same way, if there are four musicians, there will be four plus one, five shares of those hundred rupees: Four for the musicians and one for the *dairedaar*.'

'Now I get it', I said happily, 'so the money gets divided among the dancers, the musicians and the person who provides the space for the business. But isn't this person always from the dancer's side. I do not see musicians running *kothas*.'

She said, 'The dancers only get a share if they are from the outside. Do you think the managers hand over the dancer's share to their own girls? No, the *dairedaar* keeps it and the *niaz* as well. Then it is up to the *dairedaar's* own conscience. God knows best! I am not one to criticize. But these days some *dairedaars* can really trick you and somehow manage to keep most of the money.'

She smiled at me and asked, 'Are you happy now?'

In general, Pami's mother did not have a reputation for being friendly, but I liked her.

She roared again at her children. Whatever I could make out of this roar, other than half a dozen swear words, was that she wanted her daughter Rozi to make us *pakorey*.

Sitting in one position on the *charpai* made my legs stiff. As I changed position I asked her, 'What about that room?' I pointed to their third room, which had a traditional latch and a big lock.

She said, 'I am the *dairedaar* of this room. I can't afford to have a front part of the property and a nice performing place of my own, but I can afford a small room that I rent to other low class prostitutes to use at night. Usually, they have no place to take a customer, so they rent my room. It's not for music. You can see it doesn't have a front entrance, but it is only for sex.'

I asked, 'Can I see it?'

'Some other day,' she replied,

'So, how much do you charge for it?' I asked, curious.

She laughed loudly and all the children turned around. They probably hadn't seen their mother laugh in ages. 'You are so full of curiosity and questions...like a child!' I smiled and waited for an answer. Finally, she said, 'Ten *paisas* in a rupee.'

'Ten per cent, then, and how long does the prostitute get to use it?' I asked.

Just at that time came the heavy voice of Ruba, a student of Ustad Gaman, informing me that his *ustad* was back. That was the last thing I wanted at that time.

'Go away,' I said. 'I'm having fun talking to my aunt here. I don't know you any more!'

I think Pami's mother liked it that I didn't abandon her right away. She said to me, 'Today you eat with us.' I agreed and spent the late afternoon talking to her and her daughters, gradually being educated by them.

# 13

# IN THE BAITHAK

I was sitting in a *baithak* interviewing two composers who were brothers. I'd been told that they were among the few *ustads* left in the Mohalla who took their trainees' education seriously. They told me they only took students who were serious about learning music and whose families were also serious about their training. They were adamant about not wasting time on girls who want only to get by and to survive on Indian film songs in their *mujra*.

Ashraf Ali, the older brother said, 'We want to make our trainees bloom. We have had God's blessing until now. Our students have done well.'

His brother, Usman Ali, added, 'An *ustad's* job is not only musical instruction. He must introduce the new artist to the right people when the time comes to get her in the field. He has to teach her special pieces and guide her on where and what to sing.'

'We call that initiating her into the professional world of music,' said Ashraf.

I asked politely whether they meant singing in the *kotha* for different customers, and Ashraf answered, 'No, I'm talking about the professional world of performance, radio, television, and films.'

Usman Ali sighed and said, 'Even if times have changed, the Mohalla's performance aspect can't be ignored. Over the years, Pakistan's best singers, actresses, musicians and composers have mostly come from here. Totally intertwined with professional prostitution, the performing arts in this area have their own distinct tradition and significance in society. Most of our great master musicians and classical singers have been associated, in one way or another, with the Mohalla. Their families maintained their own musical traditions, but their close association with Shahi Mohalla's activity contributed to their development. In the same way, they contributed to maintaining a standard of performance over the years, but that standard is now only found in a rapidly dwindling number of *kothas*.'

Ashraf Ali continued, 'Remember that we *ustads* don't belong to *Kanjar* families and have no direct link to prostitution. We're only involved with the musical aspects of the bazaar. As the whole context for classical music changed, the stigma attached to the Mohalla has become more and more of an issue for all of us. Many children have come to feel that the Mohalla was not a 'respectable' place to live any more, and so they want their fathers to move to Karim Park, (a neighbourhood not far from the Mohalla, but outside the Taxalli Gate).'

I mentioned the famous *guru* of classical music, the late Ustad Amanat Ali Khan, and his brother, Ustad Fateh Ali Khan, saying I had visited them at their home in Karim Park. 'I understand that Ustad Fateh Ali still sometimes comes to visit his students in the Mohalla,' I asked.

'Of course!' agreed Usman Ali, 'He belongs to the Patiala *gharana* of classical music. He continues the tradition of classical music, but chose to move out of the Mohalla. Hamid Ali, their younger brother, and Asad Amanat Ali, Ustad Amanat Ali's son, have done justice to their teachers. Both are good classical performers. The next generation is already being trained in classical singing.'

Usman Ali said that *Ustad* Bade Ghulam Ali Khan was also a *sapardari*, meaning a musician who plays or who played in the past for *tawaif* or high status courtesans. He continued, 'He has many students in this area. For me having students who can keep the name of their *ustad* alive is a blessing. Personally, I like living here among my students and others who understand music.'

'Certainly!' I agreed. 'I had been visiting Master Inayat Hussain and I had the same feeling talking to him. He was very satisfied with his achievements and had no problem living in this Mohalla. He lived in Kucha Sethian, close to the Tibbi Thana. He said he moved close to this Mohalla because it was very convenient for him professionally.'

A big smile lit up Usman Ali's face when he heard Master Inayat Hussain's name, 'Master Inayat was a composer of such a high stature that he's unequalled in the entire Pakistani film industry. He composed several famous songs..."*Ulfat ki naee manzil ko chala*" [1], "*Aiy dil kisi ki yaad main hota hey beqarar keyoon*" [2] ...'

Ashraf Ali added, ' "*Jan-e-baharan rashk-e-chaman*" [3] and "*Tark-e-ulfat ka sila pa bhi liya hey main ne*" [4] ...What a composer!'

We shook our heads, intoxicated by the songs he had composed in his career.

Usman Ali went on, 'Few *ustads* live here anymore because their children don't think it's respectable....'

'But we have no plans to move out,' laughed Ashraf. 'We're proud to be a part of this place, so rich with music and arts. This is the birthplace of Pakistan's top artists. I've introduced three top singers into the film studios. Isn't that a big credit for an *ustad*?'

Two young men were roaming around, and I didn't know if they were helpers, students, musicians or servants. Ashraf called one of them and asked him to bring a harmonium.

I asked him if he only taught girls.

He said, 'Actually, I have no restrictions, but you know where we are! All my students are girls. I am a composer myself, and take students for singing and not musicians who are learning an

---

[1] Song from the film *Qatil*. Lyrics were by Qateel Shifai and the singer was Iqbal Bano.
[2] Song from the film *Ek Tera Sahara*. Lyrics by Qateel Shifai and the singers were Naseem Begum and Saleem Raza.
[3] Song from the film *Azra*. Lyrics by Tanveer Naqvi and the singer was Saleem Raza.
[4] Song from the film *Dil Mera Dharkan Teri*. Lyrics by Qateel Shifai and singer was Mehdi Hasan.

instrument. If I was also teaching a particular instrument I would probably have boys too.'

He looked at his brother, 'What about you Usman sahib?'

Usman laughed and said, 'I have two boys, very young. But most of my students are girls.'

The harmonium was brought in and put in front of Ashraf Ali. Just then, two musicians I knew well entered the *baithak*. We exchanged informal greetings. They had come to request Ashraf to take them to the studios to find work. One of them played the *tabla*, bongo and *nal* and the other played almost all the stringed instruments, but he was best at the *sitar*.

Finally, as Ashraf Ali was getting ready to play something, one of the musicians, Ruba, leaned towards me and asked, 'Have you met the pocket size singer yet?'

I did not want to start talking and interrupt Ashraf Ali's singing, but I was interested in what he was saying. I shook my head to say no.

Ruba said loudly, '*Ustad ji*, haven't you introduced your youngest student to Doctor *sahiba* yet?'

Irritated by the interruptions, Ashraf Ali said, 'Later, later.' He went into a 'Hummm...' directly and then said, 'This *ghazal* is my own composition'. I thought it was well composed, but the praise of Ruba and his friend was so exaggerated that it was obvious they were joking.

After the *ghazal*, the brothers asked if I could meet them another day at one of their student's homes. I happily agreed. This particular *Kanjar* family was among the Mohalla's older inhabitants. Their student was the main dancer, but they were also teaching her younger sister, Andila. They had high hopes for both girls.

Suddenly, Ashraf said, 'Oh! We have to be at the studios now. Wajahat Atreh (a famous composer) will be waiting for us. We're doing some work together. Then we're going to Madam's house. She's not well.'

He meant Madam Noor Jehan, Pakistan's 'Queen of Melody', who was alive at the time. Merely saying 'Madam' is enough for anyone to understand for whom it was meant. She was the country's most popular singer.

After they left, Ruba and Jaji began to laugh. Ruba said, 'Dr Fouzia I also beg leave as I have to meet Javed Sheikh (a famous actor). He's been begging to see me for a month and I told him that I'd do him the honour today.'

Jaji giggled, 'I gave time to the Prime Minister, but, for you, I'll cancel that. He'll just have to wait for another day.'

We all laughed, but I was embarrassed since the two assistants were still there. Ruba noticed my embarrassment and called one of the assistants. 'Doctor *sahiba*,' he said, 'meet the only ripe pumpkin of our bazaar'.

The assistant was embarrassed, but liked the attention. He was dark in complexion and very fat.

Ruba continued, 'He is one man who would not show in your photographs. Why don't you try it? Why don't you take our photo?'

'Stop it!' I cried with embarrassment.

He wouldn't quit, 'The only way you can see him is if he laughs. At night, we can only recognize our friend when we see him laugh. We see a string of teeth and we say, "Here is the pumpkin".'

Jaji laughed loudly, 'But that is only if he has cleaned his teeth that month.'

They continued joking about the pumpkin…whatever his real name was. As I was putting my things in my tote bag, I asked Ruba, 'What do you think will be the price for Laila's *nath utarwai*?'

'*Nath Utarwai* is for virgin girls, not for her,' he answered carelessly.

'But they say she has not been married yet,' I said.

'That's true. She's not married yet, but do you think the singing she has been doing at her own *kotha* all year was only to entertain the ears and eyes of the customers. She is not that melodious,' he laughed, 'and the customers are not that *parsa.*'

Both Ruba and Jaji laughed. Jaji hit his hand on Ruba's and said, 'Yar, you are something.... Parsa! No, they would not be there if they were.'

'You people are always making fun of them,' I went on, 'but they are seriously looking for someone.'

'Yes, they are', said Ruba. 'They cannot lose face in their biradri. They can't say that she never got married and, because the family needed the money, she started to work just like that. They have to save their face. Somehow they'll have to find a real fool who will not know that she's not a virgin.' Both young men burst into laughter.

Ruba continued, 'Who am I to say anything? These days they wash themselves with phitkari and they are as good as new again. They can fool anybody.' He paused and continued, 'Do you know that Pami's father is also looking for a fool...I mean a man.'

'For Pami,' I said innocently.

'Oh! Please, no, no...are you out of your mind? For her younger sister, Razia. Their so-called father is a very bad guy. I don't know why Pami's mother doesn't kick his ass,' said Ruba.

'She seems to be a strong woman,' I responded.

Ruba nodded and said, 'I just don't like him.'

Jaji re-entered the conversation, 'I'll tell you, Dr Fouzia, why he doesn't like this man.'

Ruba threw a pillow at Jaji and said, 'He'll bullshit you now.'

'Why, Ruba, do you have secrets from me?' I joked.

Jaji quickly moved forward and said, 'He likes Pami's younger sister. You know what I mean?'

'Which sister? She has so many,' I asked.

Ruba said immediately, 'The best one.'

'Number two, number three...which one? I don't have the eyes of your heart,' I said.

Jaji said, 'The third one, Razia. These days her father is looking for a good proposal for her. I've been telling him that we can all take a contribution and he can apply for the job. He could go in as a long-term customer and just live there. With such a nice father-in-law he wouldn't have a thing to worry about.'

'Shut up!' Ruba was getting angry.

'My God, this is serious,' I said, surprised, 'is there any chance of talking to her father?'

Ruba threw the pillow back and ruffled his hair with his hand, 'Never...never. They would never even let me close to her if they found out my heart's desire. I'm a *Mirasi*. We live with them as oil and water.'

Jaji interrupted, 'Well, they can't claim to be pure *Kanjar*. Her mother was a *Domni*.'

In the business of prostitution, being a *Kanjar* is the same as claiming the right to the trade by birth. Other ethnic groups are considered inferior. Pami's family was not pure *Kanjar*, but they always pretended to be and behaved as if they were. Her mother would not like someone calling her a *Domni* who are women from small occupational groups who earn their living singing and playing a small percussion instrument called a *gadvi*. They can be found performing in small groups at weddings or with other folk entertainers, like puppeteers. Some have moved into prostitution.

Curious to know if Ruba really wanted to marry Razia or was just infatuated, I asked, 'What would you like? Leaving the constraints aside, if you had your way what would you do?'

Ruba looked around. One of the assistants was still hanging around in the distance. Ruba got up, hit him on the back and said, 'Get going, son.'

He came back and sat close to me, 'I would take her far away from this place, far away from her family of vultures. They just want to suck her blood. She is too good for this place.'

Jaji laughed, 'He watches too many Indian films.'

'Shut up, you mother fucker,' Ruba yelled, 'I'd be better off without friends like you.' He seemed truly angry and that suddenly put Jaji in a serious mood.

'Aren't they only interested in money?' I asked, 'if you offered them some money, would they accept you?'

'Accept me as what?' he asked, tilting his head, 'they want to sell her first night.'

I said, 'But they do go for long-term relationships if you keep paying them monthly or something.'

'First of all, they'd rather die than make a link between their girl and a *Mirasi*,' explained Jaji. 'Then they'd put her to *dhanda* to get a regular income, no matter long-term or short-term. Do you think Ruba could tolerate that? He can't win. It's never happened.'

'What about her?' I asked, 'is she in love with him or is it one sided? She seemed a very quiet person to me.'

Jaji got another opportunity to pull Ruba's leg, 'Believe me she doesn't even know, and if she finds out, she wouldn't go with this nobody. She'll do what her dear mother tells her to do.'

'You keep your ugly face out of my life,' said Ruba, irritated, 'She does know. I know it in my heart. I just know that she knows how I feel for her.'

'He's been beaten by our *ustad* several times, but he doesn't stop talking about her. *Ustad* Gaman says, oil and water don't mix,' said Jaji. He got up and said, 'Come on Ruba, *ustad* will be waiting for us and on the way we can stop over at your "in-laws"...'

Jaji quickly picked up his slippers and ran out. Ruba ran after him and tried to hit him hard on his back. He missed. He came back with his head down and a long face.

I didn't know what to say, but I had to ask one thing, 'Will you tell her about how you feel for her?'

'Some day!' he said without looking at me. 'Come, I'll walk you to your car.'

'No, thanks,' I said, 'I'm not going back right now, but you can walk with me to *Ustad* Gaman's *baithak*. I'm to meet him there.'

We walked through the bazaar talking about other things, but I knew he still had that girl on his mind.

## VIEWS

### Sarwat Ali, a music critic

Sarwat Ali writes frequently on music in newspapers and is considered a well-versed person on South Asian performing arts. One day, sitting in his house, we started discussing the underlying paradox of the phenomenon of prostitution. I found his views and analysis quite interesting.

He said, 'Our films, music, poetry and visual arts have all been fascinated by the theme of the courtesan. Prostitutes and courtesans have always been the fantasy of men. At home, they have a wife, a woman who guarantees fidelity and the survival of his lineage, and in the bazaar they have a mistress, a woman who excels in charms and creativity. She is the culmination of all his fantasies. She is beautiful and highly accomplished in the arts. She sings, dances, and, at times, even recites her own verses. All men want her.'

'I've been fascinated by Umrao Jan Ada,'[1] I said. 'Both Pakistani and Indian film industries have made "super hit" movies of the novel.' I laughed, 'The Pakistani version of Umrao Jan couldn't have Umrao sleep with anyone except the hero, and then only after he married her. We changed the story to keep her virtue, but the Indians accepted her as a prostitute with many customers.'

Sarwat said, 'It's not just Umrao Jan, it's Anarkali, Pakeeza and actually every other movie that shows the glamour of a courtesan. It helps filmmakers use the kotha as a context to add beautiful songs and dances to their films. But the interesting thing is that they always turn the story around, to somehow show that the pretty young dancer is in a sinful life only because of difficult circumstances and misfortune. They try to prove that she was originally a middle-class family's daughter who fell on bad times. Then, eventually, a hero arrives to save her.'

I agreed, 'In Pakistani movies, the hero has to save her before she gets her first customer, because otherwise, the story writer can't deal

---

[1] Umrao Jan Ada was a story of a courtesan from Lucknow written by Mirza Mohammed Hadi Rusva (1857-1931), first published in 1899.

with her anymore. She can't marry the hero and has to either commit suicide at the end or die in some other manner. Writers and directors are incapable of imagining a prostitute as a film heroine. It doesn't match the society's ethics.'

Sarwat said, 'Some brave directors have made movies that are closer to reality and not the romantic image of most movies about prostitutes. For example Mandi and Shyam Benegal's film... What was the name...?'

'Bhumika,' I reminded him.

'Yes, it gives a realistic image, but which movies make more money? People like seeing romanticized versions of prostitutes and then are satisfied when the young dancing girl is saved from the pimps and manipulative naikas by a brave hero, before she too becomes a prostitute.'

'What do you think is behind this contradiction?' I asked.

'Our men are attracted to the glamour and the talent of these women, which they don't find at home, but when they get too closely involved, they want to reform them and make them virtuous like the women in their families. If they really want virtuous women they already have them at home, but they don't realize what attracts them. Men are confused by this paradox without realising that it exists.'

I think it is this obsession that the films thrive on. They provide an opportunity for people to fulfil their fantasies of being attracted to a beautiful dancing girl, winning her heart, and then reforming her. So, regardless of this tour of fantasyland, they retain the obvious mainstream values at the end. Even those who don't go to prostitutes' kothas experience the scenario through films.'

'These films really draw the audiences, don't they?' I asked.

'Yes,' he replied, 'our society is full of contradictions and hypocrisies, but it doesn't want to look at them.'

# 14

# THE ACADEMY OF
# PERFORMING ARTS

I was sitting in *Ustad* Gaman's *baithak* one day when Chanda came in. Even though she was a student of *Ustad* Sadiq, she sometimes went out on performing assignments with Ustad Gaman, and she respected him as if he were her own *ustad*. Swaying in her light blue chiffon outfit and her big dangling earrings, she asked me when he would return. Hearing he was expected soon, she joined me in waiting for him. Chanda seemed in an exceptionally good mood and sat singing to herself one song after another in a low voice. She spread her *dupatta* on one arm, untangled it from her bracelets, and then pulled it up to see how she looked. She kept playing with different ways of draping her *dupatta* on her shoulders and arms. The long dark hair flowing down her back looked more beautiful than ever.

Leafing through my notes, I casually mentioned that I wanted to see *ustad* today because he was going home for a week. Chanda sprang up with surprise, 'Oh, is he going home? Have you been to his house?'

'No,' I said, thinking that he'd never extended me an invitation.

Chanda moved a bit closer, 'They keep their homes very unapproachable, and never take anyone home. Once in a while *Ustad* Gaman brings his ten-year-old son along for a few days. That's all. But I got to go to his house once.' Her voice shook with excitement.

'How was that?' I asked with surprise.

'We were in that area doing a show at a place not too far from his house. When we finished it was 3.30 in the morning. *Ustad* Gaman thought it was too early for the local restaurants to be open and since everyone was too tired to start for home without a cup of tea, he asked everyone to come to his house. When we got there, we all stayed out in the street. His sons brought out some chairs by the van, and his wife made us tea. I went in though. As a woman I could have that privilege, and I didn't want to miss the opportunity. The house was very small and dark. He had a lot of children. I don't remember how many, but I did meet two of his daughters, one was about my age, or a little younger, and one about twelve.'

'I guess it's the older one who is getting married!' I said, smiling.

'So that's why he's going home?' asked Chanda with delight. 'She really wanted to learn music and become a singer. She said she had picked up a lot from what her father taught her brothers about music and thought that she had a good voice. She told me that the desire to sing was very strong in her heart, but she wasn't allowed to pursue it.'

'Why so?' I asked.

'These *ustads* don't teach their daughters music. I could see envy in her eyes when she met me. She clearly thought of us as "bad" women, but was still full of envy that we get to learn from her father and have the opportunity and freedom to pursue singing as a career. She actually made me sing during that short visit. She took out a harmonium and said, "Sing a little for me." She was afraid of her father so she whispered all the time. She told me she'd always dreamed of becoming a singer, but she knows that she's not even allowed to sing at the family gatherings. I sang for her in a low voice. I still remember how she smiled.'

I told her, 'I've learned through my research that these performing arts are peculiarly gender biased. Only men of *Mirasi* or other families that play musical instruments are part of the culture. Female family members of these musicians don't enter the work. The regular musicians keep their families away, and maintain a *baithak* here in the Mohalla only for themselves and their colleagues. They teach only their sons how to play, never their daughters.'

Chanda agreed, 'Yes, the *ustads* rarely teach their daughters music. If some do, it's not so they can perform. *Mirasi* daughters, like most other Pakistani girls, are considered economic liabilities to be married off as early as possible. They're not the ones taking on the family tradition of music or earning an income. Sometimes, when the daughter is bright and has learned music well, she might help her brothers in composing and improving their singing. If she marries a singer or a good musician, she could help him in the same way, but never to appear on stage with him.'

'I know,' I replied, 'among the living great masters, only *Ustad* Salamat Ali, from the *Sham Chaurasi* family, allowed his daughter to play a *tanpura* in a concert. She played in the background as the men sang classical music. This "liberal" attitude probably came from his exposure to elite society members and especially to foreigners. He's an exception, though.'

Chanda exclaimed, 'Ask *ustad* when he gets back why he wouldn't teach singing to his daughter.'

'Okay!' I said, 'we'll both quiz him. Now, you tell me why you all are excited about singing and not about playing any instrument. Why don't any of you women play *tabla* or *nal*? The harmonium is the only instrument I see any of you playing and that's only to accompany your own singing.'

Chanda sat motionless for a while, frowning. Then she looked at me seriously and said, 'I don't know. I never thought about it.' After a pause she smiled with a new idea, 'Lets ask *ustad* about that too. All I know is that it's not done.'

I asked about her ambitions. With dreamy eyes Chanda said, 'I want to become a famous artist. So many good singers come from our area.'

'I'm looking at the contribution this Mohalla and other red light districts of other cities have made to singing. Except for folk music, most of our top singers are associated with this Mohalla.'

Throwing her *dupatta* to one side, she said, 'Yes, all of them. Mention the top names and they're all from here. Like you said, this Mohalla has made a big contribution, and I plan to be one of the top ones too.' Her eyes shone with a spirit of determination.

Then she added, 'Often, when someone from a family becomes really popular as a singer, they all give up prostitution and try to live off that fame. They try to get other daughters into singing only and then marry them off to the *shurafa*. Once they become famous they want to move to a suburb right away.'

'Are you telling me your family's future plans?' I asked.

Chanda giggled with embarrassment as if I'd caught her by surprise. 'I don't think so. I like my work,' she replied. Lots of people from our area are singing in the film industry. You know, I have already sung for some good composers. One of these days I'll get my chance.'

'You've got a lot of role models! I consider this Mohalla an academy of performing arts, and it's produced great music masters, actors and dancers.'

Chanda shouted, 'and singers! All the most popular singers have come from this Mohalla or places like it in other cities, especially the female singers. Madam is the best. Any budding singer would have her as an idol. She's certainly the most popular.'

I went on to tell Chanda more about her and other singers. 'Madam Noor Jehan, is the most legendary singer of our time, and she rules equally over the hearts of audiences and her fellow musicians. Her career spans over fifty years. It is common knowledge that her family was associated with the Bazaar of Kasur, a small city of Punjab. She was taken out of Kasur when she was very young, and was never allowed to go into the traditional business of the area. She was groomed by the best *ustads* and was considered a precious discovery for the film industry. Before Partition she acted as well as sang, but later she concentrated on singing only.'

We continued talking for quite a while about many of the famous singers who had been associated with the Shahi Mohalla. Chanda seemed stimulated by the positive examples of women from the area who had succeeded in the past, so I asked her, 'If you made a list of all the successful artists this area has produced how long do you think it would be?'

'Very long!' she answered, 'but not long enough to convince the government that the place needs attention. The situation is deteriorating, and if conditions remain the way they are, the Mohalla will start churning out only trashy artists for the country. Our family is among the few that still pay attention to musical quality. My mother pays for two *ustads* for me. *Ustad* Sadiq manages my performing career, but I also have a dance instructor and I go to *Ustad* Ashraf Ali sometimes for my singing. I see what is happening to my friends, they can't even distinguish between *bhairvin* and *bhairon*.'

'Yes,' I agreed, 'training in music and dance produced stars for the films, provided talent to radio, television and theatre, and so much musical instrument making was concentrated here. Chanda, maybe our country wants the Mohalla to disintegrate, but I don't think they've thought about any alternatives for producing and training good artists. I guess most people don't really care about the quality of their own art, being quite happy listening to Indian film songs and whatever they can find on cassettes and CDs. But there really should be some systematic thinking by key institutions and people who consider themselves the custodians of Pakistani culture. We need an alternative to this mindless destruction of such an important cultural institution!'

Just then, a young boy rushed into the *baithak*, sifted through some of *ustad's* personal belongings, took a box of cigarettes and rushed back out. Chanda shouted after him, 'Where is *Ustad* Gaman?'

'He's coming soon! He wanted me to get his cigarettes. I have to run!' the boy answered as he disappeared.

Chanda made herself comfortable and looked at me, 'So, *ustad's* daughter is getting married next week.'

'I should think of a gift for her,' I said.

'Here you only give clothes or cash. I am sure all the mothers of his key students will be giving that,' said Chanda.

'I want to give him something different. I don't think he'd accept cash from me anyway.'

While we were discussing gift ideas *Ustad* Gaman came in, followed by the young boy. He seemed rather exhausted, and asked his young student to get us all tea. Chanda and I declined, but the boy ran out again, rupee note in hand.

After Chanda finished talking business, *Ustad* Gaman relaxed and moved to recline against the wall. Now Chanda became impatient for me to ask the questions we had talked about. She prodded me again and again to get me to speak. Finally, I asked *Ustad* Gaman about gender discrimination in music. He looked at me with surprise on his face and repeated, 'Gender discrimination?'

I quickly explained, 'Why women sing, but don't play musical instruments; why *Mirasi* men play instruments and also sing, but don't let the women of their families perform?'

*Ustad* Gaman thought for a while and then gave us his explanation, 'Women who practice the performing arts come from *Kanjar* families or those who have worked as professional prostitutes in the past. They sing and dance because these arts are believed to be attractive to customers. Instrument playing was never seen as something that, by itself, could help them win a customer's heart. That takes the poetry of a song or the gestures of a dance. That's why you rarely see a woman playing an instrument or composing music. The only exceptions are *tanpura* or harmonium, which a woman can play while singing. Women also occasionally play the *sitar*, but not professionally. So, even when she does play an instrument, it is to support her own singing and not to accompany other singers.'

Becoming very involved in his own explanation, he sat up and continued, 'The division of roles reflects the traditional norms of the two major groups involved here. The *Kanjar* have long been involved in prostitution. The women of this ethnic group play the crucial role in the profession, and their men exist more like parasites than partners. On the other hand, among the *Mirasis*, the traditional music providers, only the men perform the supporting role for the prostitutes in their dancing and singing. *Mirasi* men want to keep a clear distinction between *Kanjar* women and the women of their own families, so they don't allow their women to be involved in music. Don't you see? This division continues even outside the traditional ethnic groups. Pakistani women rarely play instruments, preferring to sing.'

He seemed to be making a serious effort to think about these things. When finished, he was silent for a while and then said he wanted to take a nap. Before he could lie down, Chanda quickly asked, 'Please, also tell us why no one in the government cares about the Mohalla when it produces so many great artists.'

*Ustad* Gaman broke out laughing, 'The government! Are you crazy child? If it could, the government would banish art from Pakistan altogether as a bad influence of the Hindus.' He laughed loudly and repeated a common expression: '"*Mula ki daur masjid tak*" (A Mullah can only run up to the mosque). Our leaders cannot go beyond the Hindu-Muslim argument. They say we Muslims are above all earthly expressions of creativity,' he added.

He then sighed and continued, 'Forget about the government. It's a shame that the whole country looks at us as a bad patch. They all want their entertainment, but no one wants to look at the injured and bruised corpse of performing arts that lies here naked.' With that he rolled over and buried his face in a pile of clothes lying next to him.

Chanda and I got up with heavy hearts. As we left I told Chanda I had a wonderful gift idea for his daughter.

My tone cheered her up and she asked excitedly, 'What is it?'

'A *dholak*. It's the only instrument women play without hesitation. Young girls huddle around it at weddings and sing wedding songs. The *ustad* did not think of it, probably because it is more of a folk instrument. When it's played professionally men take over. But women of all communities in Pakistan play

Making a *tabla* in the musical instrument market

Putting the screws on the *dholak* for tuning

Setting the keyboard for a harmonium

23

*Ghungroo,* or ankle bells, hanging in a musical instrument shop

The primary customers of the musical instrument market are the local musicians and performers of the Mohalla

it in one form or the other. I too love to play the *dholak*,'
I concluded.

'So do I. Yes, it really is our thing!' Chanda thought it was a
great idea.

We planned to go to the nearby market to order a *dholak*.
Since it would be a gift for an *ustad's* daughter, I didn't dare
buy it off the shelf. *Ustads* always have instruments specially
made for them. Continuing that tradition, I thought we should
go to the market only to find out where *dholaks* are made.

The main market for musical instruments stretched from the
Main Bazaar Chowk into the Langa Mandi. Some shops were
close to Thana Tibbi, the area's police station, at the opposite
end of the Shahi Mohalla, but most were concentrated here in
this long market. You couldn't miss the *dholak*, *dafli* and other
instruments hanging in front of shops on both sides of the road.
Since most professional musicians either live in the Mohalla or
are linked to it, they depend on this market for their own
instruments. It also attracts others interested in learning to play
any musical instrument, as it's the only place in the city where
all kinds of instruments are available. *Tabla*, *dholak*, *nal*, *sitar*,
harmonium, *dafli*, congo, *ghungroo* and many other instruments
are made here.

The traditional red light districts in the other big cities also
buy from this market. So Lahore's Shahi Mohalla is one of the
centres of instrument making. Percussion instruments are a
speciality of this bazaar. Gujranwala is more known for
harmoniums, and Sialkot exports clarinets, saxophones and
bagpipes, a tradition left over by British military bands. Some
instrument making has shifted to other parts of Lahore, but the
families are the same and maintain a strong link with the people
and the businesses of the Mohalla.

Anxious to order a *dholak*, Chanda and I were told to first go
to a factory to have a wooden shell made. The shells are made
by a group of craftsmen different from those who put on the
leather sides. Many factories were recommended, Baba Farid's
in Taxalli, Alla Rakha's in Malipura, Hero's in Kasupura,

Yamin's in Malikpura and some outside Lahore. We chose the closest one, Baba Farid's in Taxalli, just across the main road.

Baba Farid himself met us affectionately, amused that a couple of women had turned up at his factory to order a *dholak*. He enthusiastically showed us around and explained the whole process of making a shell for a percussion instrument. His family had been making wooden shells for percussion instruments in Taxalli for the last thirty years, his father having started this work in the early sixties. He used to make game boards, platters, bedposts and other things on order. As there were many instrument makers around who needed a factory with a commercial saw and lathes, they moved into making musical instruments. Now Baba Farid's son, Mohammed Iqbal, was taking over the work.

He took us to a stack of wood cut into rough rectangular shapes, and told us that *tali*, *sheesham* or *aam* wood is used for these instruments. He asked us to select the piece we wanted, explaining that instruments like *dholak* are best made from the *gulli*, inner wood from hollowing a bigger shell. Determined to get the best quality, I asked for that. He took a smaller piece that was quite dark and asked Iqbal to scrape it for us. It took about half an hour to hollow out the piece with an electric lathe and shape it into a smooth rounded shell. They informed us that it used to take eight days with a hand lathe to do the same work. They used simple tools to clean the shell and for finishing. Chanda and I were as proud of the outcome as if we had made the shell ourselves.

Baba Farid told his son to colour our *dholak* so Iqbal put it back on the lathe again and painted bright coloured lacquer stripes on it. We were ecstatic to see our *dholak* completed. I quickly ordered another one for myself.

Getting the skins made was not difficult. Giving the shell to a well-known percussion instrument maker who specialized in this job, we returned the next day to pick up our instrument. He told us to heat it or use kneaded flour to change the sound as we wanted.

*Ustad* Gaman was very surprised when we gave him our gift for his daughter. He wasn't sure how to react, but after a few moments' hesitation he told us that he appreciated our gesture.

Chanda and I walked away feeling very happy. I looked at her and said, 'Well, the debate about which women can perform and which cannot will continue, but meanwhile the *dholak* symbolizes what little remains for most Pakistani women to express themselves musically. It's all we have. The *dholak* and a chance to sing and dance at weddings.'

# 15

# A VISIT TO THE FILM STUDIOS

The Shahi Mohalla has made tremendous contribution to the art of acting and dancing. Just as most professional singers of both classical and popular music are associated with Shahi Mohalla, or similar traditional bazaars, so are almost all female actresses and some of the male actors of the film industry.

Budding actresses in the past did their best to disassociate themselves from their origins and many moved out of the Mohalla before they became successful. They usually made up a story about their past and introduced their manager as their mother or aunt, which in many cases, was the truth. After becoming famous, whenever interviewed by the media, the actresses would totally deny their origins or any link with the Mohalla.

Many of the stars were brought up in boarding schools or raised in suburban residences before their jump into the world of fame. By saying that these actresses were born in Shahi Mohalla doesn't at all imply that they were prostitutes before joining the film industry. Sometimes their mothers took great pains to resist the pressure from their families to get their daughters into the profession. Film acting has long been seen as an effective transition from the Mohalla and into the mainstream, a way to gain respect through wealth and popularity. However, despite the romance and charisma associated with films, the industry shares the same taboo as the red light districts. It is commonly said that because so many of its artists come from red light districts, 'chaste' members of Pakistani society have little desire to join them.

The family ties of all the famous actresses link them to various Mohallas. Only a few exceptions, like Shabnam, Nayyar Sultana, Musarrat Nazir and Samina Peerzada, had no such association and came into the industry simply because they wanted to pursue acting. Sabiha Khanum came from a family of theatre actors.

During the 1960s, a few actresses slipped into the film industry from a segment of the rich urban elite, which considered itself 'modern' and copied the night-club culture, complete with western music and dancing. While they allowed women to interact with men in this context, it was still frowned upon by the larger society. Actresses like Husna and Neelo, examples of this minority sub-culture, became popular dancers in the film industry.

Some famous actresses or singers also came from the highest class of courtesan, called *tawaif*. In the old days of *rajas* and *maharajas*, they were well-groomed artists who associated with only one customer throughout their careers. They enjoyed high status as successful businesswomen and were not equated with prostitutes. Some of these women married rich men at a young age and were allowed to continue singing or acting. Some became our most graceful singers and performers.

Interestingly, unlike the heroines of the past, many new film stars don't seem to feel the need to disassociate themselves from their roots. They have not only been quite open about their origins, but continue their profession in the form of *mujra*. They usually do not choose to live in the area as they prefer modern suburban living, but their lifestyle and circle of friends is an extension of the Mohalla culture. Many now bring their sisters and brothers along with them to the studios and get them non-acting jobs in the industry.

In Pakistani films, a pretty face, and a generous producer who provides the opportunity and publicity is all that is needed to become a star. Unlike music and singing that require rigorous training, acting is associated more with glamour. Some actors like Allauddin, Talish and others progressed because of hard work and the versatility of their performances. However, looking at the most successful actors and actresses one cannot say that it was only the high quality of performance that took them to the top. In films at present screen beauty and dance talent count more than acting ability, especially for women. In Pakistan, acting is not considered an art that is formally taught. Acting is thought to be easily learned on the job through a good director who assumes the additional role of a teacher.

The biggest market for actors is the film industry. Television provides some opportunities, but is considered more as a vehicle to attract the notice of film producers or, perhaps simply to satisfy a creative urge. Television acting is not seen as economically viable. Stage acting, interestingly, pays better and is a safer route to popularity.

I made several visits to film studios to glimpse a world that attracts thousands of hopeful actors, taking a few fortunate ones to the heights of fame while leaving most crippled like moths who burned their wings by coming too close to the flames of a candle they did not understand. They spend the rest of their lives crawling around that candle, hoping for another chance to fly.

I was attracted not by the lives of the super stars, but by the cultural milieu created by the variety of performers and technicians associated with the studios. I was fascinated by character actors, women who have been playing mothers for over three decades, and by stuntmen, set designers, composers, musicians, chorus singers, and, of course, the young hopefuls who hover around the directors, hoping to gain access through scores of agents who have long since mastered the art of human manipulation.

I arranged to watch the shooting of a dance sequence of a new film being shot at Shahnoor Studios. After passing several layers of guards, I entered the shooting compound. The shooting area was arranged to look like a park in one of the many studio courtyards. A beautiful young dancer, wearing little more than a flowing blond wig and blue contact lenses, was the centre of attraction on the set. There was a big fountain on one side and a park, with an arch of trees on the other. Film shootings may

The theme of dancing girls is quite common in the South Asian film industry. Film star Anjuman playing the role of a prostitute. *From the collection of Ijaz Gul*

The film industry has portrayed a glamorized image of a prostitute: Kavita in film
*Naam Mera Badnaam. From the collection of Ijaz Gul*

Despite the sad stories of the prostitutes in the movies, their characters are used to
jazz up the film with seductive dances. *From the collection of Ijaz Gul*

Film star Neeli (top) and Shabnam (right), though playing dancing girls are trying to meet the standards of sophistication and elegance that were a reality a century ago. *From the collection of Ijaz Gul*

A dancing girl who is unwilling to succumb to her customer's desire. A film scene
*From the collection of Ijaz Gul*

Advertisements on the facades of movie theaters reflect the way
women are portrayed in movies

sound interesting, but actually watching them can be extremely boring. You can spend hours and be lucky to see more than two scenes recorded. A scene might be shot over and over, and may end up lasting only a few seconds in the film. I enjoyed watching the dance director, who despite his masculinity danced more gracefully than the star herself.

The film director, an actor himself, was perched on a chair as if he were a god. I had seen other, older, directors who engendered fear in those around them, but was surprised by this fellow's attitude since he seemed too young to have such an aura about him. I was no judge, but he had not yet made his first film. His entry in the film industry was easy since his parents were a famous actress and a very well known film director. On that day, he was wearing black clothes and a red band on his head and looked rather strange. I asked a few musicians about him and they said, 'Fouzia *bibi*, these days whoever gives us work is a good guy. We don't look for teamwork or respect anymore. Some directors respect us and know that we've been around for decades. They treat us as family, but these new kids think they've fallen from the sky and everyone else is a fool.' I didn't push that line of questioning further. I met a writer who had come on the set to meet a producer. A friend introduced him elaborately, identifying some of his films. I asked why all the films he wrote were so similar. He replied, 'For an audience like you, all Pakistani films must be similar.'

Though this was quite true, I still replied, 'I'm not putting the film industry down, but why this formula?'

'Everyone is looking for guaranteed success,' he replied, 'so, if a movie with some vulgar dances, some romance, some action, one or two rape scenes, a comedian, several flashy songs, dances, and lots of fights is successful, every film should have that. No one wants to make the mistake of not putting in all the right ingredients. Who wants to lose money? Only recently have films started making good money again. We've all gone through hard times. The video industry ate us up. I don't think we'll ever really recover from that.'

'Don't you think over-use of this formula could have caused the downfall of Pakistani cinema?' I asked.

'No!' he replied sternly, 'video took over our business. People watched smuggled Indian movies in the convenience of their homes for only ten rupees. Families went for that, watching three to four movies at a stretch, and not even stepping out of their homes to be entertained.'

I asked him about how new faces were hired from the Mohalla, in the past and present. He was quiet for a while and then suggested I ask a director.

'But I want to hear from you,' I retorted.

He acquiesced grudgingly, 'Nowadays, the girls who come here to work are very much aware of their talents and beauty. They think they know everything. Earlier, when a director or a producer picked up a young girl from the Mohalla, they groomed and refined her for the films. Look at our older actresses, how graceful and polished they were. They learned about acting and respected their senior colleagues. They knew that they had a lot to learn, and they listened to the directors. The standard of acting was a hundred times better than now, when money has become more important than art.

'Films used to extract the best out of the Mohalla: The best singers and actors, the most beautiful faces. The industry still takes the best the Mohalla has to offer, but unfortunately, what it offers is no longer very high quality. It's just bloody vulgarity. Don't mind my saying this, but that's what people pay to see. I don't only blame the directors and producers. Very few women are like Samina Peerzada, who come from outside these circles, who are beautiful, talented and brave enough to maintain their high acting quality and make it in the industry, without giving in to the pressure of vulgarity.'

A song was playing in the background on the set that was obviously copied from an Indian film song. The music was exactly the same and so were most of the words. This was hard for me to take. I am overly sensitive about pirated songs. I knew that the Indian song itself had been 'inspired' by an old American song, but still it upset me.

Listening to that bastardized tune, I remembered Master Abdullah, one of the most creative composers of Punjabi film music, and my personal favourite, telling me how he hated such 'inspired music'. He argued that this was why great composers couldn't get any work, 'First, we come up with original compositions so we take our time and charge more. The composers who only choose songs to copy can write the music for two films in a week. They charge very little and are more economical for low budget films. Second, since our compositions are original, the singers have to learn them and we insist on rehearsals. This requires a bigger investment in terms of the time of the singer, musicians and the director. People don't like this. A singer could sing several copied songs in a day and get a handsome payment, while, when I compose, one song may take three days to record. The producer does not like this because it costs him more. The singer does not like it, because she is paid per song. With a pirated song she can listen to a tape and sing it after a few trials. The irony is that audiences also sometimes like to hear familiar tunes composed over and over in many variations.'

He made another interesting point. 'Low film budgets are the single biggest factor which have caused the deterioration of the standards of film production. We used to use what we called piece music in our compositions. We could use whatever musical instruments we wanted. Now the producer wants us to do everything with two rhythm instruments and a harmonium. It's not possible. Listen to our old compositions. For only a few seconds of music I could rent out a piano and a musician to play it. Harps, *tanpuras*, flutes—we could get whatever we wanted to add dimensions to our music, but now this 'sisterf...r' synthesizer is getting on our nerves. Either the producer wants every song with only *tabla*, *nal* and harmonium or he wants a synthesizer to exactly reproduce the tune that has been copied. Just look at these bastard senior actors and senior directors. No one is ashamed to use this copied music. How do they live with themselves? They are thieves. One day I got so angry at my honesty and starvation that I took out all my awards and photographs and burned them. I don't have a single photograph of myself any longer. What is the use of this honesty and creativity when it can't earn me *sukhi roti* for my children.'

Mushtaq Gazdar, a renowned Pakistani filmmaker, analyses the ups and downs of the film industry in his book *Pakistan Cinema*. He believes that the industry had to face such dire circumstances during most of its fifty years that creativity and risky innovations became extremely rare commodities. As an example, he noted that after Ziaul Haq established military rule in 1977, he passed an ordinance which cancelled all the censor clearance certificates for Pakistani films made prior to that date. In Pakistan, a film requires a clearance certificate from the Government Censor Board before it can be screened in the theatres. General Zia's action, he feels, was 'a death warrant for the film industry of the country.' Banning all the films made in the previous three decades created a vacuum that was quickly filled by cheap productions made for easy profit. The gap in the production also attracted those who invested simply to make quick money.

## VIEWS

### Faiza's Mother

One morning I talked to my aunt, Faiza's mother, about my discussion with Sarwat. I spoke of the paradox that men are attracted to certain women for their singing and dancing, but later want to change them. She listened to me quietly and said, 'I'm not an intellectual who examines these things, but I do know that men don't feel comfortable if their own women are involved in music and dancing. I wonder why?'

She looked as though she was going very far back into her past, and she told me a story. 'When I was in college, I participated in every extra curricular activity. I had a beautiful singing voice, and sang at college functions. It was a women's college of course so my parents didn't worry about it. Once I performed in a college play with outside guests and was identified as a new talent. Radio producers approached me for auditions. Getting permission was such a big challenge for me. My elder sister and other friends convinced my father that no one would see my face, but would just hear my voice. After a lot of begging he agreed. When I started working at the radio, I took off like a rocket. Radio was very popular in those days. There was no television and people used to listen regularly to all the plays.'

'Was your father happy then?' I asked.

'He was always concerned, the way fathers are. He was afraid I wouldn't get a good proposal for marriage. Families looking for a daughter-in-law don't approve of a woman who practices any kind of performing art. Men don't like it. I've allowed Faiza to take fine arts because that's acceptable, but no music or dancing. I'm worried about my daughter's marriage just like my father was about mine.'

'What happened when you did get married?' I asked.

She answered with a sigh, 'What happens to many talented young women? I had to stop singing. Much later, I read a newspaper article about radio artists. The author wrote, "Whatever happened to the famous radio artist Shabana Akhtar? After her marriage, no one knows where she went." I was very happy to read that because I was remembered, but I also felt sad, because I'd really enjoyed working at the radio. People loved my voice.'

I could very well imagine that. She sings at our family weddings with other aunts and cousins and has the sweetest voice I've heard. She is but one example of many women in Pakistan who stifle their talents or never even explore their artistic side, unless they happen to be in areas that society approves.

I remember the first argument in my family about dancing. I'd always been fascinated by folk dancing. Seeing a dance just once, I could pick up the steps and style perfectly. I used to dance for my family and later at college (women's only, of course!). Once I performed in a big college programme where outside guests were invited. There were no men in the audience, but a professional photographer was taking photographs. My father found out and was afraid he would display them in his shop, as photographs of women dancing were a rare opportunity. My mother sided with me, but after a big family argument we agreed that I would dance in 'safe' environments only.

# 16

## ENTANGLED RELATIONSHIPS

Laila was quite upset with me. I hadn't visited her house for ten days. She felt I was getting too familiar with other families in the Mohalla. I was apparently not giving her enough attention and she had lost her sense of monopoly over me. She loved introducing me as her close friend from Islamabad, especially to her customers.

I had a hard time explaining to her that knowing other people did not mean I was not her friend, but her childish temperament allowed me to settle the situation easily. She always relented if I took her out in my car for an icecream. Her childlike approach to life came out most clearly when she either did or did not get what she wanted. She was ecstatic over the mere idea of going out of the house on an ordinary trip for icecream. Rather than get permission from her mother to go, and get ready, she picked up the telephone and spent at least one hour calling different customers to brag about this outing. I did not mind waiting for her at all. Her telephone conversations were always of great interest to me.

The first person she phoned was Javed, whom she called Javed *Sahib*. She must have called his shop since she kept referring to the market. She spoke in somewhat formal Punjabi using the word *tusi*, which is a formal way of addressing a person. Her voice frequently sounded like a child who wanted to be pampered. First, she asked what he was doing, and when he returned the question, she went into a long description of our plans. 'I have this friend, you know, very close, a real *pakki seheli*. She comes to Lahore to see me. She has her own car, a Toyota Corolla, a very nice car, with a tape deck in it also. She takes me out and we have a lot of fun. She's taking me to have ice cream on the Mall.'

The telephone had a long cord and she carried it around the room with her. First, she lay on the sofa, then she got up and plunked herself in a chair and finally stretched out on the floor. She seemed to think the man could see her through the telephone, as though it were a film scene, and a camera was shooting her.

'My friend is a real friend, not like you,' she said, 'where do you take me? Nowhere! You are an embarrassment to friendship.' She laughed, 'What? What about permission? If you had *dil gurda*, you could get my mother's permission. I love to go out!' She lay down on the sofa with her version of a seductive smile on her face. Unfortunately, Laila's seductive smile was more like a child forced to smile in front of a camera.

After a long pause she said, 'Which friend are you talking about? I don't remember. I was so busy looking at you I didn't notice who else was in the room. I only have your image in my heart,' she said in a husky voice and then laughed in a naughty manner. 'So, if I go out with you what will you buy me? Whatever I ask for? Is that a deal? Don't back out later, I'm telling you. Better not back out!'

She put the phone down and said to me, 'My mother said I should use the phone more to keep in touch with these bastards. The one I am calling now is very funny. Listen to this one!'

Despite her protests, I could see a prostitute in the making. Laila was less upset with her mother and brother's pressure and was becoming more accustomed to using the skills required to entice a customer. She had clearly started to give in and was beginning to enjoy her role to a certain extent. She dialled the next number with excitement, and began the same conversation about the ice cream trip and me. Then she said, 'What do you do all day at your shop?' She gestured to me to come closer with a hand and had me put my ear on the other side of the receiver so I could hear a little.

The man replied, 'I sell things in my shop, what else?'

'All day?' she asked in a childlike voice.

'Yes,' he responded, 'that's my job.'

In her most seductive voice, Laila said, 'And when do you think about me?'

The man loved this comment, appreciating her words as if she had recited a verse, and answered, '*Mar jaun aap ki adaon pe.* (I want to die for what you said). I think of you with every breath.'

Laila came back to her normal tone of voice and yelled in a threatening way, 'If you think of me so much, is that why you call me so often?' He started apologizing. She made him feel guiltier and he apologized some more. Finally, she said, 'Okay, I will get a new *jora* from you.' He readily agreed, so she added, 'And bangles for my younger sister.' He agreed again. She said, 'When...when...tomorrow! I will choose it myself. You'll take me to the market and get me a *jora*.'

I suddenly saw her pattern. She had worked me the same way. She made me feel guilty for something I didn't think was important and then got me to promise her ice cream.

Laila's mother entered the room and said, 'I didn't know you were here. How are you? Did they get you a cold drink or something?'

'I am not a guest here,' I replied, getting up and hugging her. We sat down together. I asked her about her health and then thought I'd better talk about the ice cream business myself.

'Laila wants me to take her out for ice cream. What do you think?' I asked.

Kaisera answered, 'You're like a sister to her, I have no objections.' I was a little surprised. My rapport with the family was a hundred times better than the first time we went out, but there was more to it than that. I could sense in her voice a renewed trust in Laila.

When we were about to leave, Kaisera told us to take the younger sister along. Laila, with strange confidence, said, 'No, Ami, that is not a good idea.' She did not even look at her mother's face, as she announced her decision. I didn't fully understand her new level of confidence, but knew for sure that their relationship had improved. The stage where a young prostitute reacts and fights back was tapering off.

Laila went inside the house, while her mother sat with me, 'Fouzia,' she said, 'don't just drop off Laila when you come back. Come upstairs. Laila's brother is home and I'd really like you to meet him.'

Trying to hold down my excitement, I responded, 'Of course! I'd like that. He does go out on long trips, doesn't he? He works for a textile company, right?'

She said, 'Laila has been talking about you a lot. He really wants to meet you.'

I was very curious about him. I had met his wife, Jamila. She never spoke a word, but always stayed in the inner part of the house taking care of the cooking and all the other household chores.

Laila and I left in my car. Laila was ecstatic, like the first time we went out. This time it was even better, as we were alone. She felt very free. She said, 'First, we are going to see my friend, Surayia.'

I disagreed. 'Laila, we told your mother we were going to the Mall. I don't want her to lose her trust for me.'

She said, 'Listen, this friend has nothing to do with our business, Okay! She doesn't even know that I live here. She was my friend in college. I didn't tell anyone where I came from. So she doesn't know.'

'Laila,' I said hesitantly, 'we could have told your mother that we were visiting your friend.'

'Are you crazy? They don't want me to have friends. I've only seen Surayia once since I left college. I visited her house once when she was sick, and met her mother. She is very nice. I can do these things with you. Please let me.'

'Okay', I said giving in again, 'but only for a short while.'

The friend's house was not too far from Taxalli, and was on our way to the Mall. I parked in a narrow street, which ended in a huge pool of standing rainwater where scores of water buffalo were enjoying a bath, completely ignoring the crows perched on their horns.

We went up a flight of steps and knocked on the door to the flat. Surayia's mother opened the door. About fifty years old, she was wearing a modest *shalwar kamiz*. She recognized Laila and invited us in. As we were going into the living room, Surayia came out. She looked at Laila and screamed with delight, very surprised to see her.

We stayed for about half an hour, which hardly constitutes a social visit by Pakistani standards. Two hours is a minimum for a good talk, but Laila felt pressured because of my hesitation, so she wrapped up the conversation quickly. It suited her also, since she couldn't be too close to Surayia. Keeping in touch was all she could afford.

During the conversation Laila was operating at a very superficial level, talking about her brother's business going well, her friends like me in other cities and her vacation plans to Islamabad to see me. She tried her best to say things that middle-class people talk about. She threw in some conversation on the latest Indian films also.

We wrapped up the conversation and said good-bye. In the car I asked her, 'How can you have a close friend and not tell her such important parts of your life. Not even as a secret.'

She replied, 'I can't. Then I know I'll lose her friendship. I can't even be close to her, or they'll want to come and visit me. Then what would I do? If my mother finds out that I still have this link she'll kill me.'

'You saw her once this year, it's hardly a link', I said, driving back onto the main road.

'You may see it that way, but it's important to me. I know that someone out there is my friend. Just like you. It makes me happy to think I have a friend in Islamabad. Do you remember when we first met, I asked you to look for a job for me in Islamabad.'

'Yes, I do,' I said with a laugh, 'but, whatever I suggested, you didn't like.'

'Yes, but I liked that I could ask you. I like having friends, but neither my mother nor my brother can stand it. They think they would not be able to control me well if I had contacts of my own.'

I looked at her in a teasing way and said, 'You seem to be doing better these days.'

'My brother came home and we had a long talk,' was her answer.

'So, have you dropped the idea of working in Islamabad or somewhere else outside the Mohalla? Do you see your future here now? Is that it?' I asked.

'I did think about it a lot, but you know I don't like working hard. I'd like a job where I get paid and don't have to do much. I just can't see myself doing nine to five types of jobs. I like my sleep, and you know how much I like watching movies. My mother says that I was not born for office work. My brother told me that in offices women have it even worse. Bosses do not leave any of their female staff alone. You know what I mean?' I struggled through the Mall traffic, unusually bad because of the heavy rain the last two days. I didn't answer since I wanted her to keep talking.

She continued, 'My brother works in these offices himself. He says women sleep with their bosses to get jobs, and then for pay raises and promotions. He says the women get money and the men get favours. At least here we can choose our customers. My mother says that I could never get up that early in the morning in any case. I was brought up with too much love.'

'I see you've discussed everything with your mother and brother. They've thoroughly convinced you. But let me tell you one thing, Laila. You can choose to do whatever with your life, but what your brother said doesn't apply to all women who work in offices. Sure, women can use sexual services for promotions. Some men abuse their power to sexually harass or get sexual favours, but the world has moved on and most men and women do work together as professionals. There are many competent women out there who succeed because of hard work and commitment.'

She was a little surprised at my sermon, and said, 'They weren't my plans, just ideas. When I get angry at their control I think about leaving and then I imagine different things.'

We were both quiet for a while, stuck in traffic. Then she said, 'You just asked how can someone have a friend and not talk about important parts of your life.'

I had no idea where she was heading, so I just responded, 'Yes?'

'I want to tell you something.' Her voice lost her usual spark and became heavy.

I turned my head and looked at her, waiting for her to say something.

'Actually my brother is not my brother. He is my father,' she blurted out.

'What do you mean?'

She continued, 'The woman you know as my mother is actually my grandmother. She just says she's my mother because she manages me. The nieces and nephew that run around our house are my sisters and brother, and actually my grandmother is not my real grandmother. Her elder sister is sort of my grandmother but not a real one.' She was very serious.

'Laila I'm confused. I just hope you are not joking with me. Please give me the whole picture. Who is what to whom?'

She went on, 'The main thing is that this "mother" of mine is like a grandmother, Okay! If you know that, it is enough.'

'Laila, if you have chosen to tell me this, you have to at least explain to me what the relations are.'

By this time, traffic started moving and I had to wiggle my car out of the jam. I told her to wait until we got somewhere where I could stop the car and concentrate. We came to an ice cream shop. I parked the car. It's quite convenient to be able to order food and eat it in your car, especially when you want to engage in private conversation. I honked to get the shop's attention. A young boy of about twelve came running over. We ordered our ice cream and he brought it for us within minutes.

I held my cup of ice cream in my hand tightly and turned to Laila, 'Now, tell me!'

Laila started eating her ice cream, and in a more normal tone of voice, she started telling me her story, 'You see, neither of the sisters had children.'

'Wait, you are talking about your mother, I mean Kaisera, and her sister in London, right?' I asked anxiously.

She said, 'Yes, Kaisera and Shamsa. So the family decided that the elder one would adopt two children, a boy and a girl that they managed to get from a poor family that were distant maternal relatives. The children were supposed to belong to the elder sister, but the younger sister ended up raising them, especially at first.'

'The adopted daughter, Kiran, was trained to be a good singer. The son, Shahid, was married at a young age and put to producing children with his wife, Jamila. The family needed more children to survive. He had his first child, a daughter, named Bobby. This little girl was about a year old when the two sisters, Shamsa and Kaisera, split. Shamsa took both adopted children and the first grandchild of the family to London. Jamila was left in Pakistan with Kaisera. Shahid kept coming back though, and eventually eight children were born. I'm the second one. The younger sister, Kaisera, took me for her own. That is why she calls herself my mother.'

I put my hand on her shoulder and asked, 'Did you know about it when you were a child?'

'No!' she exclaimed, 'not till I was taken out of college and pressured to start working like this. That was when I learned who my real mother was. My real mother was who I thought was my sister-in-law, and my brother was my father!'

I asked softly, 'How do you feel about all this? I mean have you accepted it?'

She said, 'They're all the same. I do feel closer to my real mother. I think she's suffered a great deal, and even I gave her many bruises, not knowing who she was to me.'

I knew that I had to get the story from Laila's real mother also. She was very quiet in that household. I had some rapport with her, but had little idea of how she saw my work and me.

Laila felt good after telling me all this. I could feel high
emotion in her voice. She asked for more ice cream, which
I immediately bought her.

'Aren't you going to have more?' she asked me. We looked
at my cup; it was full of milk, and we both laughed.

I said, 'No, one is enough.' I drank it down. Laila took her
time to finish her second cup, fully concentrating on it. She
didn't say anything except for an occasional remark about
passers-by, something that she loved to make.

Starting my car after paying the bill, I asked Laila, 'Are the
two women real sisters or not?' I was suddenly aware of the
assumptions that I was making about relationships, taking them
at face value. I knew I needed to explore more to understand the
family dynamics.

She said, 'Yes, same mother, but she married their father
after they were born. I mean their father is not really their
father. He came into the picture later. Do you understand?'

'Yes, I do,' I nodded.

Laila had ten other ideas for things she wanted to do and
several things she wanted me to buy for her. I had to be very
strict to get her back home. I couldn't afford to lose the trust
that I'd built with her management and destroy all the chances
of taking her out again.

# 17

# MEETING LAILA'S FATHER

Laila was very happy when we got home. She ran into the house before I did. I stayed in the living room as she barged into the inner part of the house. I sat alone for a short while. Then Kaisera and Laila's 'brother' came out to meet me, whom I now knew to be Laila's adoptive grandmother and her real father.

Her father, Shahid, was a good-looking man, about thirty-five years old. He was wearing a well-ironed brown *shalwar kamiz* that gave him a well-groomed look. Younger than I had expected, he had black hair, a black mustache and a slightly overweight body. I sensed that a strange air of formality had entered the living room with them. Something was odd about how Kaisera invited me for refreshments and, later, the way Laila held herself. Both were acting in a peculiar manner, the way young men and women often change their behaviour in the presence of an authoritarian father. I could tell that Shahid held the power position in the family. I was surprised since the traditional power structures of *kothas* run by *naikas* have hardly any important positions for men. Even when they become pimps, they have no managerial role, but are only agents who can be scolded by the woman manager for not doing their jobs well enough.

We started with the usual small talk, comparing Islamabad and Lahore. He told me how impressed he was with Islamabad's nice, clean roads while I expressed delight in the charms of Lahore's rich culture. After a while, the servant, Bhuba, announced the arrival of some guests, three large men in starched *shalwar kamiz*. Looking like typical Punjabi men from Lahore, they had big moustaches and big, heavy bodies. All were in their early thirties. The purpose of their visit was unclear. They were introduced to me as Shahid's colleagues, but when I asked specific question about their work, they answered vaguely, saying only that they worked with Shahid at the factory. Laila's grandmother was very attentive to them and I could tell they had come to discuss something but could not talk to Shahid in my presence.

After about fifteen minutes, I made up an excuse for Kaisera about an appointment and said I'd be back in an hour or so to meet with Shahid. She agreed and I left the four hefty men behind to discuss their business. I had no appointment, but I went to visit an older woman who had once invited me to her house.

My new acquaintance was in her sixties, a hefty, modest looking woman, but very alert. Whenever I met her, she seemed very content with her life and I wanted to know more about her. I found her at home. She lived on the second floor of a tall building, with a relatively small performing area, and a few rooms at the back. It was not a large apartment, but she was content to have her own *kotha* and not be dependent on others for performance space. She was happy to see me. I sat with her on the white sheets spread on the floor, pulling up a pillow to rest my back. Only one of her daughters, Meena, was at home. The other had gone to meet a customer in a hotel. I politely asked how she was and got more details than I had expected.

'I cannot ask for more from my life,' she said. 'I am a woman to whom God has been very gracious. I have everything I could think of. At this age also, I say again and again, I am one of the most contented women in this bazaar.'

'What would you consider 'everything'?' I asked.

'I did well as a young prostitute,' she began. 'I'm from a *Kanjar* family and not, God forbid, a *Mirasi* or a *Domni*, as are many of the other women here. I obeyed my mother. By God's grace I have two daughters, who both listen to me and are doing well.' She picked up her *paandan* and started making a *paan* by putting lime on a wet betel leaf. She continued, 'I ask you, Fouzia, that in this day and age, having obedient children is a miracle. My daughters do well. Just yesterday, they were taken by their *ustad* to a Variety Show where they were both paid two thousand rupees. Many other mothers would have complained, but not me. It's not bad. One should never say no to *rozi* that God sends us.'

She passed me the *paan* she had made. I politely refused, saying, 'You take it. I don't eat *paan*.'

She put it deep in her mouth on one side and began talking again, 'I am the same way with the customers. People here argue a lot on the rates, fight with the pimps, but not me. I take what they offer. It is a sin to say no to *rozi* that God sends us. The greed of more never ends. It is like a disease.'

'Who else lives here with you', I asked, concentrating hard to understand her with the *paan* in her mouth.

She answered, 'Me, my two daughters and my husband. I don't have a servant. My husband is good at housework. God has given me a husband who does cooking, everything. He doesn't let me put my foot down from the bed.'

'When did you marry him?'

'With God's grace, when my eldest daughter was thirteen. I took on a second daughter from someone else, very poor people who could not afford to bring her up. My husband is very nice to my daughters. It's all God's grace, nothing else.'

'Is he from this area or from outside?' I asked.

'He used to work for different people. I met him at a *mujra* and he fell in love with me. I used to be very beautiful, you know. God had given me an abundance of beauty. I had a good career. He started seeing me. When I arranged my eldest daughter's marriage, I thought I should settle down with him. He really takes good care of me. If I have a headache, he massages my head all night. He washes all my girls' clothes and does all our shopping. I made a good choice. It is just God's blessing on me.'

I was interested in men's role in the bazaar so I asked her more about that, 'Does your husband help you in making deals with your daughters' customers?'

'Sometimes,' she answered, 'sometimes I take him with me when I have to go to other towns, but usually he is too busy doing the housework to really have contacts like that.'

'So, who brings your customers?' I asked directly.

'They are sent by God. He is the provider to all his creation. There is some sharing of food so every living being can survive. That is the law of nature. Even stray dogs are fed; the cats on the street find food. All humans are provided with one or the other form of livelihood,' she answered.

I insisted, 'Yes, I understand that God gives us all livelihood and our incomes to survive, but I'm curious whether the men from the area help get customers or agents outside the Mohalla.'

She replied that the bazaar is an open market, 'Anyone can come,' she said. 'I used an agent when I was looking for a good proposal for my daughter's *nath*. I knew him from the Mohalla. I trust people from the area. I couldn't rely on outsiders. He's a good lad, a nephew of a friend of mine. He helps out when we are tight, and has arranged good customers at times. But he isn't doing us a favour. If he brings us a good customer, he gets his share. When people simply take our stairs and come up, we owe nothing to anybody. We only thank God for sending them and I never say no.' Pointing to another *paan* she was making, she insisted, 'This is a sweet one especially for modern girls like you. You can't refuse this time.' I took the *paan* from her hand and put it in my mouth. She grabbed a spittoon from one side of the room and spat in it. She came back to her tube pillow and sat comfortably.

'Most boys run away from here. It's very unfortunate. Some who stay don't really know what to do with themselves. Some become pimps or open some kind of a business, like a video shop. We don't let men from our *biradri* mingle too much with the musicians. I can't complain; the musicians also have to make a living. I'm very straight with them so I never have problems. My girls go to their Variety Shows quite a bit. The musicians don't like taking me along, but when it is our kind of a performance, a proper *mujra*, at least two or three of us go.'

'Who would that be?' I asked.

'I take a friend of mine with me sometimes. It is good to have more than one manager, to keep the customers from playing tricks on you. I take my husband along too. He's good for that. He's a six-foot tall man with a big build. He scares people.' She laughed.

I thought I would ask her about Laila's family, 'Laila's mother is looking for a good proposal for her and so is Pami's family. Why are they having difficulty? Can't they approach some pimps and get a good customer?'

'Who knows? I don't know about Laila's family. Both mother and son have been trying quite hard. The girl will be old before she is married off, but who am I to say? As far as Pami is concerned, her family doesn't belong to our biradri; they are from a lower caste. Lower caste people don't have standards to care about. She can put her daughters on the streets if she wants. Someone from our *biradri* could never even consider that. We have our traditions; we have a *biradri* to face, so we have to be careful of our actions. The people who have just entered this business know nothing about the traditions of our profession.'

While talking to her, my mind kept going back to Shahid. I wondered about his childhood. What position does he enjoy in the household? Where does he go on these long official tours? Is he really employed or not? Her comment on 'both mother and son have been trying' made me think. He is involved with this profession, in one way or the other. Otherwise, Laila would not have been so influenced by his talk. When she talks about her anger, she mentions both the father and the grandmother together. He must be a managing partner.

I bid good-bye to my hostess, promising to come back to meet her husband. I went straight to Laila's house. Shahid and Kaisera were in the living room. They welcomed me and I sat on the sofa across Shahid, 'I have been told that you work at Lok Virsa,' he said, and asked if I had a card. I got out a visiting card and handed it to him. He looked at it and said, 'Usually an institution provides their employees some kind of an identification card.'

I held back my instinctive reaction to his efforts to check up on me and remained calm, took out my Lok Virsa identity card from my purse, and put it in front of him. He picked it up, read everything carefully and gave it back to me. Then he began questioning me about when I had joined Lok Virsa, what my father does, where I live in Islamabad, and so on. I kept my patience, noticing that Kaisera, sitting right next to him, was listening very carefully, as if he was verifying everything that she told him about me and she had to pass that test.

When he was satisfied, I started asking him questions. I asked for his card. He provided a visiting card, which did not state his job title. When I asked about his specific job, he said he was into marketing. After checking up on me he relaxed and became quite friendly.

He said, 'Laila told me that you do not take tea.'

I made sure not to give him too friendly a signal, so I answered with a serious face, 'Yes, that's right.'

I asked Kaisera where Laila was. 'Taking a nap,' she answered quickly.

Shahid shifted to the edge of his chair, coming closer to me. 'They all talk very highly of you and trust you. I have a proposal for you.'

'Yes, I'm listening,' I replied. I knew something was up, and I imagined that he would ask me not to see Laila any more, or not come to their house again, or not to mention any of the data I had collected from his family as a part of any research. But these were only my own fears. I was totally unprepared for what came next.

'I move around a lot and know the real world,' he began, 'I know the kind of demands our business clients have. I deal with them all the time. Our girls cannot fulfill those demands. We need educated girls in this business. You know what I mean.'

All ears, I was trying my best to comprehend his point.

He continued, 'Our sisters and daughters are not educated. Even if they go to college they are not polished enough. High-level customers require educated, polished women and we can't provide them that. I was wondering if you would be interested in helping us out...'

My eyes popped but he continued, 'You have such a vast network of friends. You know many young women who speak fluent English, and, believe me, the demand for English-speaking girls is very high. It's a totally different clientele—politicians, businessmen. It's a different class, and big money.'

I looked at Laila's grandmother. She seemed nervous. Noticing my expression, she quickly jumped into the conversation, 'We're not asking you to do it yourself, necessarily, but your cousins, friends, or anyone you know...just part-time.'

I took a deep breath and calmed myself down. 'I'm here doing research,' I told them. 'I'm not interested in any business deals. Please don't expect this from me.'

Shahid listened and slid back in his chair, looking at his mother as if he were really surprised that I'd turned down his offer. They'd apparently discussed it thoroughly and had hoped that I'd agree. I suppose that since business was going badly for them, they couldn't understand why anyone would refuse such a good deal.

Finally, Shahid said, 'You have all the time in the world to think about it and, who knows, you may meet a friend who is looking for extra money. Let's just leave it at that.'

# 18

## LAILA'S REAL MOTHER

It took me over a week of hovering around Laila's real mother to piece the whole story together. To do this I had to enter the family's private domain, an area typically off limits to outsiders. I had to go there because her mother never came out and anyway it was time for my presence to be accepted in every part of the house.

On the other side of a worn sheet that barely served as a curtain to divide the performance area and living room from the family's personal lives was a dark, crowded, smelly and run-down part of the house. Directly behind the curtain was a narrow room with a door that opened onto a long balcony. A bed was placed against one wall and a *charpai* along the other. The walls were covered with posters of film actresses, pictures from old calendars and some photographs. A television and video recorder sat in one corner. On the balcony, which ringed the building's inner courtyard, one could get some fresh air, but inside it was quite stuffy and hot.

Kaisera had divided the five-storied building into several sections that she rented out to different people, keeping half of the first floor, which faced the road, for her own family. This gave her a big performance room with direct access to the stairs from the front street and three rooms with a small kitchen as the living space.

The kitchen was the main living space for Laila's mother, Jamila. Once I found the opportunity, she easily opened up to me. I hadn't expected this because she seemed very introverted and reserved. When I began talking to her, she quietly said, 'You listen to everyone's life stories and how they feel and what they do. I would like to talk about my pains, things I've buried so deep that sometimes I forget them myself.'

According to the story I pieced together, Jamila came from a small village near Lahore. She belonged to a very poor family of the occupational castes. Her father died and left her mother debt-ridden. Having trouble surviving, her mother felt the burden of a grown-up daughter of marital age. Since daughters are considered an economic liability, parents traditionally try to marry them off as quickly as possible.

Shamsa approached Jamila's mother at this vulnerable time, having found out about the family through connections in the area. She personally took her son's proposal to Jamila's mother. Marrying off a daughter is another burden, as the family generally must have a dowry to present to the in-laws along with their daughter. In this case Shamsa said clearly that she did not want any dowry and was sympathetic about the girl's father's death, a great relief for Jamila's mother. She considered herself and her daughter fortunate to have such a good proposal from the city with no dowry to be given. Other villagers congratulated her and said that Jamila had brought good luck. No one had a clue about Shamsa's family background. In their modest celebrations and prayers to thank God, they had no idea where Jamila would end up. The wedding took place and Shamsa took Jamila to the city.

Jamila was only about fifteen years old at the time, and had never left her village. Several days passed before she could figure out where she was. Jamila was never allowed to visit her mother, but after a few months her mother came once to see if she was happy. She had not heard from Jamila at all and could not believe it when she found that she had married her daughter to a family of prostitutes. Devastated, but having a hard time surviving herself, she felt completely helpless. She cried a lot, blamed her and her daughter's fate on bad luck, and left, never to return. Jamila had not expected much from her, but with her departure, her only light of hope died. In addition to her own pain, she felt guilty for giving her mother such lifelong pain.

Jamila had two mothers-in-law, the two sisters who together ran the business. The elder sister, Shamsa, who had adopted Shahid, was her actual mother-in-law, but the younger sister, Kaisera, acted in the same way. Jamila found it confusing.

Shamsa told her she would remain in *purdah* and never be pushed into the business. She told her that as daughter-in-law Jamila was the honour of the family and that her role was to take care of the house and bear children.

Her husband was about eighteen years old, too young to do much for her. Her mothers-in-law, and not her husband, had brought her in. She spent the whole day obeying their commands, and saw him only late at night. She was instructed never to come into the living room unless called.

She also had a sister-in-law, Kiran, Shahid's real sister, who was also adopted. Jamila never learned about her husband's real parents. The mothers-in-law were quite brutal towards her, probably, she thought, to establish in her mind that if she wanted to survive she had to be obedient. The message was so loud and clear, and she was at such an impressionable age, that she almost stopped speaking. She was seen in the house but never heard. The older women acted like royalty while her husband, Shahid, acted like one of their servants.

The family celebrated the first daughter's birth in a grand manner, lighting oil lamps and distributing sweets among the relatives. They arranged a big gathering of music and dancing that continued all night. The sisters accepted the child and celebrated her birth as if she were their daughter, totally sidelining Jamila. Not only was she excluded from the celebrations, she was ordered to prepare the food and wash the dishes, despite having just given birth.

A year later, the two sisters fought, with Shamsa deciding to leave the country. Among the stories I heard, the most likely was that she fell in love with a customer and followed him to London.

Their father had given his property, this big building, to both daughters. Shamsa divided it by constructing a wall between the two halves before she left for London. As the two children,

Shahid and Kiran, were hers; she decided to take them along. Not only that, she decided to take the granddaughter as well. She did not want to leave such a prime asset. Jamila featured nowhere and was left behind.

Kaisera Begum was devastated, as she had nobody to work for her. She was just beginning to assume a management role. She could continue working herself for a while, but not for too long, as she was getting old. She convinced Shahid to keep coming back, and by good luck Jamila became pregnant before he left. Kaisera patiently waited for nine months and Jamila gave birth to another girl. Kaisera was thrilled. This time the golden egg was hers. She named the girl Laila. Having suffered the great loss of Kiran, Shahid's first daughter, she now had hope again. Kaisera declared that Laila would be raised as her own. The future seemed somewhat secure. Without young female offspring, a prostitute is really vulnerable, and could even end up on the streets in her old age. Her future is secured only if she marries or if she has young girls to continue the business.

Jamila was once again left without a child. She had already lost her first daughter, and never saw her after she was taken to London. She could take care of Laila, but could never tell her of their relationship. She could never decide anything for her daughter, but was like Laila's maid. Shahid visited from London and made his wife pregnant every year. Kaisera was financially responsible for Jamila and her children so it was quite clear she had sole rights over Jamila's children. Jamila was just a vessel; a reproductive machine. The children belonged to Kaisera.

In the beginning Shahid maintained an ambivalent immigration status in London. Later, when he filed his case, it took a long time to decide. To move the process faster he married a British woman. The British government saw through his fake marriage, however, and rejected his case. He was sent back to Pakistan.

Kaisera was happy when he returned since she needed help managing her business. While Laila was being trained, Kaisera maintained her *kotha* by getting other dancing girls to use her space. Shahid had gained some experience as a pimp in London and thought that his overseas experience made him sophisticated enough to leave the local pimps behind. Kaisera was also pleased because she needed his reproductive potential. To secure the family's future she wanted more children from him and Jamila. Unfortunately for Jamila, Shahid was a brutal husband and not a responsible father. Jamila bore eight children, of whom six survived: four girls and two sons. Bobby and Laila did not know their real mother, but Jamila could tell the other children she was their mother. However, it was very clear that they belonged to Kaisera.

Laila was sent to school, and even for two years to college. This was most untraditional, usually a young prostitute's education lasts only up to fifth or at most eighth grade. The belief is that if a girl gets too much education she'll have more awareness than she needs to properly fulfill her role. Kaisera and Shahid took this chance as they felt that times had changed and she needed some education to survive in the competitive market.

After two years of college, Laila was told she had to start her career. At first, she seriously resisted, whether as a result of an education that gave her some awareness through exposure to mainstream morals, or from the usual teenage rebellion, I cannot say. Whatever the case, her management came down on her quite hard. This happened at a time when Shamsa came back from London for a visit. She saw the tussle between Laila and Kaisera, and was very upset at how weak her sister had been in keeping control of the girl. She wanted to show the *biradri* how well she could handle business. She took charge temporarily and announced that she would handle Laila's rebellious behaviour.

She first scolded Jamila for tampering with Laila's thoughts. Jamila swore that she had never talked to Laila except to provide for her needs. Shamsa, in a rage, threw Jamila out with all her children, including Laila, and sent them back to Jamila's mother.

The crisis was too much for Laila to handle and something within her shattered. This is when she found out who her mother was. She didn't know what she was feeling. It was as if she had betrayed her own mother. She felt as sorry for Jamila as for herself, since everyone had treated her like a servant. Being quite spoilt, she herself had been very rude to her at times. Seeing the cruel behaviour of those who Laila had thought cared for and loved her, she grew very close to her own mother.

When they reached their maternal grandmother's house, they found that she had no home, but lived with another family. She worked at their house as a maid and had only a corner on the verandah in which to sleep. She couldn't keep them, having hardly any money to survive. The family she worked for gave her food. Besides, in the traditional context not only is keeping a daughter and her children a problem, it also involves serious loss of face. South Asian in-laws typically use this tactic to pressure a daughter-in law to conform to their demands. Shahid hardly played a role here, never having had an important position in his own family anyway. He was simply an agent who was used for reproductive purposes.

Laila, Jamila and the other children spent one night in the village with some distant relatives and returned the next day. Jamila explained to Laila that they had no choice but to obey. Laila wasn't sure whether the idea of becoming a prostitute bothered her or if she was merely reacting to the control of her grandmother and father. She thought that was what really got to her. But the sex trade was also an issue. She did not like society's disapproval of prostitutes and wasn't happy that she would have to hide her background all the time. She could never tell her friends at her college where she lived or what her family did.

The family returned. Shamsa was very proud of herself and the business started up again. She told Kaisera that management was an art and that she had to do better at it. She had said, 'For *rozi* you have to work. You can't just expect to make money sitting around. Hard work brings money. And why not, one should have *halal ki rozi* (legitimate income, acceptable to God).'

Shamsa returned to London. Laila went through her ups and downs. She became more protective of her mother. Her own

behaviour towards Jamila changed and she influenced her
siblings, who were used to treating their mother like a servant,
to give her more respect.

Jamila did not think much about her future. Her life was
intertwined with the family in this very complex way. She had
no way to survive without them, knew no other option and had
never thought of leaving. She wondered, though, why God had
written such a fate for her. She had never intentionally hurt
anybody and had only served others, but all she knew was
cooking, cleaning and washing for this family, in addition to
humiliation and abuse. Her entire universe was the apartment's
three inner rooms. That had been her life and she imagined it
would probably remain the boundary of her experience to the
end of her days.

# 19

## MORE ABOUT MEN

Shahid was like an adviser to Kaisera, but she was clearly the one in charge. Shortly after he asked me to find English-speaking girls to serve as part-time prostitutes, Shahid disappeared once again. No one could or would give me a clear answer when I asked where he had gone, but Kaisera clearly became more affectionate towards me. I didn't know if it came from guilt and embarrassment or because she thought that some day her link with me would bear fruit and I would help boost her business.

From then on, I started observing the Mohalla's men more carefully. They certainly seemed like second-class citizens, especially in the *Kanjar* families. As far as the business and the traditional set up of the bazaar were concerned, *Kanjar* women clearly ruled. However, as I looked more closely it became apparent that the political figures who were busy taking control were all men. Hardly any *Kanjar* women were involved in local or provincial politics. Any platform concerning issues outside the area was taken over by a few men, like Mudha Kanjar, who had fought against their traditional upbringing as second class humans and had learned the power games of the outside world.

The *Mirasi* group was mostly men as only a few resided with their families in the area. Although they had a higher status than the women of their ethnic group, they were considered socially lower than *Kanjar* men. This social impediment really was only apparent within the Mohalla itself. *Mirasi* men were becoming very adept at dealing with the outside world, demonstrating their ability by taking control over the newly emerging 'Variety Show' business.

One day, Kaisera was in a particularly happy mood. Laila
had done well the previous night with a 'party'. She was smiling
when I arrived. She hugged me twice and asked me many times
to drink or eat something. After our initial small talk, I opened
conversation about changes in the management of their business.
I asked her about the Variety Shows.

'It's a new thing,' she explained, 'we used to get proper
invitations for a *mujra*, with a whole tradition around it. Now,
people have become so cheap.'

I asked her to tell me how it used to be.

She stared at the black and white portraits on the wall and
smiled as she said, 'A "party" would approach our parents, or
whoever the *naika* was, to make a formal request to arrange a
*mujra* usually for some occasion, like a wedding. The *naika*
then negotiated the rate. Even the negotiations were done
politely. The managers insisted on their terms, but it was done
in a respectable manner not like the business talk these rotten
upstarts use these days.'

'Are you referring to the *Mirasis* or pimps?' I asked.

'These *Mirasi* have become agents for organizing the "Variety
Shows". They tell us they can pay this much, take it or leave it.
They say, "We have many other girls begging for a chance to
perform." Then they make an offer as if they are doing a favour
to our forefathers.' She mimicked them, "What do you say,
what do you say?" These bastards have been living on our dry
bread, they are like dogs who got food at our doors and now
they hire our girls as if we were beggars.' She mimicked
them in a male voice again, '"*Ki kende o!* What do you say, we
have many girls who are willing to go, so what do you
say?"...Bastards!'

I could tell she was very angry with them, and very angry
that the *Kanjar* are losing control of the business.

'Do you know what Laila's *ustad* paid her for this Pattoki
programme?' she asked. 'He paid her two thousand rupees, and
that is all. And these bastards do not negotiate. That is what
makes me very angry. We have to accept whatever they say.'

She hit her chest with her hand repeatedly and with her head stretched high with pride, she said, '*Asi khandani Kanjar aan, khandani* (We are true *Kanjar* from our lineage) not those who have jumped into the business for the money. Our generations have done this work and carried the tradition.'

Acknowledging her pride, I asked politely, 'When a *mujra* was arranged before how was the negotiation carried out?'

'Through a go-between. Either a pimp or the management would designate a person informally to talk to the party. This avoided the embarrassment of either offer being rejected directly. For example, if a *mujra* invitation was sent to me for my daughters, my sister would go ahead and talk to them, saying, "Let me talk to my sister, she does not accept *mujras* when we have to go so far away from Lahore." Then she would come and talk to me. She also played an essential role in negotiating the *nazrana*, the fee. To raise a party's offer she'd say, "My sister doesn't agree, but if you raise it to so much I may be able to convince her to accept your invitation." She'd be the one to tell them stories about our daughters' *mujras* at the big nawab's houses and how popular they were and how well they sang, you know, promote them a little in front of the "party". So, in a way, she played the game from their side, by pretending that she was trying her best to get a good deal for them, but actually she was one of us. This kept the negotiations polite and decent, and no one lost face. These guys today don't know how to make a deal. They are only good for playing instruments and that is all. They negotiate as if they were hitting the other person on the head with a hammer.'

I couldn't help laughing. I had never seen her so involved in telling me something, using actions and mimicry.

She continued, 'I have never told anybody about our business so openly. We don't talk about our trade secrets.'

'I understand', I said with a smile and asked, 'Do men get into this role of intermediate agents?'

'Of course. Anybody from the management could. Sometimes if a party had come through a contact, man or a woman, that person became the go-between and thus, earned his or her fee.'

I asked, 'So, how come these invitations are offered to the musicians now?'

'People are not doing regular *mujra* any more,' she replied. 'They want a Variety Show, like they see on television. They want music, comedy, and dancing, and a shoddy stage show. The days of enjoying a regular *mujra* are gone. You need a certain environment for dancing, and you create it, building it with one song after another. You communicate with your audience. You take them high and then low. A *mujra* is very complex. In these three-minute items, how can we get anything out of the customer? In the past, we'd set the right environment for enjoying music and the company of beautiful dancers over a period of hours. The *mujra* has its own requirements. By the time it was over many hearts had been wounded by our dancers. How can this happen in such fast moving shows, where each artist is trying to out-do the other? This whole scene is ridiculous.'

'Where do pimps fit in?' I asked innocently.

She seemed surprised at my question and asked, 'What do you mean?'

'I mean don't they get the invitations for *mujras* or these Variety Shows. Who are they and what do they do?'

'That is another story, *beti*, but in complaining against the musicians I still must say they are very smart. They try to build their own contacts with customers who can help get them into the entertainment business. That's how they're getting more and more control. They bring these deals to us but make the main deal with the customer. So, they're the ones who make the real money. We're only like labour, hired by them and taking what wages they determine.'

'Why do you accept these offers if they take control away from you?'

'This damn business is getting so bad that we are struggling to survive. We have to take their offers in hopes of getting some customers for ourselves from the audience. We have no choice. They're right! If I turn down their offer, someone else will snap it up. The musicians are playing on our downfall. They know

A man putting in wicks in an oil stove

Taking care of young children is usually assigned to the man of the house

Cooking and other domestic chores are done by the men or daughters-in-law

There are few job options for men in the Mohalla. Vending cloth, flowers or cigarettes are one of them

As opposed to sons, daughters are highly prized assets in the Mohalla

Unlike the *Kanjar* (prostitutes) community which hardly has a role for their men, the *Mirasi* (musician) community values their men highly

we've fallen on bad times and if they're smart enough they'll take a lead in the business.'

'But I am sure the business of *mujra* still goes on. Or has it all transferred into the demand for Variety Shows?'

'No, no! We still get invitations for *mujra*, but most of our work revolves around getting invitations for other services from individual customers, mostly from the business sector. We do the best we can with the kind of customers that are left around. The best customers have all been taken by those girls who moved into the Gulberg area.'

'Do you use pimps or agents for your business?' I asked, waiting to see if she would be honest enough to tell me the truth.

Turning around and getting up from her chair, she declared, 'No! I just trust in God. I get what He sends me. That's why I have not moved anywhere. I have this property. Where should I go? How can I leave it here? The way things are, if I rent it and live elsewhere, people would take it away. You do not know how people are these days. There is no honesty left. I can't go anywhere. I have to trust in God to keep my family and me alive and send my *rozi* here.'

I wasn't sure why she was getting up. She didn't seem to want to talk about the role of pimps in her work. She went into the house and came back after a few minutes with a few photographs in her hand. She put them in front of me. They were black and white photos of her and her sister. She went back to her seat.

She said, 'Look at these, how well-mannered we used to be. We knew our business and the proper way of doing it. This vulgarity disgusts me. Look at all the girls who've made it in films. They should have been the best from this Mohalla, but they're so vulgar.'

She touched her ears with her hands and said, 'I never thought that I would have to face such challenges to survive. It's hard to do what these women do with the directors and producers to get parts in the films, but if you don't, you might as well shake hands with death.'

'Do you want Laila to go into films?'

'I just want to have a decent living, sitting here in our house, that's all.'

Noticing that she was not very forthcoming on information about the pimps, I asked again, 'How do other people contact pimps to get better customers?'

She said, 'I never leave the house. I don't know what other people do. I wasn't brought up like that. I was told just to concentrate on my own family and not to go around visiting people. Tell me, you have been coming here now for many months. Have you ever seen me go out? Have you ever found me out visiting someone? *Beta*, I never go out, so I do not know other people's business.'

I wanted to ask her about Shahid's role, but thought this was enough for today. I didn't want her to close down. I saw she wasn't very willing to talk about how she had tried to boost her business. She was truthful about not wanting to leave this area and was one of those who had made the choice to remain. Many families like hers had long ago stopped hoping for any improvement in the situation in the Mohalla. They grew tired of the police and their harassment and had moved to Gulberg, a posh residential and commercial area of Lahore. Over the years, families moved there for many reasons.

Usually a family that gets an opportunity in the film industry wants to break their visible link to the Mohalla. They want to portray the new movie star as a product of mainstream society. They're not pressured to make this pretence for their peers or the people in the industry, but only for the fans and the larger public. Others move because they find it cumbersome to maintain the traditional style of prostitution with music and dancing and opt for the cut-throat business of being call girls. I was following some families who made the switch from Shahi Mohalla to Gulberg. Their network of agents and the pimp support they had was far more complete than in Kaisera's business. There the pimp's role was vital since it's much more difficult for women, either the girls or their management, to be seen openly soliciting business.

In these Gulberg families, the pimps really take charge of the whole venture. The more educated call girls maintain a stronger partnership with the pimp; however, those who become dependent on them are at their mercy. The power balance between the *naika* and the pimp is a sore point, which often keeps shifting. While it can turn into a crucial power struggle, on the surface it usually looks like a good partnership. In some cases it really depends on the personalities of both partners.

The pimps supply customers on a regular basis to one or more households. Their interaction with the *Kanjar* families in Gulberg is almost like that of a family member, but one whose intentions are not quite trusted. In the crass brothels being set up in many parts of Lahore that are not linked to Shahi Mohalla households or its traditions, the dynamics are quite different. There, the pimps take over as managers.

The customers for these call girls are men from all walks of life, from politicians to small shopkeepers. Sometimes they go to commonly known spots in the suburbs where they can find an agent or they try to contact women they suspect are standing on the streets for that purpose. Some bus stops or markets are known to have prospective prostitutes waiting for customers, although it's not as open as in western countries.

In the Mohalla, the male customers usually come in groups. If a customer decides on a woman, he generally makes an appointment to come back alone during the day. However, a separate room is usually available if the man wants to leave his friends for a while. Men don't bring women along with them even if they come to the Mohalla just to listen to music. It's strictly a male activity. If a woman does come along, it is usually a foreign tourist who wants to explore the area with her friends or someone crazy enough to try doing research here. Kaisera was right that most customers in the Mohalla just walk in to the establishments on their own, but many, I found out later, do depend on agents who roam the streets. In crowded public places pimps hang around and ask potential customers, in coded language, if they need their service.

Kaisera asked her servant Bhuba to bring her *paandan*. Bhuba had a peculiar swing to his walk, wobbling to one side as he dragged himself from one place to another. His head bent forward, swinging like that of an elephant. She prepared a *paan* for herself and offered me one. I asked about Bhuba, 'Who is he and why is he like this?'

'Like what?' She raised her head and looked at me.

'You know! He doesn't look normal,' I said turning my head towards the door, making sure he had left the room.

'He's a distant relative. *Gin da saya e ude te* (He has 'the shadow of a ghost' on him). He's been like this since his childhood. Little kids used to beat him and he never did anything, but just laughed. He is *jhalla*. He was the son of a *Kanjari* who was a distant relative of my mother. His mother married a *Mirasi*. You know what a shameful deed that is. It ruins the family honour ... drags it in mud. Her family was very hurt and angry with her. They tried to get her out of the situation and finally brought her home by force, but, by then, she was about to give birth to this *Mirasi's* child. Bhuba was born, but his mother didn't survive. God knows whether she died or the family got rid of her! They raised him for a few years, but had no use for him since he reminded them of the shame his mother's relationship had brought to them. They said that it was her bad deed that left her son like that. My father had a good heart. Once he visited them and brought Bhuba back with him to live with us. He was four years old at that time. My mother was upset since she didn't want more mouths to feed, but my father said that Bhuba would work for his daughters. My father was very fond of us, and Bhuba has been working for us since then. He does not have any brains, but he knows the housework. He can deliver simple messages, cut vegetables to help Jamila and go to the market. This he knows because it's all he has done since he was four years old.'

So, there was another role for men in this area. Bhuba had many counterparts in this community. Some, like him, lacked the sense to understand their own humiliation. Those who did left as soon as they became capable of surviving on their own.

# 20

# KOTHA AND KOTHI KHANAS

In my search for more data on transitions in the Mohalla, I made plans with Mehmud Kanjar to visit a few *kothas* together with him. He agreed and said he would bring another friend of his along with us. His friend was also a pimp. As we walked down the street from his place to the *kotha* we were going to visit, both men, dressed in white, heavily starched *shalwar kamiz*, walked with their chests puffed out and their arms pulled back. Their walk had a swing that displayed a sense of pride, as though they were on an inspection tour of their land. With these two six foot men at my side, I felt a little overwhelmed. I also straightened my back to make my diminutive five foot two look at least an inch taller.

Mehmud told me that his friend would take us to a ground floor *kotha* on the Main Bazaar road which had some young dancers. A few wide steps led to a small landing and a set of large doors, about 5 ft wide. As we were about to enter the door, a small boy blocked our way. He had beautiful flower garlands hanging on a thin stick and tugged the corner of Mehmud's *kurta*, 'You buy them from me today?'

Mehmud smiled, 'Send them inside', going ahead as his friend and I followed. I noticed a small boy, about twelve, sitting close to the stairs with a glass case full of small rupee bills to change the customers' bigger notes into small bills. The customers give dancers small bills, controlling the pace of payment to the dancers to make them work for it. Giving it all at once would take away the fun. The dancers enjoy getting money from a customer by making gestures of affection to speed the flow of money. They can show their skills in slyly extorting money out, rather than just receiving it as payment.

A third man welcomed us all. He sported a big curled moustache, but he was not quite as big as my companions. He offered us a seat on a sofa. The room had a carpet covered with white sheets. He excused himself and said he would get a singer for us. A few minutes later another small boy, about eight years old served us soft drinks sent by a shopkeeper on the street. I saw the little boy with the flowers, peeping in. He seemed a little concerned about whether or not he should come in. Mehmud saw me looking at him, and with a smile he called the boy in and bought ten garlands from him. He passed two to me and put the rest on one of his wrists. The boy was happy to get his money and smiled at me. He then sat in a corner, waiting for the show to begin.

The host returned with a petite, fair complexioned young girl no older than thirteen. Wearing too much make-up, she looked like a schoolgirl pretending to be an adult. Her big eyes added to the very innocent look on her face. She was wearing a light pink *shalwar kamiz* with her *dupatta* spread over her shoulders. She came and sat on the floor on the white *chandni*. Three musicians followed her with harmonium, *tabla* and a *nal*. The girl greeted us, but did not look anyone in the eye. It was clear to me that she hadn't been brought up in the area and wasn't used to this set up. I could hear her voice get lost somewhere in the middle of her greeting, and waited for her to look at me so I could smile at her and try to put her at ease.

When the host told her to start singing, she looked at him timidly and asked what he would like to hear. With a grim look on his face, he said loudly, 'Why are you asking me? Ask your guests.'

She turned her head towards us and asked the same question in the same tone without looking at us. Mehmud answered, '*Ghazal*, a good *ghazal*.' He looked at the host and said, 'our guest has come from Islamabad. She has good taste in music.' The host laughed.

The girl began singing, without looking up. Her hands were trembling. From time to time, she put a plastic smile on her face as if she was afraid to show her fear. Mehmud threw some money at her. I hadn't the courage to put money in front of her. When she finished, I got up and sat next to her. She looked at me with curiosity. Perhaps used to big men drooling over her, I was probably the first woman who had come to hear her sing. I spoke to her affectionately, 'You sing very well.'

She thanked me in a voice so low I could hardly hear it. 'Do you practice a lot?' I asked.

She shook her head no, but our host said, 'Of course she does. I make sure she practices every day. Hard work makes an artist good. We have an *ustad* for her and I make her practice regularly.'

I noted he was getting uptight with me because I was talking to the girl. I asked if I could talk to her another time, and he immediately turned to Mehmud for a clue. Mehmud sat with a blank face, leaving him to decide. The host said, 'She gets up late and she spends a lot of time practicing. She hardly has time, but you can try coming some time if you want.' His answer was quite clear, he wasn't comfortable with me talking to her. The girl kept looking down. Mehmud asked me if I wanted to hear more. I answered, 'Let's move.'

I had been hearing about *Kothi Khanas* from the old *naikas* as they grumbled about how the pimps had gathered prostitutes from outside the Mohalla and were running their own businesses. A traditional set up in the Shahi Mohalla has the sex trade run according to the old traditions by an older woman, the *naika*, who has close family ties. Even in cases where girls have been adopted, they are raised in a family environment, given basic education and taught the arts of singing and dancing, and they observe the prostitution business from childhood.

Unlike the traditional *kothas* run by women, in places like those I visited with Mehmud, the pimps have set up a different sort of business. They get girls from many places and manage the *kotha* themselves, with rarely any close family linkages. The girls are usually not brought up by their managers from birth, but rather are brought into the business in their teens when they can begin to work immediately. People in the traditional prostitution world, especially the old hands, refer to this new kind of *kotha* as *kothi khanas*. Sometimes a pimp might keep an older woman with him to create the picture of a typical *kotha*. This woman would not have much power, however, and would just be paid a share of the earnings as determined by the pimp.

Those who have maintained the traditional practices hate such business. They say it's the trend of prostitution outside the Mohalla where music and dancing have nothing to do with the business, sexual gratification being the only aim. In the Mohalla, they claim to provide all round entertainment. The government, perhaps inadvertently, encourages this trend towards *kothi khanas* by suppressing traditional prostitution. The claim of the traditional managers is that as the traditional business has declined, the pimps, especially the most brutal who respect no tradition, have flourished. They make lots of money with very little overhead, giving no importance to the women themselves. They get the most out of a girl and care nothing about her future. They get what they can and throw away what they cannot use. The system is designed to make quick profits so the pimps can easily survive if they are discovered and closed down by the police. They merely gather new girls, move to a new place and start over.

In contrast, managers in the traditional system claim to take care of their women as best they can. Even when young daughters are pressured to start work in their early teens, it is viewed as a part of their training for their future. As a girl's career as a dancer and prostitute comes to an end, the traditional system trains her again to become a manager and gives her all the skills, contacts and the human resources she will require to support herself and her family for the rest of her life. It is like a social security system. They claim that they pamper their girls and never force a specific customer on them.

Those who want to uphold the traditional system also claim they do not turn every girl into a prostitute. In the same household some do not wish to pursue this career while others are married off. Some stay in the household, only bearing children. There are old people and grandchildren. A girl can enjoy all relations and family ties. In addition, the larger families and the *biradri* members are also there to help maintain the traditional standards.

One day while discussing the traditional system with Kaisera, I asked her about all the problems that young prostitutes have with their mothers and other managers. I told her that not all the young prostitutes I had met were happy; some felt trapped and forced into the business. I wanted her to talk about the loopholes of the traditional system. She answered, 'Why don't you first defend your family system? Should I tell you all the humiliation and abuse your women suffer? Should I tell you how suffocated a woman feels when her parents declare that she may not marry whom she chooses? Should I tell you the abuse that happens within families, where fathers with big beards rape their own daughters? You think I do not know about the incest your society experiences. What about all the runaways, divorcees, and suicides because of the fights and tensions within the family? Should I say that your family system should be abolished because it is evidently not working.' She paused and continued, 'All systems have their problems, because so many people are involved. Parents think that they are doing it for the good of the children, whereas children see it all as manipulation and control.'

'I cannot argue with you on that,' I admitted, 'because I agree there are many problems with our social control through families. However, one does work towards improving the system, fighting against the abuse and the incest, improving communication between parents and children and weeding out harmful traditions like *karo kari* (murdering women over a point of honour).'

She answered, 'So, we can also work towards improving this system. Why finish it? Why shift to the pimp and become totally money oriented, with neither any family relationship nor respect for any tradition? In our system women control the household. Now that the government has started harassing us and trying to force us out, the pimps are taking over. Do you think they care about the girls when their career is finished?'

'Why is that? Can you please explain it to me? Why this trend towards brothels?' I asked.

She answered, 'We *Kanjar* people operate as a community, and all depend on one another, but as we are forced out of the Mohalla and spread all over the city, we cannot operate as a support network in the same way. The pimps take over because their domain is outside the Mohalla. When we move out of here, we have to let go of the music and dancing. The business goes into hiding, and the focus is only on sex. So, without music how do we attract our customers: only through pimps. You hear about girls on the streets and in the markets. What kind of a vulgar option is this society choosing by giving up a more honest option where we are what we are? Listen, Fouzia, when the profession was restricted to us *Kanjar*, it was only in our *biradri*. Now every *dala* has jumped into it and is making hundred times more money than we *Kanjar* ever did.'

'Do you think you will leave the Mohalla at some point?' I asked.

'I hope I die before I see that day. It is not only my property that I care for. We'll have to change our whole philosophy, our manner of working. No, I may starve, but I will not leave the Mohalla, *e pehere Yazeed kine julm keran* (regardless of the hardships that these bad *Yazid* give us).'

The phenomenon of brothels is spreading like wildfire. Pimps who had been working with the management of *kothas* are anxious to set up their own businesses rather than work through the tedious systems of the traditional *kothas*. They focus on two aspects, recruiting women and finding customers. For both, a wide network is required.

How these girls enter the business is not very clear. Some of the stories about them echo the myths associated with the prostitution business. Pimps or their agents often spot runaways. They know the look of a vulnerable girl and frequently succeed in getting them to come back to their brothel with them. *Rickshaw* drivers, paid by the pimps, forcibly take young female passengers to the brothels. Men sometimes marry village women with the intention of selling them to pimps. These stories are repeatedly reflected in our dramatic films. While they do closely resemble the recruitment methods of a *kothi khana*, they don't reflect the process typically involved in maintaining a traditional Shahi Mohalla set up.

There appear to be four basic methods for recruiting women into the brothel-based prostitution business. One common way is to marry women from Swat and other tribal areas along the border with Afghanistan. This area, in North West Frontier Province, still has the tradition of bride wealth. People commonly call it bride price, but that term misconceives the system. People think that in the Frontier Province tribal people sell their daughters, which is not true. Actually, the tradition is of bride wealth. The husband bears the expenses of the wedding and, in a modest way, compensates the parents for the loss of a valuable family member. Later, after the wedding, he is responsible for the women's economic requirements. This tradition has its roots in the Middle East. The tribal cultures in the western parts of Pakistan in Frontier and Balochistan are closer to the Middle Eastern traditions. In Punjab and Sindh, culturally closer to other South Asian cultures, the tradition of dowry exists. This tradition puts most of the economic burden of getting a daughter married on the family of the woman. Not only do the parents of a woman bear most of the wedding expenses, but they must also prepare a dowry including all the items of household use, clothes for the bride and the groom, jewellery for the bride and the in-laws and sometimes even cash to support the groom's initial business.

Because of the dominating position of Punjabi culture in the country, compounded with the influence of the more educated Urdu speakers who came from India at the time of Partition, an impression has developed that the tradition of the more 'civilized people' is to give dowry with their daughters. The tradition of bride wealth is seen as somehow primitive. Educated families in the Frontier Province categorically say they do not accept money for their daughters; they give them a dowry. This shows only

their embarrassment in following their own traditions because
of the common misconception about them. So they follow an
even worse tradition of giving dowry, just to conform to the
more accepted social trend.

Men from Punjab think that bride wealth is like selling goods.
They go to areas like Swat and pretend they are looking for
wives. They impress poor families, pay the bride price, and
bring the Pushto or Kohistani speaking women to the cities,
making their parents happy as they think their daughters will be
living in cities with more facilities and less poverty. These
women are then sold to the brothels or are used by the
'husbands' in their own business. The women from these distant
villages totally lose their orientation in the city and remain quite
helpless, often speaking no Urdu or Punjabi.

Reports of similar activity come from rural Sindh and rural
Punjab. The concept of bride wealth doesn't exist, but the drama
of marriage can still be effective. In Swat it works better for the
pimps because, in that tradition, once daughters are married
their families expect little communication from them. Women
brought into the business in this manner are kept in secret places,
and their links with their families completely severed.

The second method of acquiring women for the brothels is
through recruiting agents. Mostly men, these agents focus on
women's hostels, government shelters for unmarried working
and, sometimes, destitute women, shanty towns where they can
find young girls wanting to run away, and around schools. They
hover around these places and try to approach women directly
or covertly, through the management of these institutions. At
times, pimps have a direct link with a customer or group of
customers for whom the women are recruited. Political
customers are sometimes served in this manner, where the pimps
conveniently share the risk with the customer, not taking upon
themselves the entire burden of bribing the police and other
stakeholders. In this case, a pimp could be regularly providing
women from a shelter, while the politician in power provides
the full protection of the state. This method could go to the
extreme where a powerful politician could literally point to an

air hostess or a college girl and tell his pimp to get her. In such cases, the pimp uses the direct support of the state machinery. This system flourished in the 1970s and later re-surfaced with certain politicians and close relatives of politicians who used the government machinery to obtain their every desire.

A third method for recruitment, an old strategy that has been documented in several earlier books, is 'befriending' a woman. An agent befriends a woman and gradually makes her revolt against her family. That ensures that she herself helps cut her family ties and makes it easier for him in case he gets caught. By seducing her to fall in love or to become sexually involved with him, he makes her very vulnerable. Our society places a high value on bridal virginity so that once a woman loses her virginity in a pre-marital relationship, she feels she must follow that man, having no other place to turn. This typifies young women from conservative backgrounds. The agents play on such guilt and make her 'run away'. Once under his control, and into the business, he binds her to him psychologically. She believes that because of what she has already done, she can never again show her face to her family and thus she accepts her fate. Drugs are also used to make women more dependent on their captors.

Another pattern of recruitment capitalizes on disasters. Brothel agents are always standing by for any natural or human disaster, where there is a loss of control. At the beginning of my research an incident occurred in Ojri Camp, a military post, when an ammunition depot caught fire. Hundreds of artillery rounds ignited and shot into the air, affecting many areas in both Rawalpindi and Islamabad. I was in the Lok Virsa office at that time. We thought a war had started; shells rained down around us for over an hour. It was a time of intense crisis for the two cities. Parents quickly left their homes and offices to bring their children from school. Normally, school gates are closed and students, especially girls, can only leave when their parents have arrived to fetch them. During this incident, however, school guards panicked and many simply opened the gates. At the colleges, the panic also created a stampede. Young college students ran out into the streets. Girls got into any car that stopped to give them refuge, asking the driver to take them home. This kind of opportunity is God-given for such agents. Many young women and girls were reported missing in the two cities after that incident.

Similar reports followed major violent incidents in Karachi. Police often use tear gas to end protest processions, and the protesters scatter in panic. This is a good time for such agents to offer assistance to panic-stricken young women. One woman I met was raped in a medical emergency van, the clamour in the streets drowning her screams. Transport accidents, especially involving trains and buses, offer similar opportunities. When women become vulnerable they can easily be tricked or trapped.

A network of senior pimps has developed over time. They do not bother going around befriending women, but concentrate on bigger business. Being big shots of the trade, these pimps rotate sex workers around the country in small groups. This system provides the brothels with security. By changing the place city of their workers every so often they can be assured that the women are not able to seek help from their families or anyone else, through their customers or in any other way. They also ensure that the women remain vulnerable since they are dealing with new people and new places all the time. At the same time the brothels can offer a variety of new bodies to the customers. This circulation of sex workers is a highly organized, regular system of exchange among peers.

I found out that low paid pimps, mostly men hang out around bus stations, train stations and other big markets expressly to recruit new customers. They assess the men they see, decide which are likely to agree, and then indirectly ask if they want any services. Getting customers like this is more common among low class brothels. Another method is to establish a brothel somewhere and leak information about the new operation in the relevant circles. Customers come on their own, but then the pimps work to entangle them in some way so they keep returning to the same place. For example, hearing of brothels in the market area in Islamabad known as Karachi Company, a customer looking for sex may go there, be identified by a pimp and shown the way to a brothel.

More established brothels have photo albums of the women available. For example, one pimp sells *chaat*, a popular snack, in Liberty Market, Lahore. For a long time, he kept photographs of prostitutes and took requests for the call girls selected by his customers. Popular markets have many such spots, which certainly requires connivance with the lower ranks of the police. Different rates of bribes to different levels of the police are arranged according to the magnitude of the business. The more organized pimps, especially those associated with politicians or who aspire to political careers themselves keep strong, and expensive, links with the higher levels of the police.

Women selling themselves directly in the streets are also becoming increasingly common. Although they seem to be working alone, they are part of a complex organizational structure. They are only the 'tip of the iceberg', but because they are seen by the public, these women are being blamed for the spread of prostitution into the 'nicer' areas of the city while the men who organize the system remain hidden and powerful.

Information on the structure of these pimps and call girl networks are a well-guarded secret. I did not pursue this aspect in great detail. My interest was just to learn enough to make some comparison with the traditional system and also to understand the transition process that some of the well established Shahi Mohalla families were undertaking in their move from the Mohalla out to Gulberg and other areas like Township and Green town.

What became clear is that even in Shahi Mohalla's traditional *kothas*, the *naikas* are becoming increasingly dependent upon the pimps to provide enough customers for mere survival. The power dynamics of the traditional set up are changing fast. Customers coming on their own to the Mohalla are decreasing in number and, consequently, the *naikas'* need for pimps to find customers is unending. As police harassment of the residents and the customers increases, the pimps become ever more powerful and the trend of brothels replacing *kothas* continues unabated. The brothels are spreading to different parts of the cities as opposed to remaining in one specific red light area. Thus, the harsh government policies today are changing the nature of prostitution, but they have no ability to end it.

## VIEWS

### Bhai Sharif, a small businessman

*I met a man who seemed to represent the 'good citizens' of the middle-class—somewhat religious, but at the same time pragmatic; not too worried about the political system and its implications and concerned more that 'zindagi ka karobar chalta rahe' (the business of life should go on). He manages a medium-sized business and occasionally leads the prayers in his neighbourhood mosque. Father of three daughters, he fully believes in educating them, but is not in favour of letting them leave the house for any other reason. He feels that society is hostile and holds his daughters responsible for maintaining the family honour. He told me about it, 'Do you know these days even in our own neighbourhood young men have nothing to do. They stand on the roadsides and make catcalls. In the buses they touch women. Under these conditions I tell my daughters it is their own responsibility to dodge these bastards.'*

*I asked him what he thought of prostitution. More tolerant than many, he answered, 'Every human being has some good inside. The pimps and other evildoers in the society are the ones who, for their own interest, convince women to sell their bodies.' He felt the problem could only be resolved when mainstream people started to marry women from the sex trade. I asked whether he thought the women would want that.*

'It's the only solution for a woman to have a life of respect. She must be taken in by a man of a respectable family and seek forgiveness for all her sins, promising to lead a respectable life. The doors of forgiveness are always open for everyone.' He explained, 'There is poverty, there is kidnapping, there is manipulation. I'm sure that given the option, any prostitute would prefer marriage. The real problem is that no one wants to marry her.'

'Are you saying that if there were no prostitutes there will be no prostitution?' I asked.

'Of course! If there is no satan, there is no sin. You probably don't know that these women entice customers. I've heard they stand on their balconies and charm men to go upstairs to their rooms.'

'Really?' I said, 'they must be very difficult to resist!'

'God forbid, these women are taught to do so by their pimps. I don't think we should punish them. We should deal with this problem with love and affection. We have to win them over and end this open seduction and enticement of men.'

At this point, his father, who had been lying on a charpai close by and listening to us, jumped up and entered the conversation with energy and enthusiasm. He spoke first in Arabic, and then continued, 'The increase in prostitution is an indicator of our society's bad deeds. When a nation's leaders turn corrupt and dishonest, Allah gives us signs of our impending downfall.'

Totally surprised by his wave of energy, I asked, 'Who do you think goes to these prostitutes?'

'Those who pretend to be Muslims, but who are kafirs in their hearts,' he declared.

# 21

## LAILA'S MARRIAGE

The jokes regarding Laila's delayed marriage were bothering her whole family. They were not getting a customer for Laila that met their imagined status, and Laila was tired of responding to the musician's snide remarks about getting old. Her family escalated their pressure on her to lose weight and to spend more time practicing her singing and dancing.

After a year's search her 'management,' Kaisera and Shahid, decided on a customer willing to make a long-term contract. The event was long overdue and the customer was not paying an amount worth bragging about, so the family did not celebrate the occasion, keeping the affair very simple. Laila, now quite comfortable with her role, was happy with the arrangement. The announcement was made by having a *nai* take sweets to other members of the *biradri* and her teachers.

The *nai* has an important role to play; he also cooks food for celebrations, functioning as a professional chef for gatherings like weddings or parties to celebrate the birth of a daughter. He knows all the relationships within a certain *biradri* and is called upon to send invitations and other important messages to *biradri* members. By ethnicity, he is a *Mirasi*. Fulfilling a specific role assigned to him by an old tradition, he receives gifts and money for his service according to the family's status. Not specific to the Shahi Mohalla, this tradition is a part of Punjabi culture.

Kaisera and Shahid accepted a lower price for Laila's *nath* because the customer was willing to pay a monthly stipend for a long-term relationship. There was something strange about the set-up. I knew there was some trap for the customer as the deal was not as clear as it usually is. My first meeting with Laila's 'husband' was odd. I went to her house and she greeted me with affection and excitement. She made me wait in the living room and went in to call him. She came back after about ten minutes and said he was too shy to come out. She decided we should both go in and meet him in the bedroom.

We went through the curtain into the private section of the house. I found him lying on a *charpai* in the long narrow room right next to the living room. He had fully covered himself with a blanket. Laila hit him a few times on his back and said I was there and he should at least say hello to me. After many blows, he finally took his face out of the blanket, said *salaam* without looking in to my eyes, and got up and ran out of the room onto the balcony. My jaw dropped. I was shocked at his peculiar behaviour and surprised at the person I saw.

He was a petite young man, about 4 ft 10 in. tall and not more than nineteen or twenty years old. His behaviour was like a child's. He was terribly shy. He had sharp features, a small face and an impression of a moustache. Laila and her mother, who was standing there, had a good laugh. Coming back to the living room, I kept asking Laila questions about him and her relationship, but couldn't get a clear answer. She told me he would stay with her. I knew that a boy his age couldn't be financially independent to take such decisions. Either he was a run away or his family lived elsewhere.

I found out that Laila's husband's name was Saleem. Son of a goldsmith, his father had a shop in Sua Bazaar, the main jewellery market in Lahore. He worked there, but had nothing in his own name. His family lived in another city where his father had a bigger goldsmith shop. An employee ran the Lahore shop and Saleem was sent to Lahore to look after the business. He had access to the income of the shop, and his family had no idea of his activities.

He had come to the bazaar with some friends one night wanting a sexual experience and was talked into this deal. Many people talked to him about it and convinced him it was better to make a long-term arrangement than pay for only a one-time event. Subcontracted agents of Shahid usually assess a customer

well before trying a specific strategy on them. Someone like
Saleem was pure sport for them. He hardly had the confidence
to take any decision on his own, and the 'honour' argument is a
very powerful one. The pimp argues that if a man agrees to a
monthly stipend, he can be sure that no one else sleeps with the
woman he loves. This works well with inexperienced customers
or those with big egos. Saleem was convinced that Laila was a
virgin. He would be her first customer and would have exclusive
rights to her for as long as he fulfilled his side of the contract,
an initial payment of Rs. 20,000 and a promise of Rs. 10,000
every month. The amount was too small to make a public
announcement in the *biradri* so the family did not talk about it
at all.

Kaisera advised Laila to get pregnant right away, the best
way to bind a customer who had opted for exclusive rights.
Besides, if she could not work with other customers, her time
should be utilized for reproducing and her 'husband' would also
meet all the costs of child delivery. Finally, a child is always a
good excuse to raise the monthly stipend.

The way Saleem hung around their house was peculiar,
reminding me of a mongoose that had found a new hiding place.
He would come in and go straight to the inner part of the house.
Without saying much, he would either get into his *charpai* or
go straight into the kitchen. I always saw him hiding in one
corner or the other, like some of the junk found in abundance in
the inner reaches of the house. I could never talk to him; he
couldn't manage any conversation. Laila always teased him and
he blushed with embarrassment. Saleem spent much of his day
and all of his nights here. The only time he wasn't with Laila
was when he left Lahore to visit his family, at least once a
month. His status in the house was slightly above Bhuba's. He
did small household chores or sat watching Indian movies on
television.

The musicians had found a new topic for gossip and jokes.
'Some people trap rich roosters, but Laila's family only trapped
a meek chicken,' was how they put it. *Chira* (male sparrow)
became his nickname among Laila's musician friends. Laila felt

people were jealous of her. The musicians told me that the drama about exclusive rights was only a way to get his money, and that she continued to work. If he found out about it, her management would demand more money to continue the contract.

Laila said she wanted to visit me in Islamabad with her husband. Not sure how my mother would react, I didn't give a straight answer. When I went back to Islamabad, I talked to my mother about Laila's wish to visit our house. My mother answered that she had no objection to my doing research on any tabooed topic and would always support me, but she did not want me to start inviting my subjects home. She preferred that I not drag my whole family into it. I argued with her that I wanted to use my research to break people's prejudices against these people and to begin to understand them like human beings. 'How can I do this if my own family is still prejudiced?' I asked. She argued that she was already doing her share by not objecting to me spending most of my time, including weekends, all my leave time, and any other possible opportunity in Lahore. That ended the discussion.

After many visits back and forth to Lahore, I had to go to Mardan for some other work. While I was gone, my mother called to tell me that my friend Laila and her husband were at our house in Islamabad. I was surprised, since Laila hadn't mentioned these plans to me at all when I'd visited her a week earlier. I apologized to my mother for their unannounced visit but she assured me that she'd take care of them. They stayed for two days, and by the time I got back they'd already gone to Murree, a popular hill station. My mother was a little shaken up, and said it was exhausting to resist all of Laila's demands. She wanted the car and the driver all the time. She wanted to go out to eat. She wanted to take my clothes and on and on. I laughed because I knew exactly what had happened. I explained to my mother that Laila had been trained from birth to extort things from people, and she did it unconsciously. My mother told me that, despite her best efforts, Laila had taken two of my new *shalwar kamiz* and my brother's travel bag.

Laila and Saleem spent only two days in Murree, all that Saleem could afford before running out of money. Laila couldn't let this opportunity pass and she bought whatever she saw. According to custom, gifts and holidays are over and above the monthly stipend. They are a bonus and Laila wanted to take full advantage of this windfall. They stayed at a modest hotel. Laila was not happy about that, and apparently grumbled about it the whole time.

They returned to Lahore with two big suitcases full of things for Laila and gifts for her family. The family thanked him for being so kind, knowing full well he had had no other choice. When I next saw her in Lahore, Laila told me all about her trip to Islamabad. She announced that she really liked my family, especially my mother, and that she planned to visit me again soon. I told her she'd have to inform me first so I could prepare my family for her.

Islamabad and my house became her new topic for bragging. With friends and customers on the telephone she inventoried all the gadgets in my house several times. A deep freezer, two refrigerators, three televisions and a computer were on top of her list. She was impressed by all this and was very proud of me for having these things.

Laila continued performing in the evening. Her husband was simply told that the performances in the evening would continue, so she could support the family.

# 22

# NARGIS IS BETTER OFF NOT MARRYING

I maintained regular contact with Laila, but spent time with other prostitutes as well. I wanted to meet a wide range to gain an understanding of their dreams, aspirations, joys and heartbreaks. I wanted to know about their economic problems and about their health issues. Most of all I wanted to connect with them as women, to understand their lives so that, in the process, I could understand my own and others like me.

Born in the Shahi Mohalla, Nargis grew up learning the art of entertaining. Her elder sister and her mother were her primary teachers. She learned both singing and dancing at a very young age. Her family was not an affluent prostitute family, and had to do everything they could to survive. As a child, she started working in theatre shows and traditional circuses, her main job being to dance between various acts or before the main programme began. She had been working like that since she was twelve. She would be sent with any party that asked for her and her mother accepted any amount of money that was offered. They couldn't afford to say no to any opportunity to earn something. She performed as a dancer in traditional theatre, magic shows, Variety Shows and all other forms of traditional entertainment including *Mot ka kuan*, the death well. She worked in the Lucky Irani Circus, Jubilee Circus and in many more small entertainment enterprises thriving around local and religious festivals. Nargis worked from about noon until late at night. The shows could go on until two, three or even four in the morning.

'I was "married" when fifteen years old,' Nargis told me.
'My parents accepted three thousand rupees, offered by a man
from Sialkot for my *nath*. At that time such an amount was
good money. Those were times when two hundred thousand
rupees was enough to build a house. After that, I started working
regularly with customers. We gave our addresses to men at the
*mela*, and they'd follow us home,' she said laughingly. 'I liked
to talk to the customers in addition to dancing. If the deal was
agreeable to my mother, and he offered an acceptable price,
I would go with him.

'Now I live with my mother. We have four-rooms: two for
living and two for the *affis*. Girls in our community are now so
spoiled that they work for two days and take four off. It was
different before. Everyone used to work very hard. Life is still
tough for me. I work a lot, but can hardly make ends meet. Just
imagine, we pay Rs. 4000 for rent and Rs. 3000 for the
electricity bill! With such rising prices, we're lucky to feed and
clothe our children. I have four brothers—two work with the
famous dancing girls, Salma and Sitara, as their agents; two just
roam around, like the *Kanjar* boys often do. I live upstairs with
my children and my mother lives downstairs with my sister.'

'With God's help, my work is enough for my children and
me to survive. At times, I get very rowdy customers who get
drunk and make a lot of noise. They grab me roughly and push
me around. I have to be very firm to control them. I say, "*Mein
tere nikah wich nain*", (I'm not married to you) so you can't
throw me around like that. See, I will only tolerate so much.
I'm sitting in my own house after all. They come for my
services. Sometimes, I just have to draw the line. If they get
violent, I stop singing and ask them to leave immediately. In
our Mohalla, my friends ask up to Rs. 5000 for sexual services.
For singing, the minimum expectation is Rs. 300 to Rs. 500,
but, typically, *kothas* get anywhere from Rs. 1000 to Rs. 3000.
I don't take less than 500 to 1000 rupees. If a customer offers
less I tell him to go to Tibbi Gali. There, the poor women even
accept a customer for 100 or 200 rupees.'

'I'm careful about my cleanliness. I don't want to be sick. Here, we wash our hands and clean up before being with a man. Women *"jerian din wich kai bethandian ne"* (those who get several customers a day), like in Tibbi, don't care. They're dirty and don't use cloth. They take one man after the other. That is why they get so many diseases.'

'What kind of diseases?' I asked.

'Infections, secretions, but they don't tell their customers. Sometimes they ask the *dai* to help them if they have a serious problem,' she answered.

'Do you know of a disease called AIDS?' I asked.

'No, there are lots of diseases. I just believe I should keep myself clean.'

I gave her a whole session on AIDS and how it can infect women like her. When I asked her about condoms, she laughed loudly and said, *"qion ona di mardangi nu hath pan lage o* (why are you hitting their masculinity)?" She knew men wouldn't like that. For her customers, using a condom would be a big blow to their manhood.

'What about your own children?' I asked.

'My friends have two opinions about children. Some are anxious to make some money first. They want a house, jewellery and savings before they take time off to have children. Others want children and have faith that they'll have enough time in their lives for business so they can get those things in any case. I belong to the second group. I had my children quite early. I had my first child at sixteen, a daughter who did not survive. Neither did my first boy. My third child, a son, survived, but I was very sad because I had wanted a daughter. I kept trying for another child and finally, succeeded. To my pleasure, I had a daughter. She is four years old now.'

'I've never used contraceptives. Having children is God's gift and people should not interfere. My colleagues commonly abort their pregnancies, but as I've had some problems getting pregnant even when I want to, I'm not too worried about it. Women have abortions if they are already having a hard time bringing up their children. Do you know Rajo? She is a nice woman. She's had five abortions and I told her she was crazy. If she keeps doing it, she won't be able to conceive when she really does want children.'

'Where can she get abortions?' I asked.

'People used to count on the local *dai*, but now women go to the hospitals. Lady doctors do it privately. It costs anywhere from 200 to 3000 rupees,' she answered.

'Do you choose the person with whom you want to get pregnant?' I asked her.

She said, 'I'd like to have a child with someone who is interested in me and not just any random visitor who comes once or twice. I want some steady relationship with the person with whom I'd get pregnant. We can't be stupid. We want him to bear the medical expenses for the child. Some men freak out when they find out that it is their child. They can't reconcile themselves to the idea that their child's future will be in this Mohalla. If the man backs out, we have to pay for our own medical expenses from whatever we've saved. Our preference is for the man—whose child it is—to bear the expenses, but if he doesn't, we're still not at a complete loss. We spend on the medical bills but we do get the child. We raise our own children. We're very happy to have girls because they carry on the tradition in the family.'

'Do you ever get emotionally involved with a customer?' I asked.

'Liking a customer is never even an issue. We're only interested in the money we make. We have children and families so we can't afford to get into these issues.'

She stopped talking for a while and laughed, 'I started working when I was twelve. I'm twenty-six now. My mother never pushed me or stopped me from doing anything. The only time she and my sister sometimes pressured me was when they felt I was seeing too much of one customer. Then they'd start getting worried about me,' she said.

She laughed as if she enjoyed them getting worried about her. She said, 'They'd say "*Je mu kala karwanai e te banda te koi kharcha chukan wala huwe. Jinu bithaya e o te tere bachian nu roti wi nai khua sakda. Je ais kam which pai e te fer apna kuj bana"* (If you have to dishonour us, pick a guy who can bear your expenses. The one you're sleeping with now can't even feed your kids. If you get into something serious, get something out of it for yourself). I totally agree with them. I think the priority is to get a house, some savings and financial security. Then you can marry whoever you like, but only after the future is secure. Our life should not be shaky like a married woman's, where she can be kicked out with nothing even after ten or twenty years.'

I smiled, reminded of comments I'd heard from married women from our society condemning prostitutes, and amused to hear what Nargis thought of married women. I asked whether she'd ever wanted to get married.

She touched her ear lobes with both hands and stuck out her tongue, a way of saying 'God forgive me'. *'Allah na kere* (may God forbid it)! What's the use of going through with a *nikah*, the husbands harass us and beat us...what is the use? Two of my friends got married. They worked so hard, doing all the housework, and then they had to listen to their husbands' foul language. Their in-laws treated them like filth. Finally, they even took away their daughters and sent them back to the Mohalla, saying they were *Kanjar* and only fit to live with *Kanjars*. What is the use of suffering like that? I don't ever want to get into that sort of mess. I work hard and want to earn a living for my children, honestly and on my own.'

Despite her strong convictions, Nargis hadn't managed to acquire a house or much savings. Her earnings only let her and her children live hand to mouth. 'Having children was my wish,' she said, 'I don't mind not having much security. I still think my life has more dignity than that of a wife who is a slave and cannot even earn food for her children. For me, in these expensive times just feeding my children with an income from hard work and honesty is enough. *Uton hakumat nu vi sharam nai andi, her chees da ret wadai jande ne. Sade warga gharib kisran bache palen?* (On top of that the government is least embarrassed. It keeps raising the prices. Now, how do poor people like me, feed their children?).'

---

## VIEWS

*Pakeeza Begum, a homemaker*

A homemaker who was quite vocal about the issue told me, 'Earlier, whatever I knew about prostitution was through the films. I thought this was the most evil thing a woman could do. But in the movies they sometimes showed her like a victim. She would fall in love with the hero and later would die for him...all that rubbish! Now, I know better. One woman in our neighbourhood, right here in the Wahdat Colony, comes from that area. Her customer married her. Now she has three children. The eldest is twelve years old. They moved here about two years ago. I don't go to her house at all. Other women in the colony go out of curiosity and when they come back they gossip. They notice all the gestures she makes or the way she talks and then they make fun of her.'

'Does she talk differently than you all?' I asked.

'Actually, I don't think that she does. She is a Punjabi like we are, but these women try to pick at little things just to have fun. I think it is better to socially boycott such a woman. I did not even go to her house for kunde during the holy days. I do not want to eat anything from her house.'

'Why do you think that she got married and left her kotha?' I asked.

She said, 'Oh, she must have fallen in love with him.'

'And why do you think she stayed with him for so long?' I asked.

'Maybe for her children, but don't you try and tell me that she is a good woman! She was a prostitute before this man married her. I've heard that occasionally she goes to her family, back there in the Mohalla, and sits through the performances of her nieces. They give her some money for just being there as a manager.'

'So, she is still "working" there?'

'Well, I don't think so, she is too old and no longer has a body that would be interesting,' she laughed and covered her mouth with her dupatta, embarrassed at what she had just said. 'But she goes, once in a while. Other women have told me that she just sits with her sister for a while and gets some money from the earnings of an evening. God knows what she does, but I do not want my faith to be shaken so I just stay away from such evil women.'

Later, I met the woman who had left the Mohalla to marry her customer and visited her often at her house. She said she had a lot of problems in the beginning. She tried very hard to hide her background, but whenever people living around her found out, they'd start to ridicule her. She said at that age she did not have much confidence, so when a neighbour would find out about her background she would cry and feel bad. Now it was different for her. She said, 'I don't give a damn anymore! I'm happy in my house and I notice that if I don't care the others don't care that much either. Those who want to be friends with me do; those who don't can go to hell. I left the bazaar to come into their society. What do they have to say about girls who are born in their households and are now on the streets, in Allama Iqbal Town and Green Town making extra money as semi-professionals?'

Initially, she had totally cut off all links with her relatives in the Mohalla. But, as her self-confidence grew, she began visiting her family occasionally. Some people think this means she is going back into the business.

# 23

## SHATTERED DREAMS

Shalo was about nineteen years old and had been working since she was fourteen when she had her first customer. She had two elder sisters and so had been well introduced to her profession. As a child she would hang out a lot with her eldest sister and closely watch how she extorted money from the customers. Shalo was very proud of her two sisters, especially the eldest, whom she idolized. Her family did not consider Shalo beautiful; she had a dark complexion and sharp features. Fair colouring is considered to be the standard of beauty. I, however, found Shalo charming, with an intelligent spark in her eye. Growing up, she had told herself that though she might be dark, she'd make sure she was good at her job. She felt that by working hard she could show her friends in the Mohalla that looks were not the only important thing. She worked hard at her music lessons, and was one of the few among her friends who paid full respect to her *ustad*, and was regular in her singing practice

Like every Mohalla dancer, Shalo dreamed of becoming a major movie star. Her eldest sister had some small roles in films, but no speaking parts. Her family knew someone at the Shahnoor studio, who hired her sister for dance scenes requiring scores of girls to dance with the heroine. Shalo had seen all of her sister's films. She also had a distant cousin who was a bit more successful in films. Not really a big name but she had done some solo dances, the sort that fill in dead spots in a movie where the hero goes to a nightclub to mend his broken heart by watching girls perform flashy dances. Shalo saw all of her cousin's films, too. She went to the studio with her sister sometimes, but didn't like how the dance director and the movie director treated her sister and the other women. She thought resentfully that, when she became a big star, she would teach them a lesson and show them how to respect an artist. She knew that in addition to hard work, luck played an important role in getting a break in films. These actresses were just like her, she felt. Perhaps she wasn't as beautiful, but she knew she could make herself look quite pretty.

By the age of ten, she was already spending hours putting on her sister's make-up and gazing at her reflection in the mirror. Her mother did not approve of her wearing make-up, but her eldest sister encouraged her. She often managed to convince her sister's customers to buy her gifts. Her eldest sister thought Shalo's performances were good, for a child. At *Basant*, she would dress up in flashy clothes, wear heavy make-up and roam around the Mohalla with her friends. Her mother never kept her from wearing make-up during the festivities. Shalo loved to see the actresses coming home to the Mohalla for *Basant*. Watching these actresses was her favourite pastime on this occasion. She would dream of becoming a star like them.

When she got her first customer, she was quite happy since she got a good price for her *nath* despite her dark complexion. Her friends were envious of her, thinking it the result of a combination of good luck and her mother's hard work. Shalo knew it was her own hard work that had paid off, however. She had attracted her customer at a gathering where all three sisters had gone for a *mujra*. After this customer, who only paid for a single night and did not establish a long-term contract, Shalo began to work officially.

People thought Shalo's family had good contacts in the film studios, but Shalo knew that this wasn't true. A connection wasn't 'good' when you had to wait for days in the studios to get a ten-second shot in a group dance. Shalo wanted a good break in films and was very anxious and confident to display her acting talents. She was willing to work hard and learn from more experienced artists. She kept working on her singing and dancing. Shalo went to the studios many times, but got only promises. She would have taken the smallest role, even as one dancer in a group of a hundred. Agents who supplied women for dances and chorus singing at Shahnoor studios, have many on their list from which to choose. Women sometimes throw themselves at the agents to get a chance. Mothers also compete aggressively for opportunities for their daughters. Shalo felt her mother had her eyes on her elder sisters and didn't pay enough attention to her career. Her mother was always accompanying her other sisters to the studios, and pushing their photographs all the time, while no one was even asked to take portraits of Shalo.

At times, she felt like going to one of the successful actresses originally from the Mohalla and saying, 'Hey, do you know what I am going through? I am like you, from the same place. I need a break, too and I promise not to disappoint you. Try me.' She could not take such a step, however, knowing the manager is the one to fight for these opportunities. As a future actress, she should concentrate on improving herself and looking for a good manager or agent to sell her art in the industry. Her job, she assumed, was to keep practicing her music and to please her customers. She was always preparing for the day when she would be tested.

Unfortunately, her mother decided that of the three daughters, the elder two would focus on careers and Shalo would produce children. Fairer and more beautiful than Shalo, the older ones were privileged not to waste their time and bodies on reproduction. It was Shalo, the dark one, who the family could spare, to reproduce, not only for herself, but also for her sisters. When she was about to have her first child, her eldest sister said if the baby was a girl she would take her. When a boy was born, the issue never came up again.

Shalo had been working as a dancer and a prostitute for a year when she found a very handsome looking customer with whom her mother said she should get pregnant. Shalo disagreed, but could not win. Her mother insisted she had to keep thinking about the future. Once, when Shalo was unusually angry and rude to her mother, uncommon behaviour for her, her mother yelled back, 'If your sisters don't succeed in movies at least an old director or a *wadera* with plenty of land will take them as mistresses, but what will you do?' Shalo did not argue after that, but thought that, while she had enough faith in her own abilities, her mother did not have any faith in her at all. Shalo really believed that she could take the whole family to a higher level by working in films, but the burden of childbearing made it impossible for her to even try. She felt helpless and did not know how to communicate her heartbreak to her mother.

Shalo was nine months pregnant when we met. She was both happy and sad about her condition, happy because her pregnancy was about to end and after the birth she'd be free to do things she had been waiting to do, and sad because she hadn't wanted a child at this stage of her life. Already resentful that her family didn't let her pursue her dreams, Shalo wanted to be a good prostitute, to get good customers and to try her luck in films. When Shalo gave birth to a second son, her whole family was very sad. I heard the news in Islamabad, and although I wasn't planning a trip to Lahore soon, I promised I'd visit her on my next trip. The second son's birth not only rendered her future bleak, but jeopardized the whole family's as well. She had shared her fears with me before, afraid of their reaction. Knowing that her mother would not be very understanding if she bore a second son, she had gone many times to the neighbourhood shrine to pray for a daughter.

For women, going to pray at such shrines, usually graves of known Sufis or holy men who are thought to be close to God, is very common. People make offerings, pray, and promise more offerings if their wish is granted. Women go in large numbers to visit different shrines during their annual festivals, when tens of thousands of people gather from all over the country. The shrine rituals reflect a blend of religious and cultural overlays the subcontinent has experienced over the centuries. Not all sects of Islam follow these more ancient folk and religious traditions. Associating these practices with illiteracy and the influence of Hinduism, some consider them an unwanted foreign influence to be eliminated because of their perceived conflict with Islam. The Mohalla dancing community are mostly Shias and go to the shrines frequently to give offerings.

Shalo had gone to the shrine of Data Sahib, Lahore's patron saint, to pray for a daughter. She lighted a candle on Thursday evening and promised that if Data Sahib gave her a daughter, she would offer eleven and a quarter rupees to his shrine and a *chaddar* for his grave. But nothing worked for her.

I could not get away from Islamabad for a while. The boy was already three weeks old and I bought some colourful clothes for him. When I went to her house, I was told that Shalo had gone to see a doctor since her elder son had not been well. I remembered her telling me he was neglected quite a bit, and when he fell sick she really had to make it an issue before she was allowed to take him to a doctor. I inquired about the newborn and was shocked to hear he had died a week earlier. The family members seemed not at all sad about it.

I decided to wait for Shalo, talking to her mother in the meantime. She didn't say much about the dead child, but commented, 'I hope she gets pregnant again so that the next child can heal the wound of losing this one.'

'What if the next child is another son?' I asked.

She said, 'God forbid, It must be a girl. God cannot be so unfair to us'.

When Shalo came back, she cried and said her newborn had come down with pneumonia. She alone tried to get him some treatment, but after getting better for a week, he had a relapse. She told me he didn't actually die of the disease, but because no one in the family cared about him. Nobody wanted him to live. Looking into her eyes, I saw Shalo's fighting spirit and belief in herself was diminishing. She seemed burdened with life.

Pushed to get pregnant with another good looking customer within two months of her son's death, Shalo suffered through the pregnancy, sick the whole time. She had stopped talking to me or her few friends. Her eyes were puffed with dark circles underneath. The charming young woman began to look like a tuberculosis patient. I met her once on the street and she told me she'd stopped dreaming about anything. Her eyes gave a

Visiting shrines every Thursday evening to light candles and give offerings of flowers and food, is an important part of the spirituality of the women in Shahi Mohalla. Their prayers are for a girl child, rich customers, or a break in the movies

Roof tops provide multi-purpose space, for storage, drying clothes, flying kites, and communicating with neighbours

A railing forms a balcony around the skylight

A square shaped skylight cuts through all the storeys in the middle of the building for light and fresh air—view from top

The complexity of spaces created by different levels of terraces and skylights allow
the lives of different families living in the building to become intertwined

contradictory message. Had she really abandoned her dreams? She could not keep fighting her circumstances. She was like a patient who was dying a slow death.

After the birth of the third son, I heard of her suicide, but was prevented from getting more information about her death. Her family refused to see me. No one spoke about it. Life went on as if nothing had happened. Her death was a non-issue.

# 24

# MOVING INTO THE MOHALLA

I was getting more and more insight into life in the Mohalla. The lives of Laila, Chanda, Shalo, Nargis and many others were helping me to reflect on the values of the Mohalla as well as those of our mainstream society. My circle of contacts was expanding and my work was going smoothly. After maintaining continuous contact with the community for several months, I succeeded in reaching an intense level of interaction with the people even though I now saw them only on weekends. Every weekend I drove from Islamabad to Lahore for two days. Sometimes I stretched it a bit longer by taking a few days off. I had good contacts with almost all sections of the community, achieving a certain level of acceptance. Only the police did not like my presence in the Mohalla.

My links with both prostitutes and musicians were becoming stronger. They had become quite comfortable in sharing intimate aspects of their lives with me and I spent many hours of the day with them. Although I lived only half an hour away, I felt I should move into the area to get into the twenty-four hour routine and observe the subtle dynamics between the different groups of residents. My ethnographic training fully justified this step. I felt that actually moving there would give me a deeper insight. I felt comfortable enough with the people to make this move.

I began my search for an apartment to rent; one I could be sure was safe for me. I wanted a central location that would give me the opportunity to experience the residents' daily life. Kaisera's building had a vacant quarter on the ground floor, consisting of two rooms, with a joint toilet shared by all residents of that floor. Three other groups lived there: two families of prostitutes and one group of musicians. The musicians usually used the public baths, but the women's families shared the same toilet.

Kaisera and Laila lived in the front half of the first floor with their family, and another family of prostitutes rented the backside of this floor. The next floor housed three more groups; a family of performers from the now defunct Punjabi traditional theatre and two families of shopkeepers. The floor above that had only one room with an open terrace, and was used by the owners for storage purposes. All the young children used the open terrace as their play area. The teenagers in the building flew their kites there, while the homemakers and servants hung their wet laundry. The building was built around a central open courtyard. This served as a multi-purpose utility space for the families that didn't have easy access to the top floor terrace.

I met my potential neighbours while checking out the vacant section. Although I knew most of the ground and the first floor residents, I didn't know the family who lived next to the vacant rooms very well. The woman, who was about thirty-five years old, was delighted to meet me. She had seen me often, but wasn't fully aware of my work. Apparently, she was usually under the influence of one drug or another, and seldom came to the world of harsh reality.

She asked my name and with a slur in her speech continued, 'Are you going to live here or just work from here.'

'Both,' I replied, quickly.

She asked where my family lived and when I mentioned Islamabad, she said, 'You mean Rawalpindi, don't you? I have a cousin who lives in Qasai Galli (Rawalpindi's red light district), but business has become very bad there. May God make these policemen rot for ruining our livelihood. She used to do quite well there, and in better days I visited her.'

I knew she was thinking of me as a colleague and I chose, for the time being, not to clarify my actual work. The conversation was fun.

She continued chatting, 'You moved to Lahore like I did. My family was also in Rawalpindi, but I wanted to take my chances in Lahore. It was my bad luck that I had a leech attached to me. I hope you've not brought one with you who will suck all your blood.'

'What do you mean?' I asked.

'*Dala*', she shouted, but then her voice dropped to a soft mumble, her eyes unfocussed and she totally disengaged from me.

I continued looking around. I met the other family and saw they had taken most of the compound for themselves. The joint toilet was my only concern, but I knew I could deal with it, since I'd lived in villages with very scarce facilities. This, at least, was a city.

I explored other places as well. A room with a small bathroom and an independent entrance was available in the back streets of the Mohalla. The house belonged to a big landlord with many buildings in the bazaar. Chanda had told me about it. Over the last two months I had developed a close relationship with Chanda, an exceptionally intelligent woman who had totally devoted herself to her business. She felt burdened with the constant pressures from her management, especially her mother, but was determined to do her best. She once told me that she wanted to work hard and succeed in her profession, so she could someday win the approval of her family and *biradri* for certain actions that some might consider deviations from the norm. She never told me what exactly she had in mind, but my general impression was that she took her work very seriously.

Chanda's family lived on the ground floor of a larger building nearby. Her two sisters, in their mid-twenties, were at the end of their performing careers. Other than her family, some business-people lived on the top two floors. Two families had small shops that rented videos and sold audiocassettes and two had shoe shops in the Sheikhupurian bazaar. After showing me the room, Chanda said, 'You do not have to worry about food, you are welcome to eat with us.'

I thanked her, but said, 'I know it's easy to get by with food from the market. Most of the people here don't cook food at home, do they?'

'We do!' Chanda exclaimed, 'except breakfast of course. No one cooks breakfast, but other than that, we do cook our own food. We have a proper kitchen.' Taking my hand she insisted, 'Now come to our house.' We went in from the back entrance, which opened into a courtyard. As we walked through, she asked me how much rent I could afford.

'Is it that flexible?' I asked.

She winked and said, 'We have good links with the landlord. We used to live somewhere else, but he was very kind and asked us to move into his building at a very reasonable rent. He sends us some of his business and political partners and we are kind to them. You know what I mean? The arrangement is good for both of us.' We entered a long narrow room, and she showed me the main entrance from Hyderi Street, where a big gate-like door opened into a living room. Set up like a performance room or a *kotha*, it had the typical sofa set and floor seating. A small door next to it was another entrance from the main street that opened into a passage leading to the narrow room. The family came through this all day. Only customers used the big doors in the evenings.

The narrow room had two *charpai* and several suitcases stacked on top of each other. Colourful posters of film actresses decorated the walls. As we came out in the courtyard again, I saw doors to three rooms and a kitchen. Chanda told me two rooms were for the three sisters. One sister shared a room with her, and the other lived with her two children. Their mother slept in the long narrow room. Chanda took me to her bedroom, very excited to have me visiting her house. Her room had a big double bed with a gigantic carved headboard, and a huge dresser spilling over with perfumes and imported make-up items. I saw all the famous brand names and commented, 'What a collection! You must spend all you earn on make-up.'

She jerked her head back and laughed, 'Not a single rupee. My customers buy me these things. I make sure I don't even spend money on my clothes. My sisters buy clothes for themselves and pay for them, but not me. If I have to buy things for myself, I shouldn't be a prostitute. I might as well sell fruit. You're intelligent, you know what I mean!'

'Yes, I think I understand,' I nodded.

'My customers are bureaucrats, good at giving gifts. They don't open up and give me much cash, but they respond to my requests for perfumes and other things very well, and they have good taste. My customers from the business world have no taste for nice things at all.'

'From the business world?' I asked.

'You know, business-people. They're generous with money, but I would rather not have them buy me gifts. English speaking high-level government officers even bring me presents from abroad. They go on official tours so they get me good stuff.'

'Aren't you going to offer your friend tea? Are you just going to stand there and talk? Why don't you sit down?' A husky voice came from behind, Chanda's mother, a heavy, fair complexioned woman. I greeted her, and Chanda and I sat down, she on the bed and myself on a chair close by. After taking a good look at me, her mother left the room.

Chanda continued, 'You know I really enjoy private *mujra*. I like meeting different types of people.'

'What kind of customers do you like best?' I asked.

'I've enjoyed it most whenever the goldsmiths have invited us. We have sayings in our language about them being misers, but believe me, they are very generous to us *Kanjarian*. They throw their hearts at us, and once you get them to compete with their friends, it is intoxicating! I can't describe the pleasure of watching them compete to shower us with *vail*. I don't really like it when they give us five and ten rupee notes. It is hard to get the *vail* amount higher. I like the money thrown at us to be 100 rupee bills, or even better, 1000 rupee bills. The intoxication of 1000 rupee bills is out of this world. Believe me, we perform with a very different motivation then.'

Her mother came back and said, 'Chanda talks a lot. If you keep listening to her you'll stay hungry.'

'Please don't worry,' I said, 'I don't feel like eating, and besides, I enjoy talking to your daughter.' I turned to Chanda and asked her to continue.

After her mother left Chanda began talking again, 'More than just going out with one customer I like dancing in front of a group. I feel I can show off my skills and I love being able to drive men crazy! That is the best proof of my abilities, right.'

'Do you always have an all-male audience at your *mujra*?' I asked.

'Yes, but recently we've heard that very rich people sometimes have a mixed gathering for a *mujra*. I performed in one, but I didn't like it.'

'Why not?'

'They look at us like objects, and there is hardly any interaction with the audience. Men don't open up and throw their money generously, because their wives are sitting next to them. Women aren't generous with their money, because they have no taste for such gatherings yet, I suppose. For me the dance is between the dancer and the customer. There is the interaction, and the customer responds to each of the dancer's moves. What to you may seem like just giving money isn't only that. It's a response to something specific that I do. If I reach his heart with my smile, or a wink or do something else, only then his hand will reach his pocket. To me that's his response, confirming that he got my message. Do you understand what I'm saying? Only if I'm good at my work will I get this response.'

'You seem to like your work a lot,' I said.

She ignored my comment and continued talking, totally involved with her explanation, 'Sometimes these "family types" get a *mujra* organized in a mixed gathering and fix our fee. Then they think that they don't need to give *vail*. A few give us a token amount, just to have some fun I suppose, but for me nothing can be more boring than that. Try to understand! If I am booked for a *mujra* at a fixed fee and no *vail*, then I could do a good job or a bad job and what difference would it make? *Vail* is a constant message for me from my customers that they

appreciate my work, and I operate on those signals. If I don't
know that I've touched their hearts, why should I continue to
send messages to them? Who wants to perform for a dead
audience, who just claps after the end of a dance?' Putting her
feet up on the bed, she made herself more comfortable. Then
she bent forward in excitement and said, 'I get my best
customers from private *mujras*. It's this communication that
makes the magic.'

Chanda's mother came in with a glass of lemonade. Handing
me the glass, she pointed at Chanda, 'She won't let you do
anything. She tells long stories. My daughter talks a lot.'

I thanked her for the drink and said, 'No, no, don't worry.
I am enjoying her stories,' and I turned back to Chanda.

'Did you like the room you saw?' asked her mother in a
husky voice.

'It's certainly one option,' I said. 'I'll be looking at another
one in Heera Mandi, but right now I want to talk a little bit with
Chanda.'

She smiled, and with her eyes on me, left the room.
I wondered whether she was nervous about her daughter talking
so much with me. I'd already talked with Chanda quite a bit,
but only outside her house. I hadn't visited her at home before.
Maybe her mother didn't realize how friendly we were. In any
case, Chanda was not so young that her mother had to guard
her. In her mid-twenties, she was getting ready to go into
management. My observation was correct. Chanda's mother did
try to get her away from me. After a few minutes she called
Chanda outside and told her to go to another dancer's house to
pick up a specific dress that she wanted to copy for Chanda's
eldest sister. Chanda asked her to send a servant or a child, but
the mother insisted that she had to go right away. The argument
was quite loud. Both of them had heavy voices, like most women
in the business.

Chanda came back to her room where I was waiting. She
apologized and said, 'My mother doesn't know you well, so
I guess she is getting a little worried. Even though I'm old
enough, she still gets nervous. I get tired of it. Once she gets to

know you, she'll be fine. Anyway, you're just a woman, what harm could you bring me? You should see how upset she gets when I see a man frequently.'

'You mean a customer?'

Well, yes and no. She has no clue of what liking is or what love is. That's the most threatening thing for them. My mother starts nagging when she sees me getting involved with someone.'

'Do you get involved easily?'

'No! I'm a good prostitute. I'll tell you someday. Just remember one thing: I am not a *dil phaink*, I don't easily fall in love, but, you know, I am human. When I'm dealing with customers, it's different. It's more like a game and both sides know it.'

I got up and said, 'I better get going. I do not want her to feel threatened by me. I prefer taking time and getting to know her.' Chanda got up with me and insisted, 'Don't worry. I'm not going to pick up that dress anyway. I'm not a child who should run around and do such silly chores. She'll send someone else. Please stay.'

I said, 'I have to look at this other room anyway. I'll meet you at the *baithak* later this evening.'

She agreed, 'Fouzia, if you don't mind, I'd be very interested to know what you find out about our Mohalla. I like the idea of someone studying our lifestyle. Would you let me in on some of your discoveries...you know, whatever you call it in your research language? I think it's exciting, and I think about it myself sometimes.'

I smiled, 'I will be ready for a discussion today at the *baithak*.'

She called me just as I started towards the door, 'We didn't even finish our round of the house. We have another room.' She held my hand and took me to the last room, a fully furnished bedroom with a red satin quilted bedcover and frilled pillows. There was a dressing table with a big mirror. She told me it was for guests. Clearly the room was for the customers. We went back into the courtyard. She was buying a little time, not wanting her mother to think she managed to chase me away. Chanda wasn't a child and didn't want to be treated like one. Both she and her mother said good-bye. Chanda reminded me that the nearby room was very convenient and that I should consider it seriously. I promised I would.

My last choice was a room in Heera Mandi, the best known of the Mohalla bazaars. A musician, Aftab, had arranged for me to see the place. We walked through the Naugaza Chowk, towards the Fort Road and took a sharp right turn onto a narrow street, with very tall buildings on both sides. On the left-hand side small, dead end streets about three to five feet wide opened like little veins on a leaf. These streets had room enough only for a motorcycle or a bike to pass through. The buildings on each side joined together with no space in between and looked like a continuous structure. They appeared to be leaning towards the middle of the street, giving the illusion that the buildings on opposite sides of the street would end up joining from the top some day. Open drains ran down the middle or sides of the streets, and curtains covered many of the doors.

Aftab took me to one of the smaller side streets, which had a strong smell of urine. He knocked at a door and a young man lifted the curtain and came out. Aftab asked for Shado Bai, and was told she'd gone to a shrine for *niaz* and would be back in two hours. Aftab asked if it was the neighbourhood shrine, but the young man said no. She'd gone to Data Sahib's shrine to offer a *chaddar* she had promised. We left and I told Aftab not to pursue this option for me, since I hardly knew people in that area. I told him I'd like to meet Shado Bai for my research though.

I felt proud of myself for coming up with this great idea of moving into the Mohalla. I'd already done my homework and had some good options lined up. I had almost made up my mind about moving into Kaisera's building. It was suitable for me in every way. I returned to Islamabad thinking that I would apply for a leave without pay and wrap up a few things so I could fully concentrate on my research. Driving back from Lahore I had already made a list of things to bring from Islamabad to set-up my rooms.

When my family heard about it, they went into shock. My mother said I'd gone too far, and was so engrossed in my work that I was losing my mind. I couldn't understand her reaction. I'd been in the Mohalla for many months and fully trusted people there. Living in another part of Lahore had been all right, but a place that is fully alive around the clock has to be closely studied at night, too. My colleagues at Lok Virsa had a similar reaction. Suddenly I seemed to be arguing with everyone. My friends were astonished and told me not to be so crazy. I kept telling myself everyone was simply biased, holding the same ideas and prejudices I wanted to combat. They thought anyone who went to the Mohalla would be pressured into prostitution or that people there would hurt me somehow. All this was ridiculous, and I was confident that after giving people, including my mother, some time they'd get used to it.

A few days later I met my police friend, Amjad Shah. I bounced my idea off him, and he looked at me with a strange fear in his eyes, asking me if I knew the risk I'd be taking. I told him I knew the people in the area and felt safe with them.

'Do you trust me?' he asked.

'Of course!'

He asked whether I'd had any encounters with the police.

'A few,' I answered, 'they certainly aren't nice to me.'

He spoke firmly, 'Listen to me. You could be cut up into pieces and tossed in the sewer and nobody will know where your body is. Bravery is fine, but not stupidity. You think your friends in the Mohalla could save you? They themselves don't know about the organized crime that lurks around there. The dangers for you are different from what a Mohalla resident faces. So don't tell me the place is okay and the people are nice. Just hear me out. Certain people don't like you going around asking questions. They consider it spying. Do you understand me?'

I listened seriously and nodded.

'Even now you are a threat to them,' he continued, 'because they don't know when you'll step onto something they don't want you to know. That makes you a potential problem. For

now, you have the advantage because you don't live there and
they don't really know how powerful you might be. Once you
move in, you'll give away that power. You'll become a resident
and will be very vulnerable. You will be under their control.
They could get you so easily. You'd really have to be very
stupid to do that.'

'Who are "they"?' I asked in a low voice.

'Police for one and organized gangsters, including many of
our local politicians, for the other.'

I breathed deeply and asked politely, 'Do you really think
it's a bad idea? You know I have picked out this very protected
two room portion on the inner....'

He cut me off, 'If you want to go ahead, don't expect any
help from me when you get in trouble.'

His last threat shattered all my plans. I'd been thinking about
setting up my rooms nicely, inviting over my musician friends
from the neighbourhood, staying up late at night to watch the
streets after one o'clock, following some of the street walkers
around as they dodged the police, but now I knew I couldn't.

## VIEWS

### A woman activist

Surayia, an activist in the social movement and mother of two, has been working in a women's-rights NGO for several years. When I discussed the sex trade with her, she said, 'You know our women's movement never really focused on prostitution. In India, women's groups have played a key role in speaking out against prostitution, especially against the system of devadasis. Here, we had too many other fires to put out.'

I said, 'The women's movement in the West is now siding with the prostitutes. They have organized themselves as pressure groups to influence policy and are struggling to be accepted like other commercial workers. They claim they are contributing to the Gross National Product and should be called Commercial Sex Workers (CSWs) – a term that is becoming quite common – and should get regular labour benefits. COYOTE (Call Off Your Tired Old Ethics) is one such organization that was formed back in 1973. They have their support circles, and in general are well received by other women's groups, but some analysts find significant differences in the ultimate goals both sides are seeking.'

'Yes, that's a paradox, isn't it!' she said. 'I'd say we are against the sex trade, but not against the prostitutes. We do not want them to suffer. I totally condemn the Government actions. The police have been harassing the residents of the red light districts and taking bribes to allow them to continue their business.'

I asked whether she'd ever been to the Shahi Mohalla or any place like it. 'No...not really,' she replied. 'I have to say I do not know much about it except for what I've read, heard or seen in movies. I know the movies have a certain self-righteous angle to their stories, but as a women's activist I should know more about sex workers.' She seemed confused.

'You know, many of our feminists haven't really come to terms with this and have mixed feelings about it. How do you feel?' I asked, 'Would you like the women to be able to carry on their business without harassment or would you like the Government to stop prostitution?'

She thought for a while and said, 'Neither! I can't say that sex workers should carry on their profession because that would mean I'm condoning the sex trade and saying it should be promoted. I can't say that. I do not believe it's just another profession. Prostitution exploits women, whether through direct pressure or socialization, just like pornography does. You can argue that women do it by choice and are paid well, but we shouldn't take that narrow view. In the larger picture, it is abuse of women and using women to reinforce the concept of 'women as sex objects.' But at the same time what the government is doing through the police is wrong. There should be some kind of a rehabilitation programme or something.'

Then she asked me, 'You're doing research on them. I hope you will be able to do something directly for them.'

'I'm not sure what I intend to do,' I hesitated, 'I don't think we need to do something with them. I think we need to do something with us. Anyway, my thoughts are not yet clear about the intervention stage. You're right that harassment by the management and police must be addressed and I can bring that to light.'

Her husband, Amir, also a human rights activist, interjected, 'People as well as the Government think human rights are only for "good" people. Deviants and "bad" people have no rights. To establish some rights for prisoners has taken us years. The common attitude of lawyers, judges, jail authorities and other relevant officials was that since they're criminals, they have no rights. Many responsible people think my organization is wasting its time by fighting for the rights of the prisoners.'

My cousin Faiza was accompanying me on this visit, and she spoke up in an irritated manner, 'We can't look at prostitutes only as workers like other workers in the trades. That seems too narrow to me. Yes, I understand that's how they earn money and it's their choice and they can pay taxes and make money for the Government as well but that's not all. Just like pornography, it has an abusive side to it.'

I asked Amir what he thought about the rights of a sex worker. He said, 'I'm not saying she should be completely free to practice prostitution, but it's an issue the society has to think about collectively. I would insist that a prostitute, like any other woman in our society, has the right to dignity and safety. No one has the right to humiliate her, beat her, rape or harass her, be it her pimp, her manager, her customer or a police officer. Government policy is very muddled. On the one hand they harass people showing that they want to stop the sex trade, and on the other hand they support it by being clients. No wonder it's spreading like wildfire.'

# 25

# MITI KHANIAN

I was at *Ustad* Sadiq's *baithak* listening to some new compositions by a recently formed music group that called themselves a 'modern band'. They had guitars, a synthesizer and a drum set. They were very excited about their innovations, especially the drum set, a dramatic addition. Most new groups used synthesizers for the rhythm. These guys had big plans to perform at weddings and other parties.

Suddenly, a loud commotion erupted in the inner courtyard of the old building where Pami's family lived. I thought a fight had broken out, and could hear women yelling and screaming at each other. I could hardly hear the music anymore, over the noise created by the neighbours. Excusing myself, I went out into the courtyard. A crowd of at least a dozen women and men were standing in the courtyard and more, mostly women and children, were on the upper balcony surrounding it. The two main players in the fight seemed to be Pami's mother and another woman I didn't recognize. In her forties, she had a dark complexion with sharp facial features and she held a cigarette in her hand. Among those standing around, I recognized Pami's younger sister, Razia, and a neighbour who lived next door on the same floor.

The fight got louder and louder. Before I could understand what it was all about, Pami's mother, standing in the middle of the courtyard like a wrestler in the middle of the ring, quickly bent down, picked up a small stool and threw it at her opponent, who was standing by a big water drum. It hit her shoulder and broke against the drum. My heart sank in the sudden silence, as the audience went quiet waiting to see what would happen next.

The woman began screaming and crying. She swore violently at Pami's mother, who, wasting no time, picked up whatever came to hand—a broom, a tong, a slipper—and threw them at the woman as she desperately sought refuge behind the water drum.

People ran forward and tried to grab Pami's mother's hands. She had planted herself firmly on the ground and shrugged off whoever came near. The shouting got louder and the swearing more complex. Everyone shouted, either condemning Pami's mother and telling her to stop or telling the other woman to go away. I stood against a wall, not sure what to do. Having no clue about what was happening, I thought it better to remain a spectator. I could hear Pami's mother screaming, '*miti khani, gashti, mein ede te trs khani aan, e minu char gai e*' (mud eater, whore, I feel sorry for her and she cheats me). One expletive she kept shouting was '*War pande wich*', I later learned means 'Return to your mother's uterus'.

I was hoping the other woman would run away or hide, but to my surprise, she suddenly screamed, ran towards Pami's mother and threw herself at her. Like a bullet hitting a tank, she couldn't move her even an inch, but literally made a dent in her. She pulled Pami's mother's hair and hit her. About five or six people surrounded them and pulled the woman back. Her shoulder was bleeding. It wasn't broken, but must have hurt badly. Finally, people succeeded in separating the two fighters. Both had let out enough steam. A few women took the other one aside and made her sit on a *charpai*. Another brought a wet cloth and put it on the wound. The other group sat Pami's mother on another *charpai* and told her to cool down.

The audience had grown to about twenty-five adults and over a dozen children. Every newcomer started by asking what happened. Someone would give a half-sentence answer, and the newcomer would start commenting on the whole situation, even giving advice to the fighters. By now I understood that the other woman was Rani, a street prostitute who had problems with Pami's mother because she failed to pay her rent. I remembered that Pami's mother kept a room for poorer prostitutes to rent when they had a customer.

It must have been around four in the afternoon, and I was confused because these women hardly do business during the day. I stood as still as a piece of furniture, not wanting to get involved.

Pami's sister, Razia, brought a hand fan and started fanning her mother to give her some air. Other than the chirping of the audience, both sides were quiet. A man in his seventies pointed to all the children watching with delight, and said, 'Look at all these children watching you. Have you no shame, using such vulgar language.' As he turned around to walk away, a slipper came flying and hit his back. He jumped with surprise. A loud voice shouted, 'Who are you to interfere, her pimp or her lover? Bastard!' The old man held his ears with his hands and quickly ran to the stairs, mumbling *'gashtian, gashtian, gashtian'*. He didn't look back.

Now that the fighters had caught their breath, Pami's mother started yelling, 'She lied to me. She tricked me. I have been so good to her for the past many years.'

Crying, Rani said, 'That bastard lied to you.'

'Shut up you *Bhutni de* (daughter of a witch)!' screamed Pami's mother.

People told Rani to keep quiet. Pami's mother, straightening her hair with her hands, began to speak in a normal voice, 'People have no fear of God any more.' She looked at Razia, who was obediently fanning her to dry her sweat. Giving her a strange look she pushed her away and said, 'Stop it! Why are you standing on my head?' Razia fell back on the *charpai*, a confused look on her face.

Shakoora, a musician who belonged to the band, said, 'Let's go back. The show is over. Before this buffalo starts hitting other people standing around, let's get out.' We made our way through the thinning crowd back to the *baithak*. The *Ustad* was sitting there. He smiled and asked, 'So, how did you like our entertainment channel?' I couldn't laugh about the situation and commented, 'You didn't go out to see it for yourself.'

He laughed, 'No, the audio was enough for me. I wasn't interested in the video. I know them both well and believe me,

I didn't need the video.' He became serious and said, 'I knew it was coming. I know what happened. Pami's mother had been grumbling about it for hours. I knew the minute she saw Rani today she would blow her top. She occasionally rents out this room to Rani. She rents her room to these streetwalkers we call *miti khanian*. They are the trash among the prostitutes. Do you understand what I am saying?'

I said, 'Go on. I'm listening.'

He continued, 'These women are supposed to pay her 10 per cent of what they make. She gives them the room for, lets say, half an hour.'

One of the musicians spoke up meekly, 'Ten minutes is what they get.'

'Shut up!' the *Ustad* said to him, and someone giggled. 'Don't interrupt me. So Rani is supposed to pay 10 per cent of what she gets from her customer. If she is lucky, she gets one or two customers. Some days she doesn't get any. Last night, she had a customer who cheated her.'

'What do you mean?' I asked.

'He agreed to give her a hundred rupees but only paid her ten when he left. She argued, but he said if she uttered a word of complaint he'd turn her in. Pami's mother got one rupee, which upset her. Today, she complained to other people and someone told her that the deal was for a hundred. Apparently, someone heard them at the corner right outside the courtyard. Pami's mother had been waiting for the last two hours for Rani to enter the compound. Oh! She is vicious.'

One of the musicians turned his synthesizer on. The *Ustad* looked at him, 'No, not that piece,' he said, 'start with the one we agreed to use in our performance.' This comment from the *Ustad* signalled that the fight break was over and we were back into the rehearsal mode. I couldn't stay long, as my mind was still on Rani. This whole fight was over nine rupees! I felt sure Pami's mother would know about customers ditching prostitutes, and wondered why she didn't trust her.

Prostitutes like Rani mainly lived in an area called Tibbi. With narrow streets and small, dark rooms, Tibbi was known for this 'low' class of prostitutes, where a man could find sex for anywhere between ten rupees to two hundred. No singing or dancing was involved; so the customers got straight to the point. One of the main streets of this area was called Tibbi Gali.

My first visit there was very strange. Standing at one end of the Gali looking in, I could feel 'death' in the air. Hardly anyone was around, as though a tornado had torn through the place leaving it totally abandoned. It was not that people didn't live there. Worn out pieces of cloth covered the doors, but there was hardly any movement. I was jolted by the crisp heavy voice of a police officer behind me. He told me they had strict orders not to allow anybody into this area, and, therefore, I could not enter. I argued politely, saying I was certainly not a customer, so why should I be stopped. Not knowing who I was, they allowed me to pass, but told me, strictly, not to talk to anyone.

I walked slowly through the Gali, looking around at the houses. The rooms were tiny. In one doorway, I saw a very old woman, around eighty years old. Quite fat, she was pale and her grey hair seemed not to have been washed for months. The room was smelly and empty, except for a torn piece of cloth under her. Sitting with her back against the wall and her legs stretched out in front of her on the floor, she was bent over her legs and her body was swaying as if she was very sick.

Ayub Khan (1958-68) banned prostitution in the Tibbi area during his reform movement and placed severe restrictions on activities in the Shahi Mohalla. Prostitutes were uprooted from the area; consequently, they moved out and spread all over the city. There was a public outcry and the Government decision had to be reversed, so people of the red light district were allowed to come back. The musicians and dancers were recognized as artists and told they could only perform at designated times. Tibbi Gali, offering no performing arts, could never reopen for the business of prostitution. Every regime in Pakistan after Ayub Khan's retained this policy, and the police enforced it strictly during General Ziaul Haq's regime (1977-88).

Women who were up-rooted from Tibbi had no place to go, except to hide out in small rooms of big buildings here and there. The sex trade still operates in the Tibbi area, but on a lesser scale and in secrecy.

A distinct social hierarchy still exists among the prostitutes themselves. The most beautiful rarely stay long in the Mohalla, being picked up early in their careers to become wives or mistresses. If they remain in the profession, they serve a special class of customers like Arab sheikhs and high-level politicians, typically setting up house in Gulberg or another expensive locality. They carry out much of their business at home, but sometimes maintain a *kotha* in the Mohalla also. They drive into the Mohalla in the latest cars around eleven at night, just in time to open their *affis*. The *kotha* also serves as their public relations office, where they maintain their contacts with a specific clientele and others involved in the business.

This category can be considered as class 'A' prostitutes. They learn to play high level games and generally have a few rich customers who can afford their demands. Some are well educated, and others succeed because of their beauty and mastery of their trade. Prostitutes of this category enjoy more freedom and control over their income than their other colleagues in the Mohalla. Those who join the world of film stars enjoy wealth as well as fame. They provide sexual services only to exclusive customers. Some continue to work to get better contracts and bigger roles in the movies. Their managers, mothers or aunts, cling to them and struggle to maintain control over their careers and personal lives. If they enter films at a fairly high level, as real actresses, they develop quickly, both personally and socially, and move way beyond the world of the Mohalla. They leave the family occupation and enter an elite segment of society. In addition to success in their careers as movie stars, they usually aspire to marry a successful director, an actor or some influential film personality.

Some continue to perform *mujra* even after breaking into films because their popularity enables them to greatly increase their fees. According to some, they can make as much in one night from a *mujra* than from all the proceeds from a film. Others consider it distasteful to continue with *mujra* after achieving such a level of social respect which they value as more important than money.

The second or 'B' category, consists of prostitutes who live in the Mohalla and run the traditional *kothas*. 'B' class prostitutes are the Mohalla's middle class. They hang on to their traditions, no matter how diluted at present. They maintain their *kothas* and perform regularly every evening from 11 p.m. to 1 a.m. This is the category I knew best. They have suffered the most from Government's reform efforts over the years, and most importantly, from selective enforcement of these reforms by the police. They are the most stigmatised, their connection to the sex trade being quite visible and up front.

Almost all prostitutes start off here; some move on to 'better and brighter futures' and others spend their lives wishing and hoping to. This can be considered a transitory category for women who eventually move up to 'A' or later down to the 'C' category. Most prostitutes, however, remain in the 'B' category throughout their lives.

The third category includes women who started out as 'B' class prostitutes, but failed to maintain a proper *kotha* due to financial problems. It included those who couldn't take care of their old age by training and 'possessing' a younger prostitute or at least owning some property in the Mohalla. They are reviled because they were considered failures in their profession. They are forced, by economic circumstances, to drop all the traditional refinements of music, dancing, appropriate dress and nicely decorated spaces. They end up surviving through prostitution alone until they die.

Those who work in the Tibbi Gali and in other dark alleys just stand outside their rooms in the evenings. If they snare a customer, they take him inside immediately. The rooms are dimly lit so the customers can't see the faces and bodies of the women clearly. These women know well the ageing process and the loss of their youth. Heavy make-up covers their wrinkled faces. Balls of wool stuffed in their blouse make their breasts

look firm. They undress only enough for the customer to satisfy
himself, usually keeping their *kamiz* on. If achieving 'A' level
status is a dream for all prostitutes, falling down to the 'C' level
is their greatest fear. Whoever knows some art of the business
tries to ensure that before exhausting her limited youth she
makes a smooth move to the management level.

Rani was one such prostitute. Forty years old, she looked
more like fifty, with dark circles around her eyes and wrinkles
on her skin as though she'd been badly burnt. Born in a village
in rural Punjab, Rani was fourteen when she fell in love with a
young man who came to her village with a theatre company.
Rafiq was about twenty-two years old at the time. His work was
not very clear; he neither acted nor sang. Not even a skilled
worker or labourer, he did odd jobs like getting food from the
market for the other performers. He had two female relatives
working in the company as dancers. They were from Lahore's
Shahi Mohalla. He played the role of chaperone for them. He'd
grown up in the Mohalla and was well aware of the sex trade.
He knew women could make a reasonable living. He was clearly
on his way to becoming a pimp.

He met this beautiful young girl in the market with a group
of her girlfriends. The theatre stayed in her village for only four
days. He fell in love with her young and innocent face, and
being quite bold, found an opportunity to talk to her. Rani
believes he cast a spell on her. He was like a hero in her
fantasies: a romantic hero who promised a world full of
happiness and adventure outside of her suffocating village. She
had often dreamt of going to the city and seeing how people
live in different parts of the world.

Rafiq convinced her that he would steal her away when the
theatre company moved on. With no thought for the
consequences, she agreed. He had caused her to rebel against
her traditions and her family and assured her that no one would
ever find her if she left the village with him. After four days the
company folded its tents and props. As agreed, Rani left with
them very early in the morning, while her family still slept. The
theatre owner discovered the elopement on the way to the next

village and ordered Rafiq to leave the caravan immediately, fearing complications with the police. Sure enough Rani's family soon learned of the kidnapping and chased after the group.

Rafiq and Rani left the theatre company and headed for the city. Rani remembers running through ditches and bushes, getting scratched and fearing capture. She also remembers running a high fever and lying in a broken bed with bugs biting her. She's not sure if that was after she got to the city or somewhere along the way. Her memories remain, but she's lost the sequence of events. Her memories are like beads from a broken necklace, scattered on the floor. They sometimes return in her dreams.

Finally, they did reach a city, but not Lahore. Rafiq never married her, but instead made some quick money selling Rani's virginity to a customer he enticed. From there, he took her to Shahi Mohalla. He managed her for a while, and then she was passed from one pimp to another. At this point, Rani's story becomes a painful mess of tangled threads. Once a customer almost married her, and she was happy to think she could settle down, but just then Rafiq appeared from nowhere. The need for money brings people like him back to their easiest source. Rani was furious and told him he had no claim on her since he'd already sold her many times. Rafiq, however, brought up in the business of buying and selling people, paid no attention, and managed her for four more years. By this time, Rani was old by the standards of her profession, but Rafiq wanted to suck out the last possible drop of her blood.

Obviously, he was not good at his profession, or perhaps had never come to terms with the fact that he was a pimp. He saw pimping as a transitory thing, just to survive. Had he been more stable and seasoned, he would have learned to sustain his business. When he could not get any more money from Rani, he beat her up and left her alone in the Mohalla by herself. She contracted a venereal disease and was very sick, unsure whether or not she would survive. The rent on the room where they'd been living hadn't been paid for six months, and when the landlord found out Rafiq had disappeared, he pressured Rani to pay it.

That night, despite her high fever, she made up her face with whatever she had. Wearing a sheer black *dupatta* that covered half of her face, she dressed in a glittery *shalwar kamiz* and stood quietly outside her room, using all her energy just to remain upright. She doesn't remember how long she stood there before a man walked up and spoke to her. Hardly understanding what he said, she took his arm and pulled him into the room. She did not let him take off her *dupatta*, undressing only as much as was absolutely necessary. She was almost unconscious and had no energy to argue about the rate. At some point she passed out and all she remembers is that when she awoke she found a 100 rupee note on the pillow. She changed clothes, gathered her modest belongings into a bundle and went to see the landlord. She gave him the hundred rupees, telling him it was all she had and that she planned to leave immediately. She also said Rafiq had left her and she had no place to go. The landlord took the room keys, but let her keep the hundred rupees, telling her she was very sick and should get some treatment.

Rani went to a woman she knew who was in her fifties and still eking out a living as a prostitute. She was very poor and lived near the Tibbi Gali. This woman never stood in the street to get a customer, but stayed inside her room peeping out from the curtain, not showing herself fully. She made the deal from behind the curtain and led the customer into her room, lit only by a small oil lamp. She lay down on the bed as soon as the man entered and simply pulled down her *shalwar*. She accepted even five rupees from a customer.

Rani stayed with her and eventually recovered. The woman hardly spoke during the day, and had difficulty moving around. She looked about eighty years old, skinny and trembling. Her head shook constantly. After she got better, Rani helped her out by cooking food sometimes, though they usually bought simple cooked food from the market since it cost less than having their own kitchen set up. Rani started working again. One day she brought home some food and found her friend dead, in a sitting

Prostitutes of the lowest socio-economic status focus on sexual favours only. They do not indulge in singing or dancing

The living conditions of these prostitutes are extremely modest

The state of health and hygiene among street prostitutes is quite poor

These prostitutes live with their families in small quarters and rent a room for business on an hourly ba

position with her body bent over her knees. Rani ran away in fear, catching a bus to Multan. She didn't know anyone there, but couldn't face the situation in her room. She had no idea how long her friend's body remained there and who finally buried her. All this became part of her painful and disjointed memories.

In Multan she stayed a few months and realized that business was even worse than in Lahore. She returned to the Mohalla, but was never sure where she would end up. She had arranged with Pami's mother to pay 10 per cent for every customer she brought to use her room. A relatively clean room boosted her chances of getting regular customers. She earned enough for food and cigarettes, and told me she hoped Pami's mother would not hold this misunderstanding against her so she could continue to rent the room for her customers.

# 26

# A VISIT TO PAMI'S HOUSE

I worried about Rani's situation and a few months after her fight with Pami's mother, I decided to visit Pami's family. Her mother met me affectionately. She was in her usual position, sitting on her *charpai* next to the door of their main room. She had a good view of the courtyard and knew what everyone was doing. Pami and her younger sister were out.

'I never find Pami home,' I remarked, 'I'll miss her this time also.'

'No, they'll both be back soon. They've gone to their *ustad's baithak*.'

'Oh, it's training time?'

'No, they go for their training later. They went because the *ustad* is taking them for a show in Sahiwal and they have to rehearse with the musicians for some new songs.'

'Are they going with the new band that their *ustad* has set up?'

She replied carelessly, 'I don't know what they do. They'll be paying us the same. New or old, what's it to me?'

I thought about talking to her about Rani while we waited for Pami and Razia. I started out by asking if there were many streetwalkers in the Mohalla. 'Yes,' she answered, 'but they should go work somewhere else. This area is for prostitutes who perform, sing and dance. These *miti khanian* have nothing, and only attract the police. I used to feel sorry for them, but now I feel they've spoiled our business too.'

She called her youngest son, who was playing hide and seek in the courtyard with her youngest daughter, Soni. In a *kurta* and underpants, he was running around barefoot. He ran to his mother and stopped at the door to hide, too shy to come near me. 'Go give this money to Masi Shidan and tell her....' Untying money from the corner of her *dupatta*, she counted it and realized that it wasn't enough. She got up and said, '*Os gashti nu kain* (tell that prostitute) I am sending the rent on time, so I don't want to hear any nagging.' The child giggled as she opened a big suitcase and bent over it, looking for money. She brought the money and put it in his hand. Suddenly, thinking of something else, she said, 'Wait, I'll send your elder sister.' She turned to me and excused herself. 'I have to take care of this first.'

She called her other daughter who was younger than Pami, and was already a working prostitute. She told her to take the money and go to the landlady's house, throw the money at her face and tell her that Pami's family pays the rent and wasn't living in the house for free. The girl looked at me, embarrassed as her mother strung a long strand of swear words in the landlady's honour. I smiled back.

Soni ran up and asked her mother if she could go, too. She laughed, putting her hand in front of her mouth, and shrugged her shoulders. Her mother swore at her and told her to stay home. Disappointed, Soni made a long face and went back in the courtyard, but would not resume playing with her brother. Soni was about ten years old, with an innocent face and a charming smile. She had beautiful sharp features and a fair complexion. Her hair had a reddish tone, making her exceptionally beautiful. She seemed to be a happy child, but didn't like her mother scolding her in my presence. Pami's mother came back to her *charpai* and sat down. Getting up, going to the suitcase and coming back exhausted her. She was breathing heavily and yelled at Soni to bring her a glass of water. Soni rushed to the tap with an aluminium cup, afraid if she took any longer, she'd be scolded again. She brought the water and stood close by as her mother gulped it down. Soni inspected me for a moment with a lovely smile and shrugged her shoulders.

As Pami's mother relaxed, I asked her about Rani. 'Has Rani been back to use your room here? She doesn't seem to have much business.'

Totally ignoring that I had witnessed her fight with Rani, she replied, 'Yes, she comes once in a while and I let her use the room, but I've heard she's located cheaper room on the other side of the bazaar. I charge 10 per cent. Do you think that is much? What must these *miti khanian* make for me to earn anything? Just keeping the room available and clean costs money. Everybody has to survive.'

I said, 'If she comes by, give her my regards and tell her I'd like to see her. She doesn't have a contact address so I couldn't get in touch with her lately.'

'Why do you need an address? She roams the streets here every night, trying to dodge the police,' she answered, looking away from me.

After talking a while longer, I went into the courtyard. Soni was still pouting, sitting on a low stool close to her sister, who was cooking. I sat on a *charpai*, in the courtyard and called Soni over. She hesitated at first but then came. 'Do you have an *ustad* yet?' I asked.

She nodded vigorously, 'Yes, of course. I go to the same *ustad* as my sisters. I'm his good student. My sisters often miss their lesson, but I never do. My *ustad* tells me that I'm a good student.' She shrugged her shoulders like a small child.

I asked, 'Do you go with Pami?'

She said, 'No, the class for younger children is earlier. We are six in my class. Today we have no class. *Ustad* has to do a show tonight so he's getting ready. We're off tomorrow too.'

'Why tomorrow?' I asked.

She threw her head back laughing and clapped her hands in front of her. With a naughty smile she explained, 'If he's given us off to prepare for a show, how can he teach us when he's doing the show, especially in another city?'

I laughed too, and asked if she went to school.

'I did fourth grade and my father said that was enough. Do you want to hear about my school and my teachers?'

Before I could answer, her mother yelled, 'Soni, why are you bothering Fouzia?'

I answered quickly, 'Could Soni go to the *baithak* of Pami's *ustad* and find out whether she will be coming soon? Is that okay with you?'

She agreed and Soni jumped up. With one hand she pulled up her *shalwar*, a little long for her, and she stretched her other arm to wrap one end of her *dupatta* tightly around her neck to keep it out of her way. She ran away quickly.

I came back to Pami's mother. She was staring into space. 'I hear you're planning to marry off Razia now,' I said.

'Who told you?' she asked in surprise.

'I just heard it around here. Is it supposed to be a secret?'

She relaxed, 'It's no secret. Her father has been keen to arrange this for a while now, but I don't like some of the men he's brought around. I don't do business with people who have recently become rich. They're not trustworthy. I'll only agree to an offer that satisfies me no matter what my husband says.'

'Is he the father of these girls?' I asked.

'You have been working here for so long. Let's not get into who is a father of whom, okay.'

I was embarrassed and tried to cover myself by asking, 'I mean, did you marry him?'

'I don't talk about him with anyone,' she said. 'He is one of a kind. You've probably heard bad things about him from other people, but he's not such a bad man. He was a customer of my cousin and he started helping me to manage my girls. It's not easy to handle this business, especially without even a *kotha* of your own. I rent these back rooms and have to make such an effort to get business. Anyway, these are our problems.'

I let her talk uninterrupted. I knew she never talked about her husband with anyone. People knew only that he was a pimp, a drug addict and a nasty person. I'd met no one who was his friend. His circle of acquaintances seemed to be outside the Mohalla, among other pimps.

She continued, 'Getting good customers for Pami was a challenge. All *dalle* want to become full partners in deals they arrange rather than just taking an agent's commission. That's not possible. I thought it was better to have him around to help me out. He's not a bad man.'

Just then Soni entered, totally exhausted from running, but happy as she had been able to carry out my bidding. She told me they'd left the *baithak* and were coming home. When Pami and her sister Razia came in, I went to talk to them in the courtyard. Their mother swore in an undertone, no doubt meaning they took too long to return home. Chatting with Pami and Razia, I noticed how very excited Soni was, how she wanted to participate in everything. She was so happy I'd given her a task, and hyped up since she'd succeeded.

I bent towards Razia and said in a low voice, 'I heard a lot of praise for you from Ruba. He told me you sing very beautifully.' She blushed, and Soni laughed out loud. She quickly leaned over me and whispered, 'Baji, he sends her letters on small pieces of paper.'

Razia hit Soni with her hand and said, '*Bukwas!*' (Rubbish)

Soni shrugged her shoulders, giggled and said to me, 'Baji, *Qasme* (I swear)! I brought her the letters and now she hits me. Ruba said mother shouldn't find out.'

'So, Ruba has made progress,' I said. Razia lowered her gaze and smiled. She was quite happy with the idea. Since the issue was so sensitive I decided to drop it then, but planned to ask Pami later what she thought the consequences could be for Razia.

When we did talk about it, Pami told me her parents suspected that Razia was in love. 'They are not sure, but my father has noticed Ruba's frequent short visits in the building.' She mentioned frequent arguments in their house about Razia's *nath*. Her father brings messages from customers who make very low offers, knowing he needs cash for his drugs. In one case, a pimp wanted to make a deal, but later arranged another young prostitute for the same customer. Her mother was angry with her husband for spoiling the deal.

Pami went on, 'My mother is furious with him for all this, but doesn't have her own contacts. Police harassment has really

forced her into the house. She says the only businesses that
flourish are those in contact with pimps outside the Mohalla.
After that guy moved in with us a few years ago, she stopped
dealing with pimps directly. He took over most of the dealing.'

Pami was not very happy with her mother's partner and
surprised that her mother listened to him. Her mother told her it
was the price they had to pay to stay in the area. Pami really
didn't want to talk much about management affairs, which she
thought were not her business, but she'd already told me a lot.

# 27

# RAT JAGA

Over time, I'd become quite involved with several families other than Laila's. Chanda and I had begun discussing my findings about Mohalla life. Anxious to know what I found in my interviews, she was especially interested in issues like police harassment, Government's blind spot to the music and dance aspect of the society and the decline in the number and quality of customers. I enjoyed talking to her; she was not merely an informant, but also a good help in thinking things through.

Chanda had organized a celebration to announce her 'brother's' renewed health with a traditional *Rat Jaga*. A man she considered a brother had regained his health after a long illness. This would be a private gathering although these were rare within the Mohalla and I wanted to be there. On the chosen evening, I stopped by *Ustad* Gaman's *baithak* at about 8 o'clock and found everyone in a high state of excitement. Four musicians were moving around, here and there, looking for one thing or the other. The artists were preparing for the big gathering. *Rat Jaga* comes from the words *raat*, night and *jagna*, to be awake, and means staying up all night and celebrating.

I moved on to *Ustad* Sadiq's *baithak* to find out if he was going. He said he was looking forward to it, in fact as one of her *ustads* he was obligated to go. Chanda had sought special permission from the administration for this party and the police were informed in advance. I planned to go with *Ustad* Sadiq.

When we reached Chanda's place at about 11 o'clock, the music had already begun and about twenty guests had already arrived. The main living room had been turned into a party room, with all the furniture and the floor coverings taken out.

The pop band had been set up on one side of the room, a beautiful red drum dominating everything. A few chairs remained on the sides but most people were standing or walking around. Two musicians were playing loud electric guitars, possibly to announce that the party had begun. The drum set and the bongos were still untouched.

All the women were dressed in brocades and silks and the men wore silky *shalwar kamiz*, the bright colours and glitter giving the room a baroque touch. Not one man in the room wore western pants, which anyway are very uncommon among the Mohalla's men and in the old city as a whole. Only young men who find work with film studios as dance directors, assistants or stunt men wear them to distinguish themselves from the other men in the Mohalla. Small girls were dressed up in bright *shalwar kamiz*, fully made-up with small *bindiya* pasted in the middle of their foreheads. These *bindiya* are a direct influence of Indian films, where most of the Indian actresses wear them. I noticed heavy blue and green eye shadow on their eyes. Looking at so many little girls, I knew that in the future the Mohalla would be full of many new performers.

Chanda was very happy, busy greeting her family and friends. *Ustad* Sadiq told me that the only customers invited were those who had become family friends. I made sure to greet her mother, with whom I wanted to develop a good relationship.

The music started with a bang, and a very handsome young man began to sing. He sang modern Indian Punjabi songs made famous by musical groups mostly working in England. The songs were very popular in Pakistan. His singing voice was extraordinary, and after a few songs the dancing began. The gathering grew by the minute, and people were now spilling out onto the veranda and into the courtyard. Chanda was the first to jump in the middle of the gathering to dance, and other women soon joined her. Unlike their evening performance, this was more like our weddings, where dancing is for people to express their happiness and not a performance for an audience. Chanda pulled her 'brother' into the middle and people started throwing money at him as well as at the women who were dancing.

Chanda and her elder sisters kept pulling people to dance with them in the middle of the, by now, very crowded room.

People started placing money on each other's heads, and a small boy who was part of the band collected what fell to the ground. Giving away money like that showed affection and generosity to the host and to the one on whose head you place the money. Many friends and family members placed money on Chanda and her sister's heads. To add to the excitement, every once in a while, people took a stack of small bills and threw it up in the air with a jerk of their hand. The rupee notes rained down all over the room. Sometimes people took a stack of notes and threw them one by one on somebody's head. As is traditional, all this money would go to the musicians of the pop band.

The celebration continued and at 1 a.m. another wave of guests began to arrive—women who had been in their *affis* from eleven to one. Chanda received them, complaining, 'You misers, couldn't you miss one day of work for me? My real friends didn't open their *kothas* today.' Some women apologized in embarrassment, while others shouted, 'But we're not as rich as you are!' I stayed until about 2 o'clock. The singing, dancing and showers of money hadn't stopped for a second. *Ustad* Sadiq told me they'd soon break for food, but I told him food didn't interest me at all. I'd seen what I came for.

A few days later I went to Chanda to thank her for inviting me to the party. We talked for a long time. Her mother was out and her sister was preparing to go on a job with a Member of Parliament. At one point I praised the singer from the *Rat Jaga*, saying how exceptional he had been. To my great surprise, Chanda started to cry and no matter how much I cajoled her, she wouldn't tell me what was wrong. Her sister turned from her dressing table and said, carelessly, 'Let her cry, what else can she do? *Os Mirasi nal phasi e* (she is stuck with that Mirasi)'.

'He's not *Mirasi*, he's a *Kanjar*!' Chanda yelled.

'Big deal, that's even worse. Look at her correcting me! She's fallen into shit. Dog shit or horseshit, what's the difference? It's still shit! tell her to come to her senses, Fouzia. She's giving us all a bad name.' She jerked her head back around and started painting her face again.

Chanda had now begun to sob loudly. I offered her a glass of water, to help her get under control. She said, 'Isn't he good-looking, though?'

'Hai,' exclaimed her sister, laughing derisively.

Chanda asked, 'Fouzia, how can you control your heart? If you fall in love, you fall in love. Did you see the *kurta* he was wearing?' I had it made for him. He looked so handsome in it.'

'Chanda, what are you going to do? 'I empathized with her.

'I want to spend my life worshipping him. He's my *devata*.' She sighed.

'*Bakwas na ker...gashti* (don't talk rubbish...you whore) ...*devata*, my foot!' her sister shouted angrily.

Falling in love was bad and always disapproved; falling for someone from their own *biradri* was as bad as falling in love with a *Mirasi*. I felt sorry for Chanda and asked her 'What does he think about this?'

'He's helpless!' she sobbed, more tears rolling down her cheeks.

Her sister stood up and turned to us, 'Helpless, no way! He's having a hard time getting rid of her. She's the one who can't control her heart.'

'Don't say that. It hurts. Please!' moaned Chanda, now weeping.

'Our mother should have strangled her by now. She's left her alone only because she knows he's not serious about taking her away. She's my kid sister and I love her, Fouzia, but she's making the whole family her enemy and is getting a bad name in the *biradri*. She's burning up my mother's blood, and mother is a heart patient, you know. For what? For a guy who doesn't give a shit about her.'

'That's not true. He does care for me and the real thing is that I love him. I love him!', she cried loudly and lay down on the bed. 'It hurts so much I can't take it. I can't leave him. No

matter what my mother or my family say. I'm in love with him.
I'll kill myself.'

'It's worth dying for someone who loves you or at least
realizes the worth of your love,' yelled her sister.

'How long have you known him?' I asked Chanda.

'Three years. He loved me a lot right from the beginning. He
was young,' she answered.

Her sister interrupted, 'Yes, she was twenty-two and he was
only seventeen. He was young, so she initiated him into sex.
She liked his innocence and he liked her experience. Now he's
become very experienced. He's good-looking; he can have any
woman he wants. I don't think he got into a relationship with
Chanda thinking it would be the love of his lifetime. That's
why we're forbidden any such link with a man of our *biradri* or
the *Mirasi biradri*. I told her right from the start. 'Sweetheart,'
I said, 'don't moon over this relationship. It's prohibited and
will only bring you pain.' He has his career. He's a great singer.
He wants to go out in the world and take his chances. Let's face
it, how many *Kanjar* men have talent? He has a right to try his
luck in the world.'

'I'd support him all the way,' Chanda sniffled.

'No, Chanda, you'd only drag him down. He won't be able to
go anywhere with a twenty-five-year-old woman from his own
*biradri* hanging on his neck. I'm your sister so I'm honest with
you. What was between you two is over. He told you the same
thing yesterday, for what, the fifth time? He wants to go ahead
in life and you've become the chain around his ankles,' she
said.

Chanda looked at me with tears still rolling down her cheeks.
'My *ustad* used to say, *ya kese nu apna kar lo, ya fir app kese
de ho jao* (either you make someone yours or you become
someone else's). These are the only two roads to true love. If
I can't make him mine, I'll give myself to him.'

A few months later I heard that the handsome singer had
moved to Karachi to sing with a band there. Chanda attempted
suicide, creating a big uproar in the *biradri*. Her family saved
her and, in her own words she continued living, 'like a corpse'.

Other friends told me Chanda gained a strange kind of a power
after she emerged from this trauma. I had a similar feeling. She
became less talkative and more reflective about her situation.
I gave her time to recover, visiting occasionally and talking
about many things, but not specifically about my findings. Not
until I started to analyse my data did I resume my discussion
sessions with her.

# 28

## RAZIA AND SONI

*Ustad* Gaman announced that he was going to cook lunch for all of his music students. Pleased at receiving a contract to compose two film songs, he wanted to treat everyone at the *baithak*, and he invited me as well. We gathered at about one in the afternoon. When I reached his *baithak*, Jaji, Amjad and four of his other students were already there. Several of them actually lived in his *baithak*. These *ustads* have generous hearts when it comes to sharing their living space and food. *Ustad* Gaman enjoyed a good reputation as an artist and actively supported other artists in the making. He always said, 'Our job is to work hard; it's up to Him to give us *rozi*.'

Gaman had a friend who'd succeeded in the film industry and was trying to bring him in also. His friend played the *tabla* and worked closely with one particular composer. The composer friend was a famous composer's son and thus had good connections in the industry. The *tabla* player had been asking him to give Gaman a chance. After three years, he'd finally managed to convince his boss to hear some of Gaman's work. The composer had too many films at hand so when a new contract came up, he decided to sub-contract two songs to Gaman as a trial, a good opportunity for Gaman to prove his worth.

The air was filled with the fragrance of food. The *ustad* was cooking everything himself, although usually one of his students cooked. These were his male students. Since his female students came from families of prostitutes, he wasn't as close to them. He believed that the dancers had given up on music; his hopes for the future were the young men from the *Mirasi* families.

*Ustad* Gaman came to his *baithak* door where I was busy talking and gossiping with Jaji and Amjad. Jaji was grumbling on and on, at the same time joking about the police. He was telling me about recent deals the police had made with a few families to receive bribes in return for less harassment. I sometimes got good leads to investigate further from his stories, but the way he joked about everything; I never knew what to take seriously. I did notice, however, that when I asked about Ruba he turned quite serious and abruptly changed the topic. Later, I cornered him and asked, 'Why isn't Ruba here? He's *ustad's* most cherished student, isn't he?'

Jaji said, 'He's gone out of town, and please do not ask me why. I'm his friend and can't talk about it, okay?'

Being away was enough reason to satisfy me. I didn't care why. They all travelled frequently between the different Punjab towns.

Jaji asked me why, earlier, I'd asked a musician about *hijras* or transvestites. He'd found that very amusing. 'Your research is about music, right, about us, so what's it have to do with *hijras*?'

The others who were sitting around laughed, and someone yelled, 'Because some of us are like *hijras*!' Loud laughter echoed in the room.

Before they could start their typical humiliating, slapstick jokes about transvestites, I explained what I was doing, 'My research is about this area and the people who live here. Most of them are *Kanjar* or other people in the sex trade; there are *Mirasi*, musicians like you all, and of course business people with shops in the markets. In addition to all that, a population of transvestites is a part of your community. You can acknowledge them or disown them, whatever, but they are part of your community.'

*Ustad* Gaman, listening to me from the other room where he was finishing up his gourmet feast, called loudly, 'Are you serious, you're studying them too?' Before I could answer he came to the door with a wooden spoon in his hand and looked at me with surprise.

'Well, I should,' I said. 'They do live here, but I may choose not to since their system and social hierarchy is so complex it

could require a full-fledged study of its own. Just doing an
overview with limited information may not do them justice.'

The discussion ended there as two junior students spread a
piece of blue and white chequered plastic on the floor and laid
out plastic plates in front of everybody. They brought two
glasses and some aluminium cups. I knew the glasses were for
me and the *ustad* while everyone else would use aluminium.
Someone got me a bottle of Coke wrapped in a tissue and
another put a big pile of *roti* wrapped in a big cloth down in
front of me. Everyone sat around waiting for the *ustad* to signal
that his dish was ready. After a while, the students started joking
that *ustad* had burnt the food and had begun all over again.
Another laughed that he had actually sent someone to the *Phaja*
Restaurant to replace his pot. Just then, *ustad* came in with his
big pot in hand and said, '*bakwas karn to baz na ana* (Won't
you stop your rubbish)'. Everyone shouted with delight.

*Ustad* put this pot of chicken curry in the middle and I was
invited to start eating. *Ustad* said to me, 'This is a *desi* chicken.
It tastes different than the city rubbish other people eat, that
*waleti kukri* (western chicken)'. *Mirasis* have a well-known
passion for traditional food, and very specific tastes. They prefer
local eggs, local chicken and locally made purified butter, called
*desi ghee*. When they work out of town, many high calibre
singers have been known to give their hosts a hard time with
their specific food demands. In their homes, they make sure
their servants never buy the ordinary chicken or eggs available
in the market.

As everyone plunged energetically into eating, I asked, '*Ustad* ji,
why didn't you invite Pami and Razia. They're also your students.'
*Ustad*, who was smiling broadly, suddenly became serious.
Everyone stopped eating and looked at me. I felt I'd said something
very wrong, but not understanding what, I smiled in embarrassment and went on, 'Or was this only for your male students?'

They all looked at each other. *Ustad* exchanged looks with Jaji
and then looked at me and asked, 'You don't know about Razia?'

'I've just now come from Islamabad, straight to your *baithak*,'
I answered. 'I've not seen anyone else yet. What happened?'

The expressions on their faces worried me, but I couldn't think of anything bad that could have happened to her. I pleaded, 'Will you please tell me what happened?'

*Ustad* said, 'Pami's father was arranging for Razia's marriage...'

'I know that and also that her mother wasn't happy with the deals he was coming up with, but then what?'

*Ustad* lowered his head and said, 'Razia ran away with Ruba two days ago and...and... last night Pami's father sold Soni's virginity to a customer he was pursuing for Razia.'

'What!' I shrieked. 'But Soni is hardly...hardly...'

'Yes, she was only ten and hadn't yet reached puberty, but that son of a bitch needed money for his drugs. He sold his baby daughter's first night for only 10,000 rupees.'

Everybody had stopped eating. *Ustad* hung his head down. He said, 'I feel terrible. Soni had a lot of potential. He could have been patient and Soni would have earned him a lot. She had a good chance in films. Even for her *nath* he'd have gotten three times more, but you have to let a flower bloom.'

'How could her mother let this happen?' I wailed.

*Ustad* said, 'She shows her power only to her neighbours, fighting around with them, like a lion in a cage. She sold her freedom to that bastard pimp. Now the son of a bitch is calling all the shots. This happens when the *dalle* take over the management. They're butchers who only want money. They think short term. He did a bad thing to Soni, to the family and to himself as well.'

'What about Ruba?' I asked.

'Razia's father has registered a police report and the police are looking for them. I'm ashamed of Ruba. He shouldn't have done that. He's put himself and Razia into real danger. Do you think that if the police catch them those wolves will leave her alone? Not at all! First, they'll have their fun, then they'll make Razia's father pay a bribe to get her back and then they'll make Ruba's family pay to get him out of this mess. In the end they'll drop the case.'

'Do you think they'll get caught?'

'I hope not,' *Ustad* raised his head and said, 'May God damn this father! That *dala* did an awful thing. The whole Mohalla is spitting on him, at least those who are in the business by tradition.'

I soon learned more about the whole heartbreaking incident. Pami's father had taken a loan for his drugs and needed to swing a big deal for Razia's virginity. He'd almost finalized the deal, but Razia didn't want to become a prostitute. Ruba easily encouraged her to leave with him. They ran away in the early hours of the morning, and nobody seemed to know where they went. The father wasn't at home when they left so it took the family a while to file a police report.

Such an occasion brings serious social shame on the family. Bad as it is for a budding prostitute to run away, it was thought worse still that Razia ran away with a *Mirasi*. This shame will be remembered for generations. The father was so desperate to get his money that he convinced the customer to take his younger daughter instead. It happened so fast that the neighbours had no chance to say anything or pressure the mother not to let it happen. They only found out the next morning.

Throughout the time I was associated with this family, they never found Ruba or Razia. They might as well have disappeared from the face of this world. Soni, however, didn't have the luxury of disappearing like Razia, and faced the reality of the Mohalla every day. She had grown from child to an adult in a single night. She was forced to start performing in the evenings with her sisters. Although little girls in the Mohalla are well aware of their sexuality, Soni seemed very confused about the tension she experienced in her heart all the time. She was torn between wanting to play with toys and her younger siblings and the requirement that she act like an adult and interact with men. One thing was obvious; she had lost her spark, and retreated into silence.

# 29

# DOWN MEMORY LANE

Something unexpected happened in Laila's family. Bobby, Laila's sister, Jamila's first born, was sent home from London to stay with Laila's family in the Mohalla. She had lived in London from the time she was two months old. Now, suddenly, here she was in Lahore. Bobby was a year older than Laila, and they looked a lot alike, except that Bobby was thinner. Her English was a bit fractured, but had a strong British accent. She had short hair and a pierced nose, with her mysterious looking eyes which were the most attractive of her features. Introverted, Bobby liked to keep her experiences, her sadness and her joys to herself. She was quiet, in stark contrast to her younger sister who called up a customer just to tell him she had a cold.

No news of her return had reached Kaisera before Bobby called to be picked up from the airport and Kaisera wasn't sure how to react. The return of the first-born girl should have been a happy occasion, but it also opened the floodgates of anger, sadness and resentment locked away for many years in Kaisera's heart. Bobby's return brought back sad memories about the days after her father's death. Shamsa, Kaisera's older sister, had a mind of her own and had always been very stubborn. When it came time to manage the *kotha* jointly with her sister, she decided she preferred to part ways. Kaisera remembered that time with a great deal of sadness. Her mother had died before her father, and he had been very close to both daughters. After his death Kaisera badly wanted to join hands with her sister and work for the family's survival. She wanted them to continue where their parents had left off, believing it to be their obligation and part of their training. Shamsa steered her life in a different direction, leaving Kaisera with a feeling of having been ditched, leaving it all to her to keep the business going.

Shamsa had always been more confident than Kaisera. The personality difference was compounded when Shamsa was given the two adopted children by their parents. With Shahid and Kiran, a boy and a girl, she felt more secure than Kaisera about her future. Kaisera remembered the saga of Shamsa's romance with a customer. She didn't want to let go of him. Shamsa was quite young and thought she had found the love of her life. Kaisera knew her sister's lover was lying to her, making false promises and playing on her fantasies. About forty years old, the man had a wife, three children and a joint family business. He could never have risked marrying a prostitute, but no one could make Shamsa see that. He said he was moving to London and apparently even promised to take her there and marry her. Shamsa had imagined herself in that new land too often to give up her fantasy, so even when, just before leaving, he told her he'd neither marry her nor even take her with him, she wouldn't accept the reality. She had dreamt so much about moving away. Rather than recognizing that he'd only been toying with her, she decided to follow him, hoping to at least stay close to him.

She made her move in a planned and confident manner; with the intelligence to know what human resources she'd need for her future. She took with her Shahid, Kiran, and Shahid's daughter, Bobby, her first grandchild—a young man, a fifteen-year-old girl and a newborn child. Her customer did maintain contact with her for a while, and with no other option than establishing herself in her own profession, she asked for help in setting herself up in London's red light district. He actually did give her some assistance before finally disappearing for good. Smart enough to start up in a new place, Shamsa had the required future resources in Kiran, and she felt that she herself was young enough to keep plying her sexual services in England.

Shamsa succeeded in completing the paperwork for resident status in England for herself, Kiran and Bobby, but Shahid's immigration case dragged on for several years. Since he still had a wife in Lahore, while his immigrant status in London was in process, he returned to Pakistan from time to time and helped the family keep growing. His unofficial duty was to produce enough children to secure the family's future, and as a result Jamila got pregnant almost every year. Shamsa over the years took two more children from Jamila to London and formally adopted them as her own.

Shamsa had some hard times at first, but once her business was established she had an array of Asian, as well as British, customers. She maintained good relationships with major figures in organized crime in order to keep her business running smoothly. Some of her customers were criminals and she often didn't charge them for her services, considering this a simple cost of business and assuming she would gain from the relationship in other ways.

It was Shamsa's idea to get Shahid married to a British prostitute to expedite the immigration process. This action eventually got his case rejected. Shamsa blamed Shahid for ruining his case and not being smart enough to handle the situation.

Kiran never really adjusted to the environment, missing her home and friends in the Mohalla. She wasn't very close to the rest of the family, but wanted familiar faces around her. She did work her trade in London, but her heart wasn't in it, and Shamsa feared Kiran would not adjust to the lifestyle she'd planned for her. She tried explaining to Kiran about all her worries as manager in getting the business going, saying that she couldn't cope with Kiran's depression on top of it all. Her half-baked efforts to raise Kiran's spirits and become interested in her work ultimately failed, however, and after Kiran had worked in London for a few years, Shamsa finally decided to send her back to Pakistan. She made it quite clear to every one in the family that Kiran was still her daughter and that only she, Shamsa, could claim her income. Kaisera, she said, would have only the rights and share of a *dairedaar*. Had Kaisera been the only one running the Lahore *kotha*, Shamsa might have hesitated to send Kiran back, but she was sure Shahid would manage Kiran's affairs well.

Kiran came back hoping she'd find her peace in the Mohalla, but she was wrong. She'd spent her childhood here, but now that she was working, she saw that the reality of the prostitutes' lives was quite different. Her childhood memories of playing with friends and watching her mother and aunt dance for customers were far more entertaining than being in front of the customers herself. She couldn't stand how they drooled over her. She was a restless soul searching for peace. She told Kaisera and Shahid that her heart was not in her work but could not tell them what she wanted, not knowing that herself. She only knew she couldn't bear this life.

Despite her misgivings, Kaisera and Shahid arranged her 'wedding' with a customer. Although she'd been working in London, she was new to the Mohalla and Shahid managed to pull off another sale of her virginity. She was given in *mulazmat*, bought by a customer who was willing to pay her a monthly stipend, freeing her from evening performances. She was not comfortable in this role either, however, and it ended after a few months. She started working again soon after the relationship ended. This wasn't difficult because she had a beautiful singing voice, and with a long slender body and long straight black hair, she was more beautiful than the average dancers in the Mohalla.

Kaisera remembered sadly how one customer touched Kiran's heart more than all the others and she fell in love with him. Only then did people around her see her happy. Unfortunately, no *Kanjar* prostitute should ever fall in love and violate the *biradri* tradition. Her act was such a disgrace that it dishonoured the whole family. Kiran wanted to marry the man; son of a jeweller, he was rich enough to take her as a second wife. Kiran took a brave step and left her house for him, telling no one. Her action reduced the whole family to a state of shock and shame. Kaisera remembered those days with great pain, considering it more difficult than coping with her father's death. Death she said was natural, something one could cope with, but Kiran had ruined their reputation, making them ashamed to face the *biradri*.

Kaisera, in her heart of hearts, was happy Kiran got what she wanted. Her sadness, however, was not only because she lost face in the larger family, but also because she believed the man would one day hurt Kiran by ending the relationship. She kept expecting to see Kiran's sad face appear again in her doorway and didn't want to lose touch with her completely. In case Kiran needed her family's support later in her life, she wanted her to have the option of coming back. Shamsa was very angry, however, and didn't want anyone to contact Kiran. Perhaps she saw her own life playing out in front of her like a movie. Kaisera explained that Kiran followed her destiny, but Shamsa blamed her sister for having too little control in her management and letting the crisis occur. Kaisera, regardless of the burden of blame and pressure from Shamsa, loved Kiran too much to cut off ties with her. She visited her secretly, always asking if she needed anything from the house. She just wanted to make sure that Kiran's husband was not abusive to her and not a miser.

Kiran had four children during the years Kaisera kept in touch with her. She continued living in Lahore. Although the man's family never accepted her, he had a separate home for her and seemed to truly love her as a wife. Kiran was very clear she would never return to her old profession or to her family. After five years, Kiran's husband forbade her to meet Kaisera any more or to have any contact with her past. Perhaps Kaisera's occasional visits threatened him. He may have thought she might some day take Kiran back to her business. Kiran asked Kaisera not to visit again, as she wanted to make her husband comfortable about her commitment to him.

No one in the *biradri* talks about Kiran anymore. She disgraced her family. Occasionally, when the conversation turns to singing, someone might recall her lovely voice and remember Kiran. Usually, no comments follow; her name remains wrapped in silence. Nor did Laila's family ever mention Kiran. I knew nothing about her until Bobby's sudden return caused so many memories to come flooding back. The pain of remembering caused the usually strong Kaisera to sit for hours crying in a dark corner of her room. Laila tried to drag her into the living room, wanting her to talk to Bobby and find out what had happened, but Kaisera wanted to be left alone, to air the wounds

she'd hidden for so long behind her firm front. She wanted to
re-visit each memory, one by one.

Relations between Kaisera and Shamsa had always been
stressed, with a sense of competition as they were growing up.
Both were beautiful, but outgoing Shamsa always got more
attention. Although they were only a year apart, Shamsa always
had the eldest daughters' privilege. At the time of *nath utarwai*,
she outdid Kaisera, and was very proud of her first customer, a
son of a nawab. His family had lost their feudal holdings and no
longer had much money, but their attitude towards life was little
changed. Kaisera's first customer was a businessman, who,
naturally, hadn't the same flare as the nawab's son.

When adopting two children for Shamsa, their parents should
have thought about Kaisera too. The eldest daughter shouldn't
have been the only one with children. Kaisera ended up stuck
with supporting Shahid's wife and most of the children, certainly
all the boys. Although she had the right to the other girls, Laila
and Yasmin, Kaisera always felt that her future security was
only borrowed from Shamsa. After all her years of supporting
the girls, she still feared Shamsa might return to reap the
benefits, a not unreasonable fear given that earlier Shamsa had
selfishly taken Kiran, Shahid and the newborn girl away with
her, not thinking even for a moment about Kaisera and her
future. Kaisera ended up as a working prostitute far longer than
she would have liked, waiting desperately for Laila to grow up.
Without her property and the monthly rent she got from her
tenants, she'd have been out on the streets. She had to manage
the *kotha* with other dancers for years before Laila started
performing. She got merely the *dairedaar* share for this since
she was only providing the space and not managing the
performances. Those were difficult days, feeding so many, and
on top of it all, dealing with Laila's stubbornness. Later, when
Shamsa had problems with Kiran she sent her back, knowing
that Kaisera would take care of her. Finally, Kaisera got blamed
for Kiran's elopement and marriage.

Shahid had been somewhat supportive, but was totally
unreliable. Sometimes he acted like Shamsa's agent and when

he had disagreements and fights with her, he ran back to Kaisera. She could never count on him fully. Kaisera felt Shamsa always had the upper hand and could manipulate Shahid any way she wanted. The two sisters fought every time Shamsa made her infrequent visits from London. Kaisera yearned for a loving relationship with her sister, but that dream never came true. When Shamsa visited around the time that Kaisera was initiating Laila into the profession, she made a major crisis out of Laila's rebellious attitude. Kaisera remembered how she cried at Jamila being sent to her mother's house with all the children. Jamila had been an obedient daughter-in-law and Kaisera liked her, and knew she didn't deserve such treatment. Nevertheless, she stood by Shamsa to show a united front. She didn't appreciate her sister flying in from London, taking control of the management and running Kaisera down for being incapable of handling young girls. This was simply an excuse to belittle Kaisera and prove she was the better manager. Although she felt it in her heart, Kaisera hadn't the nerve to tell Shamsa she was the one who couldn't handle her girls.

Now Bobby had arrived. Shamsa had taken her away when she was only an infant. After she grew up, Shamsa put her to work in London; now there were problems and she sent her home to Kaisera. Kaisera sobbed, the world had not been fair to her. Engulfed in fear, she thought, what if Bobby was pregnant; what if she'd fallen in love with a man in London; what if she was on drugs? Kaisera didn't have the strength to take on another problem case. A day after Bobby's arrival Shamsa called, sounding not at all apologetic or thankful that Kaisera had taken Bobby in. With a crisp tone in her voice she spoke like a boss instructing her junior. She told Kaisera that Bobby repeatedly got into trouble because of a severe drinking problem. She ordered her to take Bobby's passport away and hide it. Kaisera did what her sister told her to do, but felt used in the process.

# 30

## ON HER WAY TO BECOMING
## A NAIKA

Laila gave birth to a son—a sad occasion. She tried to console herself by thinking that, after all, it was her first child and she had now become a mother. Laila liked the idea, and enjoyed having a child to take care of. Jamila did the difficult chores of course, bathing him and looking after his needs, but Laila was happy to cuddle and play with him. Kaisera was very upset at the birth of a son since she wanted a secure future for Laila. She felt all her efforts to get Laila a long-term relationship and getting her pregnant had failed and she was disappointed that Laila had lost almost a year's income and career development for nothing. She was silent about her concerns, however, and only prayed that the next time Laila would have a daughter.

Having Saleem's child was certainly a good justification for the family to pressure him to increase the monthly stipend. Kaisera wanted at least that benefit from a male child, and she complained quite loudly. Whenever Saleem came to the house, she nagged him about the rising prices and the money spent on the child. Once, when I was visiting and Saleem was lying in his usual *charpai* behind the living room, Kaisera asked me in a loud voice whether I knew the price of baby formula.

'I've no idea,' I replied.

She said, 'I give money to Bhuba for one thing and I find we're out of something else. Babies have so many expenses for milk, clothes and medicines. I can't bear them all. The father should pay for this. Laila was my daughter and I looked after her. Now he should take care of his child's expenses. Are you listening to me, Fouzia?'

Knowing full well that this monologue was not for me, but for the one in the room next door, I answered, 'Of course I'm listening.'

'Laila's monthly stipend was determined a year ago,' she continued. 'Tell me, how much have the prices gone up since then? You know Laila. Like a child she wants everything for herself. I spend so much money! And she's not working with anyone else to make extra money. How can I survive like this? You're like my daughter. That's why I am telling you this.' She came close to me. The volume of her comments suddenly dropped and she whispered in my ears, pointing to the next room, 'His parents have found out what he's been doing in Lahore. His father is here and has taken over the shop. He found out about Saleem getting money out of the shop for Laila and he's stopped even his modest stipend. The fellow has nothing left.'

'What do you think will happen now?' I whispered back.

'He'll have to get money from somewhere. *Rotian toran sade bue te aa janda e* (He comes to our house to eat). He has not paid for the last two months.'

She raised her voice again and said, 'Look, *meri bachi*, an obedient son should not get into such relationships. These lifestyles belong to families whose generations are rich. But getting into it, one must take a stand. After all, what belongs to your parents belongs to you. And when you yourself become a parent, you also have responsibilities.'

I heard Laila calling Kaisera from the next room. She wanted her to give money to Bhuba to get some vegetables that Jamila needed. Kaisera went in grumbling. As she went in, Saleem rushed out and charged towards the main door. She stopped for a moment and looked at him in surprise; shaking her head with disgust. Saleem stopped and turned towards me with scared, embarrassed eyes. He looked like a little child who had not yet learnt the ways of this world and seemed to have fallen out of his mother's lap right into Laila's. He surely had no confidence and his thin body was shaking in his loose *shalwar kamiz*. I wondered how he had got into this situation. He stood for a brief moment looking at me as though imploring me to help him out of his terrible and stupid situation. Suddenly he turned and ran out.

After a while Laila came into the living room and sat close to me. I'd been interviewing business people in the area all morning and was sitting on the carpet, labelling my audiocassettes. She put her hand on my knee and asked, 'See what is happening?'

I nodded and she went on, 'Ami has been after him from the day my son was born. She got him to pay 15,000 rupees for the hospital expenses, but still complained. I don't like this at all. What can he do? His parents have found out about us and have taken the finances of the shop away from him. He used to take money from there. Now what can he do? He didn't tell me where he got this 15,000 rupees.' She started crying and I held her shoulder. 'I kept asking him, but he didn't tell me. My mother pressured him so much he had to get the money even if he stole it. She was humiliating him like anything,' she sobbed, 'I don't like this at all.'

Kaisera walked in and saw Laila sitting next to me, crying. She also sat down. She looked at me and pointed to Laila, speaking in a soft voice, 'Just look at her, as if I'm talking to Saleem this way for myself. If she were smart, I wouldn't even have to talk to him. She should be the one to get her stipend raised.'

Wiping her tears Laila answered loudly, 'Leave me out of this. You made the deal with him; you handle this business.'

Kaisera said, 'If a horse becomes friends with the grass, what will he eat? She doesn't learn. We can't be nice to the customers and say, "You get everything from us, but it's okay if you can't keep your end of the bargain". Laila doesn't have responsibility on her shoulders yet, so she can afford to sit and cry with you. I'm the one who has to deal with all the problems. I pay the money for the vegetables that will be cooked today. I take care of all the children that are being raised in this house and all the adults who eat here, including him.'

Laila got up and left. Kaisera turned to me, 'If he can't pay for Laila he should just back off. He has no right to waste her time. There are other customers. If he wants his son he should take him.'

I looked at her, surprised, 'Really, if he goes away will he take his son?'

She laughed, 'They never take their children. All these men pretend to be so honourable, but they leave their children here. They don't have the courage to face their families and these children would never be accepted. We have, in this Mohalla, the children of...you wouldn't believe...' she raised her voice, 'The biggest political leaders of this country.' After a pause, she sighed, 'They don't take their children back; they're cowards. They want all the pleasure, but not the responsibility.'

I asked, 'Would people here let them take their children back? I mean if they wanted them.'

Kaisera smiled and said, 'This is a bazaar. Everything is sold here. They have only to offer a price the management finds acceptable. You've been studying this place for a while now. Don't you know that everything has its price? Many would hesitate to give away the girls, but all things can be bought. Believe me, they won't do that. They're all hypocrites. Those who speak loudest against us are the ones with many children here.' She got up. 'Forget it!' she said. This profession has always been here and it will stay. Why curse the customers? After all, they're the ones who help us survive. I have to go see Laila's son. He has an upset stomach.'

Months went by. Saleem tried his best to sneak some money from one sale or the other. His visits were now shorter and with longer gaps in between. Saving face in front of Laila and her mother drew him back; the relationship had lost the thrill and lust that initially lured him in. Kaisera continued pressuring him, while at the same time she was looking for other options for Laila. Laila kept dancing in the evenings, but they were only getting, on average, two customers a week for music, with perhaps one in a month who would stay over or come back for sex. Kaisera had to think of other ways of boosting her business.

She even tried to get Laila into Variety Shows, but those appearances rarely generated much income. Laila was not very good at coaxing *vail* from the audience.

Finally after dragging his feet for another six months, Saleem gave up. Caught taking one more tranche from the jewellery shop, his father threatened to turn him over to the police. Saleem had to promise his parents that he would never return to the Mohalla. They took him back to their hometown and forbade him to leave. Laila was depressed for a few days, but Kaisera got her involved in exploring options in films. Every dancing girl in the area dreams about the film industry, and Kaisera, knowing that Laila was already over twenty-one years old, thought she'd make one final effort to get her into a film. Laila kept on gaining weight. Her singing voice was considerably below average and her dancing skills were mediocre. She had a good heart, but that alone could not get her any work in films.

Kaisera told me she had asked a favour of someone and was hopeful at first, but Laila never actually met any director or film producer. Their few contacts could only get them to agents of agents of agents, people who promise the sky and keep milking their clients with no results. Kaisera was a smart woman. She consulted some other people and got the message that she shouldn't waste time on Laila any more, but should focus on Laila's younger sister Yasmin. She was young enough to stand a chance.

Kaisera let Laila know her decision after Laila had already started dreaming about the fame working in films would bring. Kaisera was in a tough mood and gave Laila a hard time. She spoke bluntly, 'Laila, I wasn't expecting any more from you in any case. You haven't spent a single day doing the hard work this job requires. Going into films isn't easy, otherwise all the girls in the Mohalla would be in the film industry.'

'It's all contacts!' Laila yelled. 'Girls just like me have made it in the movies. They had contacts that you and Shahid *bhai* don't have.'

'You're lying, and you know it,' Kaisera shouted back. 'I've been telling you to eat less, to get up early, to practice your dancing.' She walked away from Laila saying, 'But you haven't changed anything about your life. I can't lose weight for you.'

Laila went after her, 'Wait a minute! What do I eat? Should I stop eating and die? I have a body that expands, what can I do? I'm a pretty good dancer.'

Kaisera, looking at her very seriously said, 'I'm not going to pick a meaningless fight with you. I've been told to focus on Yasmin and give up on you. You brought this fate on yourself. You seem to have made up your mind to never learn.' Finished, she turned and walked away.

Laila yelled at her, 'I'm pregnant again!'

Kaisera's eyes turned red with rage, she pivoted and said, '*Did kara lia e* (you have got yourself pregnant)! Which month?'

'Second,' answered Laila.

'And we were looking around for work!' Kaisera exploded. Suddenly, she calmed down and announced, 'We'll keep the child.'

Laila was angry at her grandmother, at all the agents she'd been meeting who'd given her hopes and dreams, at Shahid for not having enough contacts, at Saleem for being such a wimp, at her unborn child, and at herself for not being successful in her life. She lay down on a sofa and turned on some music. An audiocassette of Indian film music started playing. She hardly listened to the music. She just wanted to drown the noises inside her.

Laila was very upset, but didn't know why. She'd never liked hard work and had been told that acting was hard work, the actresses working long shifts repeating the same thing over and over. Still, she couldn't convince herself that she didn't want it. She dreamed about seeing a coloured photograph of herself on a magazine cover! She'd love to see herself in several poses on the coloured pages of *Jang* newspaper. She was sleepy. Her tired mind took her on a fantasy ride where she imagined herself in a Lux soap advertisement, saying, '*Mere husn ka singhar Lux sabun* (the secret of my beauty is Lux soap)'. Somewhere in the middle of her daydream she fell asleep.

A big bang at the door woke her. She jumped up and saw an old woman entering the room. She had been too deeply asleep to understand what was happening. She wasn't sure how long she'd slept. She heard her mother yelling and telling the woman to get out. She also heard little kids, her siblings, squabbling around her. There was a lot of fuss and then it subsided. Everybody went back to whatever they'd been doing. At the end of this uproar she heard her mother grumbling, 'She was a courtesan from a good family and look what she's become—a beggar! She doesn't even know she's breaking into people's home without permission. It's tragic what happens to women who fail here.'

Laila dozed off again and woke after a while strangely afraid. She suddenly realized she'd missed the bus. The age to work on moving out of the Mohalla or up within it had passed. Her youth was gone. Totally engulfed in fear, she saw her whole life pass before her eyes and wondered what to do now. Until that moment, she'd always thought things would work out for the best and had never thought seriously about her life. She'd occasionally toyed with getting a job outside the Mohalla and leaving the sex trade. She dreamed of some Prince Charming who would take her away. Recently, she'd thought she'd become a film industry superstar, but the reality of life now hit her for the first time and she realized that none of her half-baked ideas had led anywhere. Having a child meant leaving work again for several months, and who knew whether or not she'd have a daughter this time? How could she wait seven months? She felt very nervous.

From then on Laila became quite serious, experiencing a strange sense of panic and insecurity. Kaisera noticed a change in her, but ignored it. She'd always thought of Laila as a spoilt child and she'd pretty much behaved like one. She had never really been serious about anything, ever. Laila was scheduled to perform the following day in a Variety Show in a village near Peshawar. She was a different person; unsure what she wanted, but she knew she had to do something about her life. She packed her best dresses and kept reassuring herself about her singing and dancing. The group included musicians, two other dancers and a comedian. The performance took place in the house of a big landlord whose son was getting married. The music programme, attended by an all-male audience in a huge courtyard, was to celebrate the wedding.

Most of the audience were tall Pathans in *shalwar kamiz* and big turbans, rifles hanging over their shoulders and their chests decorated with cartridge belts. Some men in the front rows were different. Graduates of Edward's Collage, Peshawar, they'd been classmates and close friends of the groom, a fellow graduate. These young men stood out from the rest. Pathans in general are fair-skinned and tall, and the groom's friends were not only handsome, but westernised as well, with the arrogant look educated Pakistani men often assume. Laila found them very attractive.

As the show began, the comedian/master-of-ceremonies started off with witty remarks about the groom and his friends, clapped and made a lot of noise. Laila told the manager she wanted to be the first dancer to go on stage. When she started dancing, this group became very rowdy. They got up from their seats, crowded close to the stage and sat around it, whistling and cheering in Pushto. Laila danced her best. Her big smile and a new radiance in her face made her look very charming. She started looking into the young men's eyes and noticed one she liked. Wearing a white starched *shalwar kamiz*, he looked like a prince to her. She gazed right into his eyes as she danced. He looked around to make sure he was the one she was staring at, and then relaxed, beginning to enjoy it. The show continued and their interaction became increasingly intense. Men were throwing money at the dancers, and this young man started throwing money at her. Laila was thrilled, knowing her magic was working.

Before the show had finished, he sneaked backstage to where Laila and another dancer were waiting for their turn to go back on the stage. He came up and told Laila he liked her dancing. He'd obviously been drinking. The meeting was brief, but they both communicated their interest in following up after the show.

Laila made arrangements with the man and told the organizer she'd not be going back with him, but would return on her own. The organizer became furious and told her he was answerable to her manager and that she had no right to jeopardize his relation with her mother and other Variety Show managers. They argued angrily. Laila was very rude; not used to hearing such nonsense from dancing girls, the *ustad* told her to go to hell.

Laila disappeared with the young man. Kaisera was enraged to hear that Laila had taken off on her own, but couldn't blame the *ustad* since she knew Laila was in a strange mood. For several days nobody knew where she had gone; and Kaisera and the entire household was becoming concerned. Kaisera asked Jamila to go to the neighbourhood shrine to offer a *manat*, promising to bring more offerings if Laila returned home safely. She couldn't go to the police, knowing they'd be of little help, and would instead complicate things more and demand a bribe to find her.

Two weeks went by with no news from Laila. Kaisera was angry that she hadn't even called home to say she was okay. Kaisera, although she had a Pathan father, feared Pathan men, afraid they'd kidnapped her daughter. She had nightmares that Laila was being raped and battered. She thought of road accidents. She prayed for her day and night.

About three weeks later, Laila turned up at my house in Islamabad around 10 o'clock in the morning, accompanied by the handsome young man. She had told him she was taking him to her friend's house. She met my mother and my brother, who were home at the time, affectionately. My mother didn't know she'd disappeared, so she thought it was simply a surprise visit and she didn't panic. She had come to accept Laila as a person, not a prostitute, a visitor to our home. My mother called me at work. Not free to come home early I talked to Laila on the phone. She sounded very happy and cheerful. I told her she could call her mother from our house if she wanted. She seemed to be in some other world, but promised to call Kaisera.

My mother and brother entertained the guests until I got home. My brother could not get over such a sensible, intelligent young man, supposedly from a regular middle class family, getting into such a relationship. He shared his amazement with me later in the evening, saying he could see himself in the man. My brother had graduated from the same college in Peshawar only a few years earlier. He told me that when the man called his mother in Peshawar from our phone he talked just like we do when we call home. He said he told his mother he and his friends had suddenly decided to visit Murree and that he was calling from there, but would soon be leaving for home. My brother and I talked about our stereotypes of people who use prostitutes. We think their main customers are gangsters or other low life characters, but, in reality, it is just ordinary men from our society who are the ones keeping the Mohallas alive.

By the time I got home from work, her friend had left and Laila was talking to my mother and was planning to stay the night. She said she'd be going back to Lahore the next day. She'd called her mother to say she was coming home. From the way she was talking and what my mother and brother told me about her conversations with the young man she didn't seem to have changed much. She still used her baby talk, but I knew something inside her was different or about to become so. Consciously getting a customer and taking off without letting any one know was not her usual behaviour. Perhaps she wanted to announce she'd now be making her own decisions or to express some kind of autonomy. I couldn't be sure. She returned to Lahore with no excuses, explanations or apologies. She went back as if nothing had happened. Noticing her mood, Kaisera did not push the issue. Laila told her they'd be doing more business in Peshawar now. She'd made good contacts with some agents there during her trip.

Time went by and Laila kept performing in the evenings in her *kotha* and in Variety Shows whenever she got a chance. She was doing all right. Some days she could make an effort, but at other times she did not want to laugh at a customers' silly jokes or even try to get them excited. Bobby was a support, but hardly a reliable one. She performed with Laila for about six months and then decided she didn't want to work any more. Neither Kaisera nor Laila could convince her otherwise, and Kaisera felt she should be tough on her, since she was, after all, living off of them. However, about this time Kaisera found out that other than the problem with alcohol, Shamsa had sent Bobby to Lahore because of her emotional involvement with a man in London with whom Shamsa feared she'd run away. Despite all this Kaisera couldn't be harsh with her. She felt Bobby should realise by herself that she needed to contribute to the family earnings since families survive that way. Laila agreed, but somehow neither could pressure Bobby. They both felt she belonged to Shamsa, and that if Shahid were worth anything as Shamsa's representative, he would discipline her.

Bobby was very upset about losing her British passport and visa papers. She was aloof and withdrawn all the time, and Laila felt that, after Kaisera, she should talk to her, to put some sense in her head. She tried many times, even sharing the thoughts and experiences she herself had early on, but Bobby refused to engage with her. Suddenly, after a few months break, Bobby started working again. Laila, pleased, associated Bobby's decision to return to work with her own modest attempts to talk to her, but no one really knew what was going on in her mind. After about a month Bobby gave the family another shock by telling them she was in love. Kaisera cried loudly and Laila yelled at her while Jamila and the younger children hid in the back rooms, afraid of the next storm.

Kaisera cursed Bobby. She didn't want more blame from her sister for yet another sin she didn't commit. She cursed herself also for her bad luck, and prayed for her own death. None of this affected Bobby. Kaisera told her to wait for Shahid to come and decide what to do. She tried her best to salvage the situation, using love, anger, guilt, anything she could, to keep Bobby from running off with the man. She said that if the man was also in love, she'd be happy to arrange a long-term deal with him so he could have exclusive rights to Bobby. She said he should pay for what he wants, and should support her economically. In anger, she shouted that if he had any ethics he should even pay for the cost of bringing Bobby up. Kaisera knew she had to try to save the situation, otherwise her sister would hold her accountable for not trying to strike a deal.

Laila was very vocal, wanting to stand by Kaisera and deal with this family crisis, part of the new role she was trying out. Bobby didn't give either of them much opportunity for involvement, however. She disappeared the next day. Kaisera was not only heartbroken, but also frightened of the blame that was to follow. When Shahid came home in the evening, he was furious. Her behaviour wasn't really unexpected, though, since Bobby had been problematic even in London. He didn't say much to Kaisera, but cursed Bobby and the man who took her. The next morning he engaged his network of agents and pimps to track her down.

Shahid discovered that Bobby had already married her lover so his options were limited. He managed to break into their house, but the man was out. He tried to convince her to come back. He abused her verbally, but before he could use physical force she threatened to cause him serious trouble if he did. She ordered him to disappear from her life, saying she wanted nothing to do with the family anymore and no one should ever look for her again. Shahid returned disappointed and hurt. He knew that if Bobby was willing to stay with the man and they were legally married, he couldn't pressure him to pay up or push him to release her.

He came back and told Kaisera, 'We have only ourselves to blame. We set a bad precedent by letting Kiran go when she wanted to get married. We're already weak. How can I fight with that man when I can't control my own daughter? Even if I dragged her home, would she work? No. She'd be stubborn again.' He told Kaisera to pray for Bobby's husband to have family problems because of his secret marriage. Only then could he be pressured to leave her.

Tired of entertaining customers all by herself, night after night, Laila suggested inviting some other dancers to join her evening performances. Kaisera agreed and they contacted Pami and her sisters and another dancer Surayia, Laila had worked with in Variety Shows. They continued performing. One day, around noon, when everyone was having breakfast, Bobby walked in. Laila's jaw dropped. Only her real mother, Jamila, ran forward with a string of questions and hugged her, crying, 'Daughter, are you okay? Was he bad to you? Did you come on your own or did he throw you out? Tell me, tell me please, are you okay?' Kaisera remained contained and reserved. Bobby had no answers. Running inside the house she threw herself on the bed, and cried till she fell asleep.

Laila was very angry, feeling that Bobby used them whenever she needed to, but didn't even bother to share her sorrows with them. Bobby's facade of silence turned Laila's love and concern into hostility. Kaisera told Laila not to push her, reminding her, 'Laila, remember when Bobby came back from London, none of us knew what had happened. She never talked about what was bothering her. She's behaving in the same way.' She began to cry, 'Shamsa's children think I have a hotel here. I shouldn't ask them anything about where they go and where they come from, but I should be available whenever they need me.' Laila agreed with her.

Household dynamics changed strikingly over the next few days. Bobby talked more to Jamila; in reaction Laila came closer to Kaisera. Laila and Kaisera felt certain that Bobby had confided in her mother, but the two were keeping the problem to themselves. Jamila knew the family well and felt the tension. She urged Bobby to talk to them, and when she disagreed, Jamila got permission to tell them something. She convinced her that if they were to live in the same house they'd have to open up a little to Kaisera. As head of the household, she had a right to know what was going on.

Jamila gathered up her courage and told Kaisera that Bobby's husband had beaten her up. Kaisera was enraged; she couldn't imagine anyone hitting a girl from her family. She cursed him loudly and shouted, 'Now you see what happens to those who get married. You girls sit there and romanticize that life is a bed of roses. But here you decide your terms and have *apni mehnat di halal di rozi* (your own genuine income). You have all the facilities and comforts. There you give yourself to one man, give up all control over your life, do his housework and then become victim of his rage. Huh! Those men have it good. They get themselves a free slave. Wives are so stupid they not only give themselves freely in slavery, but they even bring dowry to fill the bastard's house, and then the children are his, too. What a system!' She looked at the girls and asked Laila, 'Are you going to be that stupid, too?' They kept quiet. The anger and crying went on all evening. Among the accusations, resentment and tears there was also a great sense of helplessness and sadness.

The next day Bobby disappeared again, and they found out her husband had sent a message apologizing and saying he wanted her back. The whole family was in shock. Jamila became terribly depressed. She kept doing housework but couldn't keep the tears from rolling down her cheeks. Laila was quiet. Sitting in front of the television, she watched one Indian film after another—her best means of escape. Kaisera brooded in the living room and felt guilty that she should have been more loving than angry with Bobby the other evening. Maybe she should have told her not to believe in his apologies, because he would surely beat her again. Maybe, if she'd hugged her, Bobby wouldn't have gone back to him. Time passed and she had to face reality that Bobby had again run away. They did not hear from her until about a year later, when she had already become the mother of a son. The family did not do anything to retrieve her.

Laila gave birth to a second boy, another disappointment. Kaisera thought God was cursing them because two women of the family, Kiran and Bobby, had violated the tradition and married. She did not know how to compensate for their sin, and all she could think of was to give a *deg* of food to the local shrine. Now she had two boys to feed. Laila was also disappointed, but she wouldn't talk to me about it and changed the subject every time I brought it up. She couldn't admit she was sad about the second boy, but it was quite evident, although at the same time she became closer to her elder son, now almost two years old.

I became involved in other aspects of the research study, and in addition, was initiating my career as a development consultant. I didn't see Laila again for a few months. I had come to Lahore once again for the *Basant* Festival and stayed a few days to see some friends in the Mohalla. I visited Laila about mid-day. She was combing her wet hair on the balcony by the living room, and met me with a barrage of complaints for avoiding her. She was mad at me for becoming a stranger and became even more upset about my short hair. She abused me for cutting my long hair that she loved, and she called me names telling me how ugly I looked with short hair. I was happy seeing her again. She said she'd been to Peshawar often, but she never stopped to visit me. She called Bhuba in her loudest voice, and gave him money tied in a corner of her *dupatta* to bring cold milk for me. I was surprised to see this since she always used to ask Kaisera in a baby voice for money for this or that. It was a major change.

We caught up on our stories. She told me about how my other friends in the area were doing, who she was speaking to currently, and who had been dropped from her list of friends. I told her I was planning to visit some other friends while I was in Lahore. After a pause she yelled at her younger sister, Yasmin, who was sleeping in the next room, 'Are you up yet?' she grumbled, 'She sleeps so much. A person should get up by twelve and start the day, but Yasmin, no, Yasmin just loves to sleep.' She shouted again loudly, 'Yasmin, Yasmin, look who's here. Come, say *salaam* to Fouzia. Can you hear me or not?'

Laila turned at me and said, 'She only likes to eat, sleep and laugh. She is not serious about her dance practice, and is always making excuses so as not to go to her singing lessons. On top of everything else, she's gaining weight. Look at her age and her figure.' She picked up the *paandan* and started making *paan* for herself. She continued talking, carelessly, '...and she does not listen to me at all. I don't want her to suffer in the future, you know, but her and her taste buds...she just sits around and eats.'

Make-over, before and after: heavy make-up and bright lights are an important part of the business

Open doors and well-lit rooms with made up dancing girls are an invitation to customers

All dressed up and practicing with musicians while waiting for the customers

Enjoying their own performance, these three young dancers entertain their customers

*Naika,* or the manager, counting the money to divide it justly among all involved in the performance

A young prostitute, waiting for the right customer

Seductive gestures, calculated to win the hearts of her customers

Rehearsing the performance

47

A young prostitute, entertaining a customer

I was so stunned hearing all this, I couldn't respond and just looked at her face. I saw this amazing transition; Laila was turning into a manager. The child in her got lost somewhere in the labyrinth of survival. She was on the road to becoming a *naika*.

# 31

# THE ONLY OPTION
# FOR SURVIVAL

Laila was totally focused on Yasmin. Although she continued performing in the evening and at Variety Shows, her basic purpose was to get her sister contacts and good customers. Yasmin was fourteen years old. Her big round face had sharp features and a brown complexion, and her black hair had a natural curl. She liked to have some curls on her forehead. Neither thin nor fat, Yasmin was generally quiet and withdrawn, but always proud of her looks. However, I could see her getting heavier each time I visited.

Yasmin thought herself as very beautiful and didn't believe she'd have to do much to attract people. She began to work in Variety Shows with Laila. Laila made sure she got the performance fee. She also looked after her since Yasmin's *nath* agreement hadn't yet been arranged. At this stage in a dancing girl's career, when she is still a virgin, their managers are most careful to protect their assets. Yasmin was constantly talking to people about getting into the film industry. One category of customer work as part-time agents. They're quite familiar with the Mohalla and other businesses that employ girls from there and often recommend musicians and prostitutes to them. These businesses could be those that provide 'extras' to the studios, dancing girls to theatre companies or beautiful prostitutes to big business ventures for their sales and public relations sections. They're not simply pimps since they may or may not do this for a living. They know the system well enough to play an agent's role if the opportunity arises. They're customers, but are shrewd enough to bring people together and take a share. They might sometimes prefer to take their payment in the form of sexual favours. Laila lacked the confidence to jump into the ocean of the film world on her own, and so ended up swimming around in ponds and puddles on the side, wanting someone to connect her to a bigger agent.

Yasmin ordinarily rose late in the morning, put on nice clothes, sat in front of the mirror for a while and then watched an Indian movie. She was also very childlike, and still liked playing with her younger sister and brother. Kaisera and Laila both scolded her now whenever they saw her too involved with her siblings in children's games. They wanted her to behave like an adult. Once, after an out of town performance when Laila was scolding her for not getting up in the morning, she complained of blisters on her feet from dancing all night in high heels which she wasn't used to. She sounded exactly like Laila.

One would imagine that Laila's transformation would have brought her closer to her grandmother, but Kaisera had no such luck. Laila remained, as she had always been with her, affectionate, but distant. Bobby's crisis had brought them closer and she also sided with Kaisera on disciplinary measures for other family members, but emotionally, she drew closer to Jamila. Coming home from her performances she'd joke with her about the customers. Her feelings about the family's unfairness to her real mother were getting stronger and stronger.

While Kaisera and Shahid were busy looking for Yasmin's first customer, Laila wanted her to flee the nest and kept her focus on building contacts on the margins of the film industry. Through a customer/friend she arranged for a photographer to make a portfolio of Yasmin. She told him to make sure that his camera had a filter to give the photographs a soft look. She had the best ones enlarged and prepared an album to show influential people in the film industry. This idea came from a customer who would give her free advice.

Laila glued herself to one particular contact who promised he could get Yasmin's photographs to the right persons. She kept pampering the relationship in hopes that it would bear fruit. He once even asked for some money as a loan, certainly out of line in this business. If anything, loans are the other way round, but Laila was willing to make this exception to their traditions. She gave him money and even free sexual services from time to time. He used her just as she had been trained to use others. He told her a certain producer was casting for a movie soon and he was trying to convince him to give Yasmin a very good role. Every now and then he told her stories about his visits to the studios and the discussions he had had with the 'right people'.

Laila was getting tired of the delays. Then, one day when she was bragging that Mian Fazul Ali would be casting her sister in his new film she heard that work on the film had already begun two months earlier. Shocked, she decided to find out what had happened, but didn't have the courage to go to the studios herself. She sent another semi-agent, paying him to do this for her. He managed to meet the producer and was told that the erstwhile agent had showed him photos of many different girls, but had been told immediately that none of them would do. This reverse manipulation shattered her. She was very familiar with the behaviour since lying to get money and to get out of difficult situations was second nature to her, but she had never before been on the receiving end. She had never paid actual money to anyone for this kind of work before. Inexperienced, she felt the incident was a big professional failure and was disappointed with herself and became bitter towards the world.

As if this failure were not enough to undermine her trust in her managerial skills, the greatest tragedy of her life occurred just a few months later. The house they lived in had been left to both Kaisera and Shamsa. Since they couldn't work together they had divided the building into two portions. One night, a fire caused by a faulty electrical connection broke out in Shamsa's portion. Part of it was rented to families and part kept vacant for her to use whenever she came to Pakistan. The fire began in that apartment. By the time it was brought under control Shamsa's entire portion was destroyed, but the firemen had managed to save Kaisera's half.

The news enraged Shamsa, who came directly to Lahore from London, staying for only a few days. She couldn't believe it was an accident, and openly accused Kaisera of conspiring against her. How else could it be that nothing of Kaisera's burned while her section of the building was ruined? The sisters seemed never to be able to build bridges. At every opportunity for better communication, a crisis ruined any good will and the old wounds became fresh again. Shamsa was also furious at Bobby, and could never forgive her for what she had done. She took Bobby's passport and other visa papers from Kaisera and burnt them.

Kaisera took the pain of this visit deeply to heart and fell ill. Her health deteriorated every day; she left more and more of the management problems to Laila. In a will she'd written earlier, she had named Laila as her heir, and gave her a copy of the will in case she had problems establishing her authority as manager. Kaisera suffered an attack of paralysis, probably a stroke, which the doctors attributed to her mental condition. Walking became difficult for her, one of her legs being almost numb. Laila was travelling for performances during this time and couldn't pay much attention to Kaisera so Jamila took on the old woman's care. Laila didn't know how to take care of her, unable to relate to Kaisera in such a helpless state. Kaisera's condition improved but not for long.

A family fight threw her deeper into her ailment, with another attack of paralysis affecting both her legs. Her medical problems began compounding. She couldn't go to the toilet, her sugar level soared and she developed heart problems. In her last few weeks she relied on Jamila for everything, with Laila too scared to face the reality that she was dying. She wasn't ready to become manager without Kaisera around to help.

Kaisera, for her part, was disappointed by Laila's distance and resented being totally dependent on her daughter-in-law. Jamila, in the final weeks of Kaisera's life, asked her to make a revision in her will, to name some of the male children as heirs. She wanted some security for herself in return for all the care she had extended Kaisera. Jamila hadn't been allowed to learn

much about the *Kanjar biradri* into which she'd married and
thought male children had a right to inherit the property, as in
the rest of society.

A few weeks later Kaisera had a heart attack. She died after a
few days in intensive care, and Laila's entire world caved in.
The darkness around her became unbearable. She could not
foresee any future, and had no hope for herself. She remembered
the low class streetwalker who had once barged into her house
and Kaisera's words still echoed in her ears: 'She was a
courtesan of a good family and look what she has become, a
beggar.' Laila couldn't bear to hear these voices, and didn't
want to face the fear that was overtaking her. She'd been doing
fine until the fiasco over Yasmin's missed film opportunity.
She needed more time to truly become a manager. She liked
playing manager as long as her grandmother was around to
handle the big problems since she'd never really gained
confidence in her abilities. She'd tried out her ideas and really
wanted to do a good job for her sister, but somehow she knew
that if things went wrong Kaisera could step in.

She felt Kaisera had left her alone too early. If only Kaisera
could have given her a few more years of training she could
have been ready. She knew she wasn't as quick as some other
girls at picking up the tricks of the trade. She needed more time.
Maybe her grandmother had been right, she should have taken
the business more seriously, and conformed to the tradition in
order to ensure her survival. She should never have thought of
leaving the profession. She'd wasted a lot of time toying with
different ideas for her life. Along with her despairing thoughts,
she heard again and again her grandmother's voice, 'This is
what happens to women who fail in the profession'. She repeated
to herself, 'I will succeed, I will succeed. I will not turn into a
beggar', but in her heart she was unsure and very scared.

Within a few days of her grandmother's death, Laila
discovered that her mother had succeeded in getting Kaisera to
change her will. Ownership of the building had been left to
Jamila's two sons and Laila's eldest son. That really threw her
off. She was angry to have been so naive as to not guard her

right of inheritance, the right of an eldest *Kanjar* daughter. She had a major disagreement with Shahid over Yasmin. When she told me about it later the details of the fight were not very clear, just that she argued with Shahid and became extremely upset. She couldn't figure out what her relationship with Shahid should be. Her grandmother had taught her nothing about in-house power struggles, or perhaps she hadn't paid enough attention. She wanted to get things under control so she could maintain some order in their family business, but she was too panicky and afraid of failing. She couldn't really deal with Shahid and still feared the hold he had over her when she was only a dancer. Since he was her real father, she had little chance of getting him to listen to her anyway.

Suddenly, Laila packed her bags and left home. Although the family was shocked, Shahid nonetheless took off again on some mysterious business, leaving Yasmin and her siblings alone with Jamila, and the *kotha* without a manager. These circumstances forced Jamila to build up her courage to start managing the house and keeping the business intact. She told Yasmin to continue the evening performances and asked her to get some other girls to join her. Jamila focused on collecting rent from the tenants and feeding her children.

Laila had gone back to Peshawar. No one knew more than that. I guessed she was trying once more to survive on her own; she was confused about whether the house and business in the Mohalla belonged to her or Shahid. At the time Laila ran away, I was getting married in Islamabad. It was an important occasion for me so I had invited many friends, including those from the Mohalla. Yasmin told me that Laila was away, but promised to pass on the invitation if she called, but I didn't hear anything from her.

On the day of my wedding, Laila turned up at my house with a gift after the ceremony was over. She spent some time with my mother, conveyed her best wishes for my future and left.

About two months later I learned that she'd returned home to Lahore. She had given herself that last chance to try to survive on her own, but discovered she had no options other than what had been carved out for her from birth. She could take that role in the Shahi Mohalla or become a pathetic beggar, something she was determined not to do. She remembered Kaisera's words on her deathbed. Moments before she died Kaisera had asked for a few words with Laila in privacy and had apologized for not giving her what was rightfully hers. At the time, Laila couldn't understand what she was talking about. Then Kaisera held her hand and told her she should never leave her house in the Mohalla. She also told her that if she wanted her daughter in the same business she should groom her from childhood.

Laila came back from Peshawar with a lot of confidence and immediately took charge of the *kotha* again. She knew she had to work hard at making a living and to make sure that Yasmin and her younger sister were well groomed to survive in the system.

---

## VIEWS

### A Stage Actor, Salman Shahid

Salman, a stage actor friend of mine, told me that women who express themselves threaten our society. Pakistani men can, to a certain extent, tolerate other women expressing themselves, but cannot bear their own woman being expressive. They fear she may get in touch with herself and want things around her to change. Pakistani men, he said, are very afraid of allowing anything to happen that could change the status quo.

'Why, then, are they attracted to prostitutes?' I asked.

They like prostitutes because they're not in touch with their own selves either. These women intrigue them. It is a very strange attraction; the prostitutes are like a mystery to them. Unlike the women they have at home whom they have already won and controlled, prostitutes are not under their rule. They are attractive beings who can fulfil a man's fantasies. Charming, expressive, and without sexual inhibitions—men love that. The minute they conquer, however, they can't handle the dancing girls' free expression. We have many examples of famous actresses who marry and immediately announce they will no longer act. Can you tell me why?'

'Yes, I know many such cases – actresses, singers, dancers.' I replied.

'Other than Shabnam, who had a progressive husband and did not belong to a Mohalla biradri, name another Pakistani actress who continued her career on the screen after marrying. Sometimes, if the husband is a director or a producer, he allows her to work, but only in his films so he can keep an eye on her. If he is an actor himself, he says she can only work with me and with no one else. It goes on and on.'

'What's the bottom line?' I asked

'I'd say control, maintaining the social hierarchy, where women remain inferior', Salman replied.

# 32

# SEARCHING FOR CLUES

The lives of the people of the Shahi Mohalla are the basis for this book. Their stories taught me lessons I'd otherwise never have learned about our own society and its values. I felt so close to them that the faces of Chanda, Laila, Bobby, Soni and Rani sometimes appear in my dreams. Nevertheless, I felt a strong need to step back from them for a while to give me an opportunity to grasp the larger pattern. I convinced myself at this point that I had to stop collecting data on the present and to journey into the past, scanning the work of other researchers for more pieces of the puzzle. Three main questions kept coming up: Why prostitution? Why such a strong stigma? and why the persistence of this phenomenon? I wanted to understand the root causes of the organized sex trade.

I prowled through many libraries and surfed the Internet for historical descriptions of prostitution through the ages. After reviewing books and articles on the topic I concluded that although most research literature didn't answer my questions, I did find some good clues I could discuss with another researcher. One morning in the stuffy, narrow stacks of the National Archives in Islamabad, I bumped into a friend of mine, Paul Amin, in Pakistan on a sabbatical to research the musical traditions in Sindh and Rajasthan. We exchanged spirited greetings and then the poor man made the mistake of asking me about my research. I launched into a long monologue, totally ignoring any look of disinterest on his face. I explained my fieldwork findings and my frustrations at the way academicians have looked at the sex trade, focusing only on the women, leaving the customers and other stakeholders invisible. I also told him about the ruling class linkages with prostitution I'd found in the history books. I would have gone on for hours without taking a breath, but suddenly I felt an unexpected, but firm, tap on my shoulder. I turned around to see the sweaty, stern face of the head librarian looking at me over his glasses. He put his finger on his lips and said 'Shhhhhh!' Paul was more embarrassed than I. He took my hand and dragged me out of the room.

We went to a restaurant downstairs and I told him, 'The literature I found mentions the authors' ideas on the causes of prostitution, but they seem to confuse the causes of the existence of a sex trade with the reasons women become prostitutes. To me, these are two very different things.'

Paul asked, 'What kind of causes do they mention?'

I said, 'most studies identify poverty as the number one cause, followed by the existence of destitute women, trafficking etc.' I smiled, 'Poverty is safely blamed for all society's problems—corruption, smuggling, wife battering, robbery etc. With poverty as an excuse we keep the focus elsewhere and need not deal with the underlying issues. No researchers explain why, over the years, highly organized prostitution has predominantly occurred with women providing the services and men buying them. Were poverty the basic cause, then it would seem that mostly women experience poverty in this world, not men. They also fail to explain why the stigma has invariably been on the service provider rather than the customer. Some studies actually say it's because some women have an extraordinary desire for sex, calling them "fallen women". The words "prostitute" and "pimp" are derogatory words in most societies, but the terms used for customers carry no stigma. The final mystery for me is why no society has succeeded in eradicating prostitution, regardless of the efforts it's made. There must be more to it than is visible on the surface!'

Paul reflected for a while and said, 'I can see you're totally involved in your work! I'll be coming every day this week. I'll be happy to have some serious discussions with you.'

His offer thrilled me because I'd always admired his analytical abilities and respected him as a social scientist. The next day I sat waiting at a table in a corner where our conversation wouldn't bother anyone. My open books, studded with post-its, were spread over the table with more piled on the chairs next to me. As soon as Paul arrived we slipped into a discussion on local musical traditions, their link to prostitution and the royal patronage provided in Rajasthan. After a while though, I felt we should be more organized, and said, 'Let me tell you what I found while looking deeper into the real causes of the sex trade. It's amazing! I can't even begin to understand the institution of prostitution without looking at the social structures and hierarchies of the larger society over the centuries. Let's take it step by step.'

Paul relaxed in his chair while I continued, 'First, I've got to tell you this: One of the most jarring studies I came across was Dolgopol's treatise on prostitution in the Second World War in Asia. During that period women were captured from occupied countries and used in well-organized brothels set up for Japanese soldiers. The costs of establishing these brothels, arranging for the capture, transportation and maintenance of the women were classed as regular expenses under the state military expenditures of Japan. Women from Indonesia, the Philippines and Korea, in particular, were taken and placed in brothels for the pleasure of the Japanese troops. Between 1928 to 1945, approximately 150,000 to 200,000 women were captured and enslaved, "recruited" by force. Military police accompanied the 'recruiters' and instantly killed any relative or parent who attempted to prevent the abduction. At one point the women were referred to as the "Special Service Personnel Group". The Japanese military was also responsible for day-to-day management of the brothels. A precise account was kept of the number of times a soldier visited the brothels and the number of the rooms he visited. In order to avoid any possible information leakage, strict control was maintained to prevent any relationships developing between soldiers and prostitutes.

'This study provided me with clear evidence of a case where powerful men meticulously developed and institutionalised mechanisms for creating and managing prostitution. It really got me thinking! I soon realized it wasn't just a wartime phenomenon. Historical literature shows a strong, consistent link between prostitution and the ruling classes of South Asia. Not only is there evidence that the ruling classes supported the women's arts and dancing by keeping them in their courts, but also that they supported the business of prostitution, in many cases institutionalising it through their governments.

Paul frowned and said, 'First, what do you mean by ruling classes, and in what time period, and then lets define this "link" you're talking about. A link can mean anything.'

I responded quickly, 'The key players in the literature who I think constitute the 'ruling class' are, first, the rulers or those who controlled state administration and, second, the leaders of the army. In many cases the first two groups were the same, so we can look at them together. The third group, religious leaders, had varying degrees of control and importance in the administration and government.'

'So, you're talking about the elite who ruled the area and imposed the law.'

'Not only imposed, but created the law and developed the regulations, official regulations through their administration and social regulations through the religions. You know that the major religions engulfed most local religious traditions after the conquerors brought them into South Asia.'

'Basically, you mean the men who had power and control of a kingdom or a country.' asked Paul.

'Precisely.'

'Now, what kind of link to prostitution are you talking about?'

'I found that all three categories of men were instrumental in developing, institutionalising and protecting prostitutes.'

Paul thought about this for a while, 'So, you are saying that studying the link between prostitution and the ruling elite is crucial to understanding how the institutionalised sex trade developed in South Asia. You're also saying this link is more of an employer-employee link.'

'Well, I wouldn't define it so narrowly, but, basically, yes. Since I'm learning that the ruling elite developed and institutionalised prostitution in South Asia we have to analyse the relationship between the two,' I said, confidently.

'That's a big claim!' Paul raised his eyebrows, 'What evidence have you found?'

'Oh', I said, 'I've found incredible stuff. Look at this,' I picked up an open book, 'Here, Joardar has reproduced an amazing text from 300 BC. Rules and regulations to manage prostitution were part of a ten-volume documentation of the government of Chandra Gupta Maurya. According to this text, the government took full control of the institution of prostitution for taxation purposes and regulated the women's activities as a part of the State property. Women initiated into sexual service were also used as an intelligence force. They owed their services and income to the State. The government appointed a superintendent of prostitutes who arranged for the women's training in music and dance and managed their business. Do you understand?' I demanded. 'This wasn't a link where the government made some deal with the managers of the prostitutes; the government was itself the manager and punished a courtesan who disobeyed the king. Do you get it?'

'I see what you mean. The government was the owner and the manager. But did this apply to only those women who worked in the court or to all the prostitutes in their area?' asked Paul.

'Access to prostitutes was restricted. The state controlled who was given this privilege. I can read you some documentation from later periods when the kings began getting worried about the profession getting out of control and common people, especially traders, benefiting from access to unregulated prostitution.'

I continued, 'since Vedic times (c. 1000 BC), India was known to have had courtesans who were highly accomplished in music and dance. The Aryans had a tradition of providing these beautiful women as "pleasure gifts" to alien kings as a mark of affection and hospitality. Vedic literature has several sources referring to prostitutes and their place in society. These suggest that prostitution existed as a well-organized institution that was socially accepted and had specific assets and obligations. Plenty of evidence, from the *Mahabharta* to recent studies, indicates that, in those days, the sex trade wasn't widespread, only existing for a small section of the aristocracy. The classification of prostitutes was well defined in those days also, reflecting a well-developed system corresponding to the strict hierarchy among the aristocrats themselves.'

Paul picked up a book lying on a chair and said, 'Why have you marked a quote from Al-Beruni?'

'Al-Beruni was a well-known scholar and traveller living around 1030 AD. He commented on the peculiar relationship of the Indian Princely States with prostitution. Why don't you read it?' I asked him.

Paul started to read, 'In reality, the matter is not as people think, but it is rather this, that the Hindus are not very severe in punishing whoredom. The fault, however, in this lies with the kings, not with the nation. But for this, no Brahman or priest would suffer in their idol-temples the women who sing, dance and play. The kings make them an attraction for their cities, a bait of pleasure for their subjects, for none other but financial reasons. By the revenues which they derive from the business both as fines and taxes, they want to recover the expenses which their treasury has to spend on the army.'[1]

'You see, he had the insight to see through the state's involvement,' I said with a conqueror's smile, and went on. 'Let me show you more. In the Indian kingdoms that existed just prior to the Mughal conquest, prostitution was a significant part of the kingdoms' administration. A policy had developed whereby most of the income the State earned from the sex trade was used for maintaining a large police force. The prostitutes

---

[1] Joardar, 1984, *Prostitution in Historical and Modern Perspectives*, New Delhi: Inter-India Publications.

regularly served the army, in addition to the aristocrats and the royalty. The ruling elite seems instrumental in creating, encouraging, protecting and/or regulating the phenomenon of prostitution. They were the key beneficiaries in any case. One can say that, practically speaking, prostitution evolved and flourished around these institutions.'

'Let's take a tea break,' interrupted Paul, 'we'll have a chance to reflect a little.'

'Okay!' I took a deep breath. Very hyped up, I added, 'Let's talk about the Mughals in the restaurant.' I knew of Paul's study on the Mughal period and his special emphasis on the performing arts.

He smiled at me and said, 'So, you think with me around you won't need to carry your books to the restaurant to discuss the Mughals.'

I laughed.

The restaurant was spacious and well-lighted, unlike the stuffy library halls. Paul ordered tea and I a Coke, thinking it hilarious that every time I ordered myself a Coke, I heard Laila's voice in my ear calling me a *'paindu'*.

Paul and I immediately started in again, as I couldn't talk about anything else in the world, but this. 'Tell me about the Mughals', I urged.

'Mughals!' Paul exclaimed, 'The Muslim Mongol invaders who came from Persia in the early part of the sixteenth century and ruled over half of South Asia. You want me to tell you all about two and a half centuries over tea?' He paused, 'Actually, it's nearly impossible for me to separate their patronage for arts and music on the one hand and prostitution on the other, because I've always seen them together. Actually, I never considered it prostitution as such, because the tradition of those days was very different from ours, or the typical western concept of prostitution.' Paul stroked his beard and looked out of the window. He went on, 'Mughals not only patronized singers and dancers, they were also great admirers of poetry, painting, music, crafts and architecture, providing patronage to all kinds of artists. Both men and women artists were championed. Craftsmen from other countries, scholars, and poets from far-flung areas were invited to share their knowledge and art. They supported great masters of classical music, men as well as women. These artists were given regular stipends and housing and were assigned to the courts on a regular basis. The women artists mostly belonged to the higher status communities of entertainers. They acquired fame and respect on the basis of their singing and dancing, but extending their entertainment of the royalty to sexual pleasures was an accepted, and even desired tradition.'

I added, 'Harems were maintained where hundreds of young women had the task of keeping the palace clean and organized. By tradition these women were available for sexual service to any men from the royal families.'

Paul sipped his tea and said, 'Yes, but I always looked at that from a cultural perspective.'

I interrupted, 'I understand the tension in your voice, Paul. You culture *walas* are torn between acknowledging and appreciating the performing arts of the courtesans and accepting the fact that the rulers had them available for sex as well.'

Paul smiled and said, 'You've conveniently separated yourself from the culture *wala* category! You're one of us. Don't you feel the tension?'

'Yes, but I'm a feminist first. I also know about the power dynamics operating between men and women and how whole societies are structured around that one principle. Let me clarify one thing for you,' I said firmly. 'The purpose of exploring the direct beneficiaries and sectors of society that helped the sex trade flourish doesn't, in my mind, trivialize this community's appreciation of music and the development of the performing arts and the invaluable contributions high level courtesans made in music, poetry and literature. But in order to understand the dynamics of how prostitution flourished and was managed over the centuries in South Asia I have to go deeper than my simple appreciation and respect for all the good that came out of this support for the artists. Do you understand what I mean?'

'Just like when I saw the great pyramids in Egypt and was awestruck by the power they represented, the unbelievable magnitude and advancement of the society, at the same time, I knew how many slaves worked on those monuments, and how many died. I get the same feeling admiring beautiful grand palaces and the heights of aesthetics they touch. I always experience some pain from knowing that they symbolize the absolute power of an elite minority over a poor, subservient majority. Being a woman maybe it's easier for me to feel the victimization of the many, hidden in the grandeur of a few. Women are quite familiar with such situations. About the Mughals, I've learned that they recognized prostitution as an institution and managed it through specifically appointed representatives of the king. All the Mughal rulers, to varying degrees, maintained control over this business.' I added.

'Yes,' Paul added, 'most Mughal rulers were great patrons of singing and dancing women; prostitution was legal and liable for taxes. Emperor Akbar (1556-1605) is known as the greatest patron of music and dancing, besides being an eminent scholar himself, while Emperor Aurangzeb (1658-1707) was the other extreme. A staunch Muslim, he tried to ban prostitution, but failed to eradicate it. As fast as he closed down the bazaars in Delhi, the courtesans moved to other areas where rich patrons protected them. In any case there were many famous love affairs and several palaces and tombs built in the memories of courtesans during that time.'

I interrupted him, 'My information is that Akbar realized that the sex trade was getting out of hand and he took special measures to make sure that access to prostitutes was not available to just anybody. Anyone who wished to take a virgin had to get permission from the court. He appointed a keeper, a deputy and a secretary to manage the quarters of prostitutes that he brought together in a community called Shaitanpura. During the seventeen years he held court in Lahore, the city alone had over six thousand houses of prostitutes.'

'Good! You have done a thorough investigation,' interrupted Paul, 'you should remember it was all guided by tradition.'

'But who controlled the tradition?' I snapped at him, 'traditions, social or religious, were all imposed by the ruling elite.'

Paul responded, 'As far as the social hierarchy and power structures are concerned, I agree. Traditions linked to those were transformed by the elite to suit their political needs.'

Moving on to the military power circles, I said, 'Since conquering new lands and defending the kingdom's boundaries were two crucial issues for the royalty, senior military officials enjoyed high rank and prestige in the courts. Women used to accompany the marching Mughal armies to provide them entertainment. Separate camps were set up for them, and the officers as well as soldiers could avail themselves of their services. The more skilled dancing girls used to entertain in the elaborate camps of the senior military officials. This link of prostitution with the ruling elite continued through the disintegration of the Royal States, but it wasn't controlled by the royalty alone. Many other important political powers entered the arena. Right?'

I didn't wait for an answer, 'Historical documentation points out that, with the arrival of Portuguese, French and English traders, prostitution flourished in the seaports of Bombay, Calcutta, Cochin and Madras. Foreign traders came to India without families and satisfied their sexual desires with Indian women. Many kept concubines. According to Kapur, purely commercial prostitution flourished in the subcontinent in the early seventeenth century as the traders became major clients of the prostitutes. From the ports it spread into the bigger cities and then to other parts of the region. Profit became more important than tradition, and, in addition, women were forced into brothels.'

Paul added, 'I understand that traders brought in women from other countries for Indian brothels near the ports where this business boomed. During the East India Company rule, followed by the establishment of the British Raj, prostitution increased and many brothels opened to entertain British men who were either unmarried or came to India without their families. This also helped give rise to the present Anglo-Indian community.'

'I just found out,' I continued, 'that in Great Britain, in 1870-71, a military budget of £40,000 was spent to provide 2700 registered prostitutes for the armed forces. Thus, the British also had the tradition of using foreign prostitutes for their soldiers.'

Paul responded with a smile, 'the *nautch* girls in Calcutta and their accompanying musicians were all Muslims. Besides the local aristocrats, these girls intrigued the British as well. Nude *nautch* girls were often used as models for drawing by British artists.'

I interrupted, 'According to oral traditions in Lahore, the famous Anarkali bazaar actually came into being because of the British. Their armies always camped outside the main cities and established what we now call cantonments. They created one outside the walled city of Lahore. To provide for their needs, a market grew up along the path from the campsite to the walled city. Soon, the soldiers attracted prostitutes who took over the second floors of the shops to set up their own businesses.'

'That's new to me,' said Paul, surprised to hear this. 'Why was it called Anarkali?'

'The grave of Anarkali, the famous courtesan whose romance with the Mughal King Jehangir became a legend is supposedly close to where the soldiers built their camp. People now say it's where the old Secretariat Building stands', I answered.

'I should pay my regards to Anarkali next time I go to Lahore,' he laughed.

'My point is that in the early 1900s the British were both clients of prostitutes and reformers of prostitution. They revised regulations to control the sex trade and trafficking of women. All prostitutes had to register with the government. One research study on the dancing girls of Calcutta includes specific questions women were asked when they applied for registration with the Commissioner of Police. Any girl below sixteen, or who was pregnant or married, but not properly divorced, was not registered. Sometimes, if a girl was a virgin, her guardians were instructed to keep her out of the business until she was older. The women were given medical check-ups and treatment if required. Their cards had space for the dates of the medical check-ups. The number of prostitutes was in the census, which documented prostitution as a legal profession. In Calcutta, the 1921 Census reported 10,814 prostitutes, the second largest group of working women after the 20,999 domestic servants. So the British clearly did little to eliminate prostitution during their rule. In many ways, their administrative practices further legitimised and institutionalised it.'

Paul straightened his back, looked at his watch and laughed, 'I guess we had a long enough break.'

I smiled, 'I guess it wasn't a break for you, but I really enjoyed our talk. It helps me clarify my ideas. You corroborated what I've found in the history books. I'd still like to discuss with you how I feel the religious elite has also supported prostitution.'

Getting up from his chair, Paul suggested that we get on with our own work and continue with our discussion the next day. We both went upstairs. Paul got lost in the aisles that interested him and I prepared myself for a talk about religious patronage for the sex trade. I lined up my books and notes I'd been making during my long search for the real causes of prostitution.

The next morning, I reached the library about nine and settled down in the same quite corner, spreading out my documents far away from the librarian. Paul came in an hour later. We said hello and geared up for our discussion. Paul said, 'Okay, shoot. Give me your argument first.'

I began, 'I have records showing how religious institutions in different parts of the world viewed, or were connected to prostitution, but most of my material focuses on the South Asian tradition of *Devadasi*. In Cyprus, King Cinyras instituted sacred prostitution. Residents had a custom of sending their daughters off to the seashore to earn their dowry by prostitution and to make offerings to Venus to help them in the future. In the Sumerian culture of Mesopotamia, women were attached to every temple as menial workers or concubines to priests. In several cultures so called "dishonoured women" of men defeated or killed in war had to serve in temples and provide sexual service.'

'Then the Romans on the one hand regulated prostitutes, registered them and collected taxes from them, but also gave strict orders not to marry into those families and denounced them socially. At a later time though, both the administration and religion accepted them fully. Herniques found that Emperor Justinian of Rome (sixth century AD) himself married a prostitute and made efforts to rehabilitate them. In medieval Europe prostitutes were persecuted and yet were considered a necessary evil, and brothels were still maintained through public expenditure. The women had to wear a distinctive dress and live in secluded sections of the city. Civil and church authorities shared the revenues equally.'

'Now, I'll tell you what I have found about *Devadasi* in Hindu religious traditions. You know about that, don't you?'

'A little,' Paul replied, 'but I know more about their musical traditions. You know they excelled in singing *bhajans* and were invited to rich people's houses to lead *puja*. The tradition came to the subcontinent around 300 AD right?' he asked.

'About then, yes. The custom was to seek *mukti* by purchasing a girl, usually from a "lower" caste and offering her to a temple in the name of god. These young women were called *Devadasi*, or in the north, *Mangalmukhis*, *Devaratial* or *Kudikhar*. Their job was to clean the temple, fan the deity and sing and dance for the worshipers. Property was put in their name and they shared income from the temple, helping the tradition to spread quickly. Literature indicates that prostitution by the *Devadasis* began secretly and then became institutionalised to the point that *Devadasi* came to mean "religious prostitute". The *Devadasi* cult flourished during the Pallava and Chola dynasties in South India, from the sixth to thirteenth centuries AD. Many historians agree that "sacred prostitution" in India reached its height in the ninth and tenth centuries and was associated with the great spurt of temple building. It was actually banned in the early twentieth century, but continued in some places.'

Paul asked whether I found any evidence of patronage by Muslim religious structures and I answered, 'No! I didn't find any documentation of hiring, managing or encouraging prostitution by Muslim religious scholars or Sufis.'

Paul stretched and said, 'This role carved out for the *Devadasis* was pretty complex. Low class and somewhat stigmatised, they still were respected in the society and had a prescribed well-accepted role. Since they were married to gods who were immortal, they could never become widowed. This was very positive and they were supposed to bring good luck and prosperity.'

'You know that's true about other traditional prostitutes too,' I said. 'They were stigmatised, but at the same time enjoyed a certain position in the society. But my main point is that just as courtesans flourished under royal patronage, *Devadasis* were encouraged and supported in the vested interests of the temple priests. Some historians argue that the popularity of many temples was somewhat due to the sensuous women attached to them.'

Paul sighed and said, 'It makes sense to me. But what about now? How does this all relate to the present?'

'Thanks for asking,' I grinned. 'I'd say the link prostitution has with the ruling class is still strong. Just look at the composition of the current ruling class.'

'Okay,' said Paul, 'let's say it's comprised of politicians, business tycoons, military and, sure, bureaucrats, also. I think the religious groups are operating through politicians or bureaucrats, so they may not really be part of the ruling elite.'

'Yes', I added, 'but we need to see the current situation as a result of the process I described. This is the aftermath. Things are out of control. A cadre was developed to entertain a small, powerful minority, but the traditions developed to ensure its stability are gone. Pakistani society is going through major changes and the turnover in the ruling class is very rapid. Things in general are out of control. Attitudes about the sex trade are only a minor element in all this. The relationship of the police towards the *Kanjar* and *Mirasi* is not so different from the attitude of the police toward people in our society in general. The harassment is just at a higher level and on a daily basis in the Shahi Mohalla. No one in Pakistan is totally free from police harassment, any more than people are free from the shifting winds of political oppression and arbitrary administrative aggravation.'

'The traditions surrounding prostitution that are manifest in the Shahi Mohalla's complex social organization are disintegrating on their own. The police and the administration are simply helping them disappear more quickly than they otherwise would, and I might add, without having any impact whatsoever on the amount of prostitution in the city. Ordinary citizens should watch this in order to understand that what is favoured at one time in history can easily be swept away in another. What the elite creates, the elite can destroy. Unfortunately, as happened with Aurangzeb, the suppression of traditional practices often results not in their disappearance, but in their evolution into other forms more difficult to control. The flourishing of *kothi khanas* filled with girls who have been forced into prostitution and the proliferation of "hobby" prostitutes, middle class girls providing sexual service either for extra money or for kicks, are partly the result of modern elite actions against the *Kanjar*. The long-term consequences of this are far worse than the traditions they are trying to destroy.'

'So, what I'm saying is that maybe we don't see the same patterns as in the past when the ruling class was the main impetus for prostitution, although some of that is very evident even today, but we need to consider the present times as the aftermath of that ancient institutional arrangement. People, in general, hang on to their prejudices and myths about prostitution, especially as practiced in the Mohalla, but the profession has been transformed into a service for the masses and is spreading like wildfire.'

# 33

## THE REAL REASONS
## Conversation with Chanda and Faiza

I felt uneasy as I wrapped up my historical research. I was still unable to resolve our society's clear-cut hypocrisy and double standards in its treatment of prostitutes. Paul Amin had already left Pakistan by that time. I needed someone else to listen to my thoughts. Why, despite all the proclaimed efforts for reform, do the very reformers declare that no prostitute can ever be reformed? From the literature I could only tell that institutionalised prostitution has always had strong links to elite classes (be they rulers, administrators, military men or religious leaders), which have alternately supported, protected, regulated or 'reformed' the profession. So much was clear, but I still failed to understand the stigma attached to it, a stigma more severe than that applied to any other social activity that violates moral sanctions.

One morning I decided to visit Chanda to discuss some of these ideas with her. As I was about to leave, Faiza asked if she could come along. Throughout my research in the Mohalla I'd often used Faiza as a sounding board to clarify my thoughts. I immediately invited her along, thinking she just might add a perspective that would be useful. We went first to her college so she could take care of a few tasks, and around 11 o'clock, we headed towards the Mohalla. On the way, I shared with her something my guru told me once. She was surprised I had a guru and I told her I had several gurus, who all give me precious advice. I said that my guru once told me that whenever I am unable to properly visualize the solution to a problem I should close my eyes until my vision is blurred, and only then would I see what is important. Faiza looked at me rather oddly, so I explained that he said that when we see things very clearly we can get so involved in looking at things that are close to us that we are distracted by the details. When we partially close our eyes and blur our vision, we can see patterns, and sometimes seeing broader patterns can be more important than focusing on details. Maybe I needed to see the bigger patterns and not get stuck in the details and exceptions.

We reached Chanda's house. By good luck her mother had gone to Data Sahib. She was barely awake, so we sat around her bed. I told her I wanted to have a serious talk with her about the roots of prostitution.

'What can I tell you?' she began, 'All I know is someone carved out this groove for us and we stayed in it, without questioning. God is a witness, we did not choose it; this role was given to us. I was told that to be a good daughter, I should do my job well and keep my mother happy. I've been doing it honestly, but I didn't choose it myself.'

'Chanda,' I answered, 'what you just said is very important. Do you know that?'

She smiled in sincere embarrassment. Straightening up her bed sheet she told Faiza to sit on the bed to be more comfortable.

I said, 'I have been doing a lot of thinking about this and reading what other people have written about it. To me it all seems to link to patriarchy.'

'What is patriarchy, Fouzia?' she asked.

Faiza spoke up, 'It's a male dominated system where men are at the centre. Right, *baji*?'

'Yes,' I nodded, 'patriarchy is a social system based on male lineage, where the man is the head of any social unit—family, neighbourhood, village, or country! Actually, the core of this system is that the man has to ensure the continuance of his genes and name into the next generation. He's developed the whole system to ensure that.'

Chanda pondered, 'So, basically, men have developed the system for themselves?'

Hesitantly I responded, 'Well, it's not that individual men developed a master plan, intentionally leaving women out, but the system has evolved over centuries under the influence of men who were in positions of power. It doesn't necessarily serve all men, but the system benefits mostly men in power.'

Faiza was concentrating hard, 'Basically, if we want to analyse patriarchy in relation to the sex trade, we could ask the question, "Who does this system serve?" The answer would be the men who are in power, right?'

'Good, Faiza, good! That's another way of looking at it,' I said.

'Now, what did you say about the transfer of genes?' Chanda asked, with a naughty smile, 'Tell me about that.'

'In a patriarchy, the lineage descends from the man,' I began, 'the children belong to him; they take his name, his status, his religion and his property. That's why a woman is moved to his house to join his family and not the other way around. She changes her name to his and all the children take the man's name. I'll share something with you. One day when I was small, my father was going through my grandfather's old things and he found a document with the family tree of the last seven generations of our family. He called all the children over to show it to us. I was very excited and kept asking, "Where am I, where am I in the tree?" To my great disappointment no women were listed in that family tree. Under my father only one name appeared, my brother's. None of my sisters were there.'

Faiza asked, 'In some western countries don't they now include wives and daughters in the family trees?'

'Yes, but the families still mostly follow the male lineage. In western societies, women have become quite professional, but most still change their names when they marry and, ironically, often keep changing it with every new husband. The tradition of taking the husband's name was exported to South Asia by the British.'

Faiza, staring in the air, remarked, 'I knew that at some level, but you know we hardly think about it. We take all this for granted '

Chanda said, 'But in our system, everything is the other way round. The mother is the one who is important.'

'Yes, Chanda, yours is a special South Asian sub-culture. We'll come to that, but let's look at the larger system first. Later, we'll find clues to why your system is different from the rest, or whether it really is different at all. Patriarchy is the system of the larger society. Now, let's ask ourselves, what does a man do to ensure the transfer of his genes to the next generation?'

Faiza exclaimed, 'He gets married.'

'Okay,' I went on. 'So marriage is created to establish a relationship where a certain woman is to be his wife, and the relationship is announced socially with rituals and festivities. It's a public announcement that the woman has left her father's lineage and has joined the man's family. She is no longer "eligible", so to speak. She is "taken" in marriage by a man.'

'Sure,' Faiza added, 'that is why, in our culture, the bride's family cries because they're losing a daughter and the groom's family celebrates because they're gaining a daughter-in-law. She literally leaves her family and joins that of her husband's.'

Chanda spoke up, 'Marriage is also an announcement that the woman now has a husband.'

'Yes, it is,' I agreed. 'If we think crudely, you see, a woman is just a vessel to produce children. Now she belongs to him and he must ensure that she remains pure and only carries his genes and no one else's. So, what does he do?'

Faiza said, 'He puts her under the burden of morality. He wants to keep her "pure" for himself. He wants her to remain confined, not go out too much, not talk too much, not be exposed to the world too much and not travel too much. He doesn't want her to become too smart, too educated or too empowered, right?' Faiza leaned back, immersed in her own thoughts. Then she sat straight up and said, 'Baji, all this preference for submissive women, especially when choosing a woman for marriage, is directly linked to this, isn't it! Men want women they can control. Whenever a family visited us to look me over as a prospective daughter-in-law, my mother told me not to speak unless someone asked me a direct question. I was told just to answer whatever they asked me, and not to initiate any conversation. Isn't that part of it?'

Chanda agreed, 'Haven't you heard that Pakistani men who go abroad like to fool around with western woman, but when it's time for marriage they run back to their mothers to look for a woman half their age who's never seen a man before and who has never left her city.' She broke into laughter.

'When I was studying in the States, that's exactly what I saw,' I confirmed.

Faiza kept going, 'Morals are for women, but nobody worries much about standards for men's behaviour. Men act as if they had the right to be custodians of women's behaviour, but women are never considered men's custodians. The reason for establishing a moral system seems to be focused on controlling women's behaviour and, most of all, their sexuality. Men are threatened by outgoing women, afraid that if such a woman became his wife, she might approach other men and become "impure" for him.'

Faiza exclaimed sarcastically, 'Oh my God! Just imagine, his vessel carrying another man's sperm!' We all laughed.

'Men created these morals to control women,' I said, 'and then used religion to help. Most religious practices only focus on appropriate behaviour for women, covering their bodies and being modest. No one talks much about religious rituals required to control men's behaviour.'

Chanda agreed, 'I like this thing you just said about morality. I always used to laugh at the religious people, *ina da islam aurtan te i mukda e* (their Islam ends at women). They're always putting more and more restrictions on women. They never talk to the press about the corrupting influence of men even though all our clients are men from the city who come here openly under their noses. They never say anything about them. One girl tries to marry a man against her family's will, her legal right actually, and you see these religious men calling her names and declaring her a non-Muslim. They're obsessed with women so they want women to hide all the time. So many taboos about a

woman's body, but when was the last time a man was punished
for leering at a woman? These religious cults want women to
cover themselves more and more. Now they should cover their
heads, then their hands, their faces, and go about wearing a
black shroud as if they were a dead body—for some they may
as well be.' She laughed openly, 'You want a prostitute's
opinion? I think they just think about women too much!'

I smiled and looked at her. 'Morality is used to control
only women's sexuality; why would they put controls on
themselves? If men come to your Mohalla and "sin", it's your
fault! They don't have to be bound by any morals. Women
should take the burden of all society's bad things. So if a woman
is harassed at a bus stop, she's the one who is told not to leave
home again, as if the fault was hers because she left the house
in the first place. No one considers that the man who harassed
her could be at fault.'

Faiza's eyes brightened, '*Baji*, so that's why we have two
standards of morality, one for men and a different one for
women. I always wondered why my brother could get away
with so much and I'd be nailed for the smallest thing. He can
laugh out loud; he can go out. I've also got legs, but he's the
one who goes out to get things, not me, even if it's just down
the road. He can be with his friends as much as he likes but
every evening I spend out is counted. I never understood why
these double standards existed.'

'If influential men are the ones who create morality,' I said,
'they can make as many sets of morals as they want, without
justifying themselves to anyone. The dilemma is that the rest of
society is socialized into following their rules without question,
because morality, especially if it comes wrapped in religion,
isn't to be questioned.'

Chanda asked, 'Is this why men can have affairs, but not
women? It's accepted if a man has sex before he gets married or
even afterwards with someone other than his wife. In male
company he'll even brag about it. But if the wife or sister or
fiancée of the same man told him about one adventure with
another man, what do you think would happen?'

Faizia shrieked, 'If it's his wife or sister, he'd kill her. If it's a woman he's supposed to marry, he'd certainly never marry her.'

'Right, because with a woman like that they'd feel threatened,' I confirmed. 'They couldn't control her sexuality. He would consider her impure. That's why society puts such a high premium on virginity. In some traditions a groom has to display the virginal blood on a handkerchief to prove his bride's purity. In Western countries white was supposed to be the colour of the wedding dress only for virgin brides. If you weren't a virgin you had to distinguish yourself by wearing a pastel coloured dress.'

Faiza jumped in enthusiastically, 'I remember when Princess Diana went through the virginity test, and we all wondered why no one makes such an issue out of male virginity. If not physically, Prince Charles should at least have taken an oath with his hand on the Bible stating he was also a virgin.'

We laughed. I said, 'virginity is very important to them and so is sexual "purity".'

Faiza said, 'They can't stand women who know something about sex. Women always have to pretend that they know nothing about it and don't even like it.'

'Well,' I said, 'they still cut off a woman's clitoris in some parts of the world. That certainly shows men's fears of their women enjoying sex.' We kept talking about the standards that determine a "good woman", one suitable for marriage. We discussed the morals that pressure women to remain "pure" for a man. There's even a further set of morals and values developed by powerful men and religious leaders to ensure that these "good" women should stay with their men.'

Surprised, Chanda asked, 'What's that?'

'You see,' I continued, 'any thinking woman would revolt against a system that's biased and full of double standards, so they bind her with traditions and moral values that keep her from leaving without suffering terrible consequences. That explains the tradition that a woman loses all respect, social status and often her economic support if she leaves her husband.

The entire burden again rests on her shoulders. This false morality binds her even for her husband's wrongdoing. Even if he beats her, it's her fault. I've been working with women's counselling organizations for a long time, but I still feel peculiar when I talk to women who've been beaten up for years and still choose to stay with their husbands. They stay because they're afraid of the false morality that will blame them if they leave and will deprive them of their place in society. Women don't even think about this; it's so deeply rooted.'

'How convenient,' Faiza said, 'the men can rest assured that their wives will stay and never even object to the double standards. Their control is total.'

'Yes, these moral traditions run very deep through our society. Behaviour is so often directed by tradition that people rarely know why they are acting as they do.'

Faiza kept pondering, 'Besides, when a woman is married, her parents send her off to *pia ke ghar* (the house of her husband). It's her husband's house, not hers. Even after twenty years of marriage he has the right to kick her out in the street literally "in three clothes"—*shalwar, kamiz,* and *dupatta*—because it never really was her house, but was always his. So if she ever leaves she loses all status in society and everything. Even if things are changing gradually, the underlying attitudes are the same. This double standard guarantees that the freedom men want for themselves don't rub off and corrupt their women. Women's lives and their sexuality are totally tied up by these moral traditions.'

I said, 'Yes, and to top it off, they created this concept of "honour". It's intrigued me for years. Men created this concept and housed it in women's bodies. So I am the honour of my father and my brother and my husband. What a man does himself doesn't affect his honour, but if "his" woman ever crosses these false moral lines, it tarnishes his honour.'

'What do you mean?' puzzled Chanda.

I asked her, 'Have you heard the story of the *jin* and the *tota* (the genie and the parrot)? The genie's soul was in a parrot. No one could kill the genie unless they reached the parrot. So the genie built a secret den in a big mountain and hid the parrot. Once the parrot was hidden, the genie was indestructible, free to move around and do whatever he liked. It's the same idea here. A man places his honour inside a woman's body and hides her away in his house, freeing himself to go around and do anything he wants, without any damage to his honour. He can come to your Mohalla, he can commit rape, and he can abuse his wife. He may even run afoul of the law and be arrested, but his honour will not be questioned.

'His honour is challenged only by something linked to his nidden woman. If any man outside the family even looks at her, his honour is challenged. The woman may do nothing "immoral". In more conservative parts of Pakistan, if some man in the street catches just a glimpse of a woman's face, her husband's honour is challenged. In the North West Frontier Province, it's an open secret that men murder their own wives and any man with whom the wife may have had a completely innocent conversation. This "honour killing", called *Karo Kari* in Sindh and *Sia Kari* in Balochistan, has societal approval. Until very recently, even courts allowed these murders in the name of "honour". Among groups where women are instructed to wear a *chaddar*, taking her *chaddar* off in an office could offend her husband's honour. Regardless of what a woman herself may think, any action of hers that offends her husband causes him to lose his honour.'

Surprised, Chanda sputtered, 'Really!'

'I'm talking about present day values in our country.' I emphasized. 'In some places a woman's own brother or uncles can kill her if she's raped. Why? Because her rape dishonours them! Ask these people to explain the logic behind it and they can't. They become much too emotional. They have been so socialized for many generations.'

Faiza said, 'Nothing happens to the rapists' honour, right, or the honour of his family? But we see this all the time, not only in these extreme cases. I know the difference in my life between my brother receiving a phone call from a female classmate and my getting a call from a male classmate at our home. For him, someone may joke, "Our son is growing up!" But I'll face a hundred questions: "who was he, what does he do, how do you know him, what did he want?" It can be very subtle, but still the control on me is very evident, and regardless of how I feel about it, my father's and brother's honour will become an issue.'

I said, 'Let's go back to Chanda's earlier point about the Mohalla. Men wanted restrictions on the women who reproduce for them, and they wanted full control over their sexuality. But for themselves, they wanted something more, so they created space for their playgrounds. They created little pocket sub-cultures for their own entertainment. Later, even more ingeniously, they labelled these as bad places, so only the powerful could take pleasure there. Having women other than their wives available has been arranged in many ways, by keeping harems or slave women, having female maids available sexually and by allowing prostitution. They created a group of women who would provide sex freely, and all the entertainment they could think of. They played out whatever fantasies they wanted. They entertain themselves with these women, but consider them very low class. In their minds, women are either "good" or "bad", or, rather, "pure" or "impure". All women fall in one category or the other. The "good" ones are mothers, daughters, sisters and wives (all relations in association to a man) and the bad ones are all whores. Even now many men have a hard time placing women in any other category. She is either in his home or in a *kotha*. That's why women working in offices and factories here are struggling to create a new category for themselves as just women.'

Chanda became very serious, and the silence grew. She seemed sad and sunk in deep thought. Finally she spoke, 'Fouzia, I knew I didn't chose this role, that it was given to me, but now I'm beginning to see that it's not simply a God-given fate. Some influential men created the system and our *dhanda* (business of prostitution), and your society accepted it.'

'Our society!' I looked back at Chanda.

She smiled, 'We've been thinking "us" and "them" for so long, it will take me a while to use the word our for the whole society.'

I saw a tear in her eye, and she shook her head, 'So social traditions long ago assigned us our place, and it's pretty well planned, well established and well protected. Look at me,' her voice rose, 'look at me, I still follow each rule.' She paused, 'But I can't understand one thing. Why did our mothers go along and instil these values in us when it went against us? Why did they socialize us so completely to play out these roles?'

Faiza responded immediately, 'In my world, a mother socializes her daughter to be submissive and obedient to her man. She knows she has to transfer this tradition to her daughter so she can survive in the system. She doesn't want her daughter to deviate and suffer. No mother wants that for her daughter. She may not understand the underlying system, but she has the responsibility to socialize her children to prescribed male and female roles. My mother is like that. She always wanted "social approval" for me. She doesn't think she's reinforcing her own inferiority. All she wants is for her daughter to survive and succeed in the system.'

'I get it! My mother always told me she didn't want me to suffer and be left behind. She taught me all she knew about surviving in this system,' said Chanda putting her head on Faiza's shoulder. 'She doesn't understand the larger picture of the social system any more than I do. All she knows is that she had to bring me up to fit into the system and not be punished by our society for deviating. She told me marrying and trying to lead a life without selling my body is against the rules and strongly disapproved of. She didn't want me to marry someone from my own biradri because it would disown me for not following the rules. She didn't want me to be left alone. All she wanted was "social approval" for me. She wanted me to play by the rules so that I wouldn't get hurt.'

After a heavy silence, I continued, 'Men wanted to distinguish between their courtesans and women they use for reproduction. That's the value of stigma. The playgrounds created for men are heavily stigmatised. Going there isn't so bad, only the women who work there are defamed. The stigma comes with well-rooted myths that maintain the status quo. First, these women are not for marriage. Their purpose is to entertain, not to carry on a man's lineage. Because of the stigma, people feel these women are "bad" from birth and responsible for society's evils. They should never be allowed to marry into mainstream society where they could corrupt other people's values and morals. Basically, the stigma keeps them isolated and distant, where they can be blamed for the existence of the "problem" and not be used for reproduction.

'Second, it ensures that they don't get out of their prescribed role as prostitutes. The stigma makes it impossible for them to even think about a different lifestyle. All the myths, like "once a prostitute always a prostitute", "a prostitute never gets accepted in society", and so on help make sure that this pool of "free women" is always available to men. Third, the stigma keeps them from mixing with "good women" and corrupting them. It reinforces the categories and creates a fear of these women so "good women" stay far away from their influence. Any woman from "polite" society who tries to express herself openly or shows an interest in the performing arts is strongly pressured to change. Her actions are associated with the "negative" role assigned to prostitutes. The stigma prevents any mixing of the two categories, guaranteeing that "pure" women remain "pure" and "bad" women stay isolated and "bad".'

'Huh!' Faiza put her hand on her mouth, her eyes open wide. 'Do you remember how scared I was when I came here with you for the first time on that New Years Eve? What was I afraid of?' she asked herself. She looked restlessly around the room and then stopped and stared at the wall, 'I was breaking the boundary of the two categories, stepping into a forbidden world, forbidden for women like me, that is, and look how I am now talking to Chanda about it!' A smile lit up her face.

'The stigma itself is an interesting phenomenon,' I added, 'Just like honour, it's mostly used to control women's sexuality. We have to ask why a woman born to the profession doesn't complain about this attitude.'

Chanda said, 'Because she's the one who is stigmatised, through her very life.'

'Yes, but isn't that ironic? She's accused of a crime for which she has no fault. Why? Anyway, Chanda, tell me, if a man comes and asks you for sex, gets what he wants and pays for it, who's responsible?'

Faiza exclaimed, 'According to the male system, Chanda is.'

Chanda turned toward Faiza, her mouth open.

'Right,' I said with a laugh. 'Even though he pays for what he wants, Chanda is the one who must be reformed, not him. I read somewhere that when Nehru was president of the Municipality of Allahabad in the 1920s, some people complained to him about prostitution and asked him to pass an order that prostitutes had to be secluded in a specific location rather than being able to work all over the city. He refused to do that and said he'd comply only if he could also create a separate area for those who visit them. Wasn't that an interesting answer?'

Chanda broke in, 'What I can't understand is why people don't see through this. Why do normally intelligent people think it's our fault that men come to us? We don't go looking for them. It's they who come after us.'

'Let me try to answer that,' I said. 'First, ordinary people aren't setting the standards. People in power establish them, and since it's not in their interest to bring themselves into the spotlight it serves their purpose to blame you. Second, two other myths are crucial here. Many historians call prostitution a necessary evil, saying that prostitutes have to be tolerated to safeguard family values. Otherwise, stray men would bother the "respectable women". The other myth is that men are biologically polygamous.'

Faiza exclaimed angrily, 'My God! I've heard that so many times. It's how they used to justify polygamy. And to justify a man raping a woman people say, "After all he's a man. You know how men's sexual needs are". What are their sexual needs? It's nice for them to create that image so they can get away with rape.'

Chanda said, cynically, 'Men have conveniently created this image that biologically they have more sexual desire and by nature need several sex partners. Fine. Keep women totally suppressed, especially sexually. Never let them talk about it, or even think about it, because that's in keeping with their biological nature.'

I said, 'That's why they call you bad, remember! When men are promiscuous, it's biological. If women even enjoy sex, they're "bad".'

Chanda responded, 'Going back to what I was saying about our lineage, our female lineage isn't something we've chosen, but because the men want nothing to do with our offspring. We're "impure" so they don't want their children who are born to us.'

'Sure,' I said, 'and they conveniently call these children "bastards". A child the man doesn't own is a bastard, regardless of the mother's ownership. He chooses to give respect or to take it away. It might seem that women run the show here in the Mohalla, but men are ultimately calling the shots. He selects you, he gives you status by association and he can own or disown you as he likes.'

Chanda nodded, 'That's right. I'm not "respectable". He can come to me, have his fun, and then swear at me, call me a whore and throw money in my face.'

Faiza murmured softly, 'Chanda, I have to apologize to you. I've been using the word whore as a swear word to put down other women. I really thought you all were very bad and the cause of the whole problem.'

Chanda gave her a sad smile, 'Sometimes we use the word ourselves to refer to other prostitutes we don't like. When we get angry at a woman, we call her "*gashti*".' She started to cry. 'This system has given us such low status that they've turned us into a bloody swear word, but still they come to us for their kicks.'

'Don't be sad, sister. I'm realizing that I do the same thing myself. Putting myself down,' Faiza spoke in a broken voice, 'Chanda, we do the same thing. We "respectable and pure women" also use the word "woman" as a swear word and a put down without realizing that we're only reinforcing the lower status decreed for us. I call my brother "sissy" when I'm making fun of his fears and his feminine behaviour. I tell my friends "go wear bangles like women and sit at home" when I think they're being cowards, not realizing it's myself I'm putting down by saying that women are cowards who wear bangles and sit at home. I use my own being as a swear word, Chanda.'

Chanda hugged her. Trying to console her, she patted Faiza's shoulder, but felt torn herself. She sensed she wouldn't be able to sit another evening in her *kotha* while customers passed by checking her out and walking away, without thinking about Faiza. Faiza, holding Chanda's hand tightly, thought she couldn't go through another marriage proposition with people looking her over like merchandise on display without thinking about Chanda.

Faiza whispered, 'Our worlds are not so different, Chanda. I'm glad we broke the boundaries for ourselves and saw through the barriers.' They looked at me, expectantly.

I couldn't control my emotions and exclaimed, 'Don't look at me for solutions. To me it's all the same, a middle-class woman cursing a prostitute who's moved to a "nice" part of town, a man making cat calls at a scared young woman waiting for a bus, a boss assuming he can flirt with his women employees, a husband beating his wife, a mother teaching her daughter that obedience is everything, all the stories propagated about what good girls should do. They're all the same to me. Your world Faiza and your world Chanda, they're the same.'

I put one arm around Faiza and the other around Chanda as we all broke into tears. 'Two sides of the same coin,' I thought. One sold in the Mohalla as a "bad woman" in the name of sin and the other sold in as a "good woman" in the name of honour and morality, both fulfilling roles laid out for them by the same patriarchal system.

# BIBLIOGRAPHY

Acton, William (1972). *Prostitution: Its moral, social, and sanitary aspects.* Frank Cass: London.

Agnihotri, Vidyadhar (n.d.). *Fallen women: A study with special reference to Kanpur.* Maharaja Printers: Kanpur.

Brody, Alyson (Ed.) (1997). *Moving the Whore Stigma. Global Alliance against Trafficking of Women.* Bangkok Thailand.

Ericsson, Lars O. (1980). *Charges against prostitution: An attempt at a philosophical assessment.* Ethics, 90, 335–366.

Ghosh, S.K. (1984). 'Changing faces of prostitution'. In S.K. Ghosh, *Women in a Changing Society* (pp. 136–155). Ashish Publishing House: New Delhi.

Golden, Aurthur (1998). *Memoirs of a Geisha.* Vintage: London.

Goldstein, Paul J. (1979). *Prostitution and drugs.* Lexington Books: Toronto.

Henriques, Fernando. (1966). *Prostitution and Society.* Grove Press Inc.: New York.

Jeffreys, Sheila (1985). 'Prostitution'. In D. Rhodes and S. McNeill (Eds.), *Women against violence against women.* Only Women Press: London.

Joardar, B. (1985). *Prostitution in historical and modern perspectives.* Inter-India Publications: Delhi.

Joardar, B. (1985). *Prostitution in nineteenth and early twentieth century: Calcutta.* Inter-India Publications: Delhi.

Kapur, Promilla (1978). *The life and world of call-girls in India.* Vikas Publishing House (Pvt.) Ltd.: Delhi.

Khalaf, Samir (1965). *Prostitution in a Changing Society.* Khayats, Beirut.

Kumar, T.B. Chandra (1978). *Sociology of Prostitution.* Kerala Historical Society Trivandrum: India.

Leeuw, Hendrik De (1933). *Cities of sin.* Harrison Smith and Robert Hass: New York.

Lerner, Gerda (1986). *The Creation of Patriarchy.* Oxford University Press: New York.

Mathur, A.S., and B.L. Gupta (1965). *Prostitution and prostitution.* Ram Prasad and Sons: Agra.

Punekar, S.D., and Kamala Rao (1967). *A study of prostitutes in Bombay.* Lalvani Publishing House: Bombay.

Raj, M. Sundara (1988). *Prostitution in Mardras: A Study in Historical Perspective.* Konark Publishers Pvt. Ltd.

Rao, M.R., and J.V.R. Rao (1969). *The prostitutes of Hyderabad.* Association for moral and hygiene in India: Andhra Pradesh.

Rozario, Rita M. (1988). *Trafficking in women children in India: (Sexual exploitation and sale).* Uppal Publishing House: New Delhi.

Scott, George R. (1976). *A history of prostitution: from antiquity to the present day.* AMS Press Inc.: New York.

Sinha, S.N., and N.K. Basu (1992). *The History of Marriage and Prostitution (Vedas to Vatsyayana).* Khama Publishers: New Delhi, India.

Trivedi, Harshad R. (1977). *Scheduled caste women: Studies in exploitation.* Concept Publishing Company: Delhi.

Varma, Paripurnanand (1979). *Sex offences in India and abroad.* B.R. Publishing Corporation: Delhi.

## ARTICLES

Adams, Elizabeth. (1994). 'Madam 90210'. *Cosmopolitan,* Jan. 1994, v216 n1, p. 154(10).

Alejandro, R.G. (1998). 'Letter from the Philippines'. *Dance Magazine,* Jan. 1998, v72 n1, p. 40(2).

Aslam, Salman. (1990). 'Dancing Girls Granted Bail'. *The Frontier Post,* 30 June 1990.

Bhatti, Mumtaz. (1989). 'Multan's Candid Courtesan'. *The Friday Times,* 20–26 July 1989.

Bhatti, Mumtaz. (1989). 'To Be Or Not To Be'. *The Friday Times,* 15–21 July 1989.

Caplan, Gerald M. (1984). 'The facts of life about teenage prostitution'. *Crime and Delinquency,* 30(1), pp. 69–74.

Dolgopol, Ustinia. (1995). 'Women's voices, women's pain'. *Human Rights Quarterly,* Feb. 1995, 17 n1, pp. 127–154.

Friedman, Robert. (1996). 'India's shame: sexual slavery and political corruption are leading to an AIDS catastrophe'. *The Nation,* 8 April 1996, v262 n14, p. 11(7) (Cover Story).

Fairclough, Gordon. (1994). 'No bed of roses: government tries to uproot prostitution from economy'. *Far Eastern Economic Review,* 15 Sept. 1994, v157 n37, p. 30(1).

Fairclough, Gordon. (1995). 'Doing the dirty work: Asia's brothels thrive on migrant labour'. *Far Eastern Economic Review,* 14 Dec. 1995, v158 n50, p. 27(2).

Gilfoyle, Timothy (1991). 'Prostitution'. *The Reader's Companion to American History,* 1991 Edition, p. 875(3).

Glover, Terry. June (1996). 'The shame game: who profits from prostitution?'. *Playboy,* v43 n6 p. 58(1).

Gup, Ted. (1995). 'What's new with the world's oldest profession?'. *Cosmopolitan,* Oct., v219 n4, p. 236(4).

Jeffreys, Sheila (1981). 'Prostitution'. *Revolutionary and Radical Feminist* newsletter no. 6, spring 1981. Kingston, Leeds.

James, Jennifer, and Nanette J. Dacis (1982). 'Contingencies in female sexual role deviance: The case of prostitution'. *Human Organization*, 41(4), 345–350.

Leuchtag, Alice (1995). 'Merchants of flesh'. *The Humanist*, March–April 1995, v55 n2, p. 11(6).

Magee, Audrey and Philip Sherwell (1996). 'For girls, few choices—all bad: seamstress, servant, or prostitute?'. *World Press Review*, January, v43 n1, p. 12(2).

Manto, Saadat Hassan (1999). 'Noor Jehan'. *Manto Nama* (pp. 244–275). Sang-e-Meel Publications: Lahore.

Marks, J.F., K.E. Nelson and D.D. Celentano (1994). 'Why isn't a commercial sex worker a prostitute?'. *JAMA, The Journal of the American Medical Association*, 19 Jan. 1994, v271 n3, p. 196(1).

McElroy, Wendy (1999). 'Prostitutes, Feminists, and Economic Associates'. Article posted at http://www.zetetics.com/mac/vern.htm

McKenney, Hobby (1998). 'Resorts of the Philippines'. *Gourmet*, March 1998, v58 n3, p. 62(5).

Sherry, A., A. Lee and M. Vatikiotis (1995). 'For lust or money'. *Far Eastern Economic Review*, 14 Dec. 1995, v158 n50, p. 22(2).

Srivastava, Vinita (Jan 1998). 'Sex here, baby. (the plight of sex-trade workers in Bombay, India)'. *Essence*, v28 n9, p. 50(3).

Stanley, Alessandra (1998). 'With prostitution booming, legalization tempts Russia'. *The New York Times*, 3 March 1998, v147, pA1(N) pA1(L), col. 5 (28 col.).

*The Economist*. 'Green-light areas: prostitution'. Nov 12, 1994 v333 n7889, p. 73(1).

*The Economist*. 'The red lights of Italy... and Hungary'. July 27, 1996 v340 n7976, p. 45(1).

*The Economist*. 'Giving the customer what he wants'. Feb 14, 1998 v346 n8055, p. 21(3).

*The New York Times*. (17 Feb. 1998). 'Visit to an ancient brothel'. (Site from first century BC in Salonika, Greece). v147, pB13(N), pF4(L), col. 6 (4 col.).

Vatikiotis, Michael, Sachiko Sakamaki, and Gary Silverman (1995). 'On the margin: organized crime profits from the flesh trade'. *Far Eastern Economic Review*, 14 Dec 1995, v158 n50, p. 26(2).

# INDEX